A Pleasant Year
with
Father Brown

A Pleasant Year *with* Father Brown

365 daily readings *in the company of* G. K. Chesterton's priest detective

Edited by

Stephen Poxon

DARTON·LONGMAN+TODD

First published in 2022 by
Darton, Longman and Todd Ltd
1 Spencer Court
140 – 142 Wandsworth High Street
London SW18 4JJ

ISBN: 978-1-915412-06-5

A catalogue record for this book is available from the British Library.

Designed and produced by Judy Linard
Printed and bound in Great Britain by Bell & Bain, Glasgow

INTRODUCTION

Gilbert Keith (G. K.) Chesterton, one of the most prolific writers England has ever produced, with some 80 books, several hundred poems, 200 short stories, 4,000 essays and several plays to his credit, is, arguably, most famous for his literary creation of the fictional Roman Catholic priest/detective, Father Brown.

A staunch Catholic himself, whose death in 1936 prompted none other than Cardinal Eugenio Pacelli to send a message of condolence to the people of England, on behalf of Pope Pius XI, Chesterton modelled Father Brown on the Rt Revd Msgr John O'Connor, a parish priest in Bradford, Yorkshire, who was involved in Chesterton's conversion to Catholicism in 1922 and remained a significant spiritual mentor to the writer.

A bumbling, modest and generally shabby character not given to taking vast amounts of pride in his appearance (black cassock, cape, matching saturno hat and wood-handled umbrella, in all weathers), Father Brown tended to shuffle faithfully and unassumingly around his parish duties, somehow becoming involved, as an amateur detective, in all manner of crimes and dastardly escapades ranging from the theft of jewels to murder.

All throughout, albeit dealing in lies and deception, and mixing and mingling with an astonishing range of villains, he retained, undamaged, a wonderfully endearing gentle temperament that sparkled with humility, humour and charm.

Much to the annoyance and frustration of police forces whose professional efforts at detection had all-too-often failed to bear fruit, Father Brown's wisdom and intuition enabled him to solve even the most baffling cases and deliver criminals to justice. The possessor of uncanny revelatory insights into human nature, Chesterton's quietly spoken, mild-mannered, biblically literate priest combined deep spirituality with large amounts of honed instinct and pastoral experience. The skills he had nurtured in the confessional and at the pulpit served him well at scenes of crime – to such an extent that even those being arrested and taken into custody often bore him no ill-will.

The widespread success of *Father Brown* as an immensely popular television series has served to present this childlike ecclesiastic to an audience of viewers who might never have read Chesterton's books. Lifting plots from the pages, TV producers have successfully introduced Chesterton's policing priest and his assorted friends in a way that never fails to convey his skill, his understated wit and his modest genius. Portrayed over the years by theatrical luminaries such as Alec Guinness, Kenneth More and, latterly, the excellent Mark Williams (amongst others), the television adaptations have entertained and amused literally millions of fans.

Undoubtedly, Father Brown's appeal lies in his self-deprecating and winsome manner. He is a priest who is beloved by his parishioners, who value and appreciate his common sense homilies and integrity. He is a man in whom there is no guile; a lamb amongst wolves in many ways, but a lamb whose intellect should never be underestimated. It is not within his nature to gloat or to boast, despite a crime-solving record that would be the envy of many police officers. Rather, he will pray, and think carefully. Therein lies the essence of his likeability. His religion is that of the mystic and the devout, yet one that is also thoroughly practical.

Having had the terrific privilege of compiling and editing these daily devotions, it is my sincere hope and prayer that those who read the excerpts will find, somewhere within them, thoughts, reflections and sentiments that will encourage personal pilgrimage. I trust they will convey helpful little messages of faith and seeds of Christian confidence. Father Brown will make us smile at times (as will the amusing range of characters with whom he associates). We will marvel at his ingenuity and we will admire his exemplary kindnesses. Above all, though, we will spend time together, as a reading, praying community, enjoying the mellow company of Chesterton's cleric. He will do our hearts and souls a power of good. He will inspire us.

S.J.P.

HOW BEST TO USE *A PLEASANT YEAR WITH FATHER BROWN*:

- **Plan *when* to read:**
  Try to read at the same time each day or night, if possible, including this book as one part of your daily devotions. An established routine of prayer can be a very helpful spiritual discipline.

- **Plan *where* to read:**
  Choose a quiet, comfortable place where you are not likely to be disturbed (your bedroom?).

- **Plan *how* to read:**
  Be still, taking a few moments to pause and relax, knowing that God is with you. Take time to become aware of his loving presence, and of his interest in your life.

- **Plan to *receive* as you read:**
  Asking God to speak to you as you turn these pages, believe that he will do so.

- **Plan to *reflect* after you have read:**
  Allow yourself a few moments of reflection, so that the Holy Spirit can gently assist you in your understanding and application of what you have read.

1 JANUARY

If we confess our sins, he is faithful and just and will forgive us our sins and purify us from all unrighteousness (1 John 1:9 *NIV*)

Father Brown flung down his paper, and, knowing the office door to be locked, went at once into the cloak room on the other side. The attendant of this place was temporarily absent, probably because the only guests were at dinner and his office was a sinecure. After groping through a grey forest of overcoats, he found that the dim cloak room opened on the lighted corridor in the form of a sort of counter or half-door, like most of the counters across which we have all handed umbrellas and received tickets. There was a light immediately above the semi-circular arch of this opening. It threw little illumination on Father Brown himself, who seemed a mere dark outline against the dim sunset window behind him. But it threw an almost theatrical light on the man who stood outside the cloak room in the corridor. He was an elegant man in very plain evening dress . . .

His face, now flung back in the lamplight, was swarthy and vivacious, the face of a foreigner. His figure was good, his manners good humoured and confident; a critic could only say that his black coat was a shade below his figure and manners, and even bulged and bagged in an odd way. The moment he caught sight of Brown's black silhouette against the sunset, he tossed down a scrap of paper with a number and called out with amiable authority: 'I want my hat and coat, please; I find I have to go away at once.' Father Brown took the paper without a word, and obediently went to look for the coat; it was not the first menial work he had done in his life. He brought it and laid it on the counter; meanwhile, the strange gentleman who had been feeling in his waistcoat pocket, said laughing: 'I haven't got any silver; you can keep this.' And he threw down half a sovereign, and caught up his coat. Father Brown's figure remained quite dark and still . . .

'I think, sir,' he said civilly, 'that you have some silver in your pocket.' The tall gentleman stared. 'Hang it,' he cried, 'if I choose to give you gold, why should you complain?' 'Because silver is sometimes more valuable than gold,' said the priest mildly; 'that is, in large quantities.' The stranger looked at him curiously . . . He put one hand on the counter, vaulted over as easily as an acrobat and towered above the priest, putting one tremendous hand upon his collar. 'Stand still,' he said, in a hacking whisper. 'I don't want to threaten you, but – ' 'I do want to threaten you,' said Father Brown, in a voice like a rolling drum, 'I want to threaten you with the worm that dieth not, and the fire that is not quenched.' 'You're a rum sort of cloak-room clerk,' said the other. 'I am a priest, Monsieur Flambeau,'* said Brown, 'and I am ready to hear your confession.'†

LORD JESUS, PROPHET, priest and king, you are always more than ready and tirelessly willing to hear my confession, and to do so in mercy. You are that kind of God. Thank you that I may confess in absolute confidence, certain of encountering indefatigable grace. You have my deep gratitude for your definite promise of pardon. Receive my prayers this day.

* Hercule Flambeau, a fictional jewel thief, at once friend and adversary of Father Brown. Flambeau had a particular fascination with stealing precious religious artefacts; bejewelled crucifixes and the like.

† *The Blue Cross.*

2 JANUARY

Come now, let us reason together, says the Lord (Isaiah 1:18 *ESV)*

The two figures that they followed were crawling like black flies across the huge green contour of a hill. They were evidently sunk in conversation, and perhaps did not notice where they were going . . .

Under a tree in this commanding yet neglected spot was an old ramshackle wooden seat. On this seat sat the two priests still in serious speech together . . .

For the two priests were talking exactly like priests, piously, with learning and leisure, about the most aerial enigmas of theology. The little Essex priest spoke the more simply, with his round face turned to the strengthening stars; the other talked with his head bowed, as if he were not even worthy to look at them. But no more innocently clerical conversation could have been heard in any white Italian cloister or black Spanish cathedral . . .

The taller priest nodded his bowed head and said: 'These modern infidels appeal to their reason; but who can look at those millions of worlds and not feel that there may well be wonderful universes above us where reason is utterly unreasonable?'

'No,' said the other priest; 'reason is always reasonable, even in the last limbo, in the lost borderland of things. I know that people charge the Church with lowering reason, but it is just the other way. Alone on earth, the Church makes reason really supreme. Alone on earth, the Church affirms that God himself is bound by reason.'*

REASONABLE GOD, GRANT me that happy knack of combining faith with reason, and to work out my salvation according to that ever-maturing balance. Teach me not to regard one as being in conflict with the other, but, rather, to embrace a sensible belief system that includes intelligent logic as well as confidence in the supernatural. In other words, Heavenly Father, grant me a heart with which to love you and a mind that follows suit.

* *The Blue Cross.*

3 JANUARY

When they came to Jesus and found that he was already dead, they did not break his legs. Instead, one of the soldiers pierced Jesus' side with a spear, bringing a sudden flow of blood and water (John 19:33, 34 *NIV*)

Lord Galloway was crying: 'A corpse in the grass – a blood-stained corpse' . . .

'We must tell Valentin* at once,' said the doctor, when the other had brokenly described all that he had dared to examine. 'It is fortunate that he is here'; and even as he spoke the great detective entered the study, attracted by the cry.

It was almost amusing to note his typical transformation; he had come with the common concern of a host and a gentleman, fearing that some guest or servant was ill. When he was told the gory fact, he turned with all his gravity instantly bright and business-like; for this, however abrupt and awful, was his business. 'Strange, gentlemen,' he said, as they hurried out into the garden, 'that I should have hunted mysteries all over the earth, and now one comes and settles in my own backyard. But where is the place?'

They crossed the lawn less easily, as a slight mist had begun to rise from the river; but under the guidance of the shaken Galloway they found the body sunken in deep grass – the body of a very tall and broad-shouldered man. He lay face downwards, so they could only see that his big shoulders were clad in black cloth, and that his big head was bald, except for a wisp or two of brown hair that clung to his skull like wet seaweed. A scarlet serpent of blood crawled from under his fallen face . . .

'Examine him, doctor,' cried Valentin rather sharply. 'He may not be dead.'†

* Aristide Valentin, chief of the Paris Police who was simultaneously annoyed by Father Brown's presence during an investigation and impressed by his logical and charming manner.

† *The Secret Garden.*

LORD JESUS, YOU died for my sake; the most brutal, blood-stained death imaginable, paying the price for my sin and waywardness. You too lay utterly lifeless, to be examined by men who had little or no idea of your true identity; the divine victim – the King of Glory meeting the most inglorious end, all for my sake. You are my God. You are my Saviour; the Lamb who was slain.

4 JANUARY

There is a time for everything . . . a time to weep and a time to laugh (Ecclesiastes 3:3, 4 *NIV*)

Father Brown's pipe fell out of his mouth and broke into three pieces on the gravel path.

He stood rolling his eyes, the exact picture of an idiot.

'Lord, what a turnip I am!' he kept saying. 'Lord, what a turnip!' . . .

He began to laugh . . .

Father Brown repressed what appeared to be a momentary disposition to dance on the now sunlit lawn and cried piteously, like a child: 'Oh, let me be silly a little. You don't know how unhappy I have been . . .

'Only a little lunacy, perhaps – and who minds that?' He spun round once, then faced them with gravity.*

GOD WHO INVENTED humour, preserve us from a faith that never sees the funny side of anything, and a Church that frowns far too often for its own good. Let us love being silly a little.

* *The Honour of Israel Gow.*

5 JANUARY

Strive for full restoration, encourage one another, be of one mind, live in peace (2 Corinthians 13:11 *NIV*)

Valentin . . . found a policeman, and said: 'This is urgent, constable; have you seen two clergymen in shovel hats?' The policeman began to chuckle heavily. 'I 'ave, sir; and if you arst me, one of 'em was drunk. He stood in the middle of the road that bewildered that –'

'Which way did they go?' snapped Valentin. 'They took one of them yellow buses over there,' answered the man; 'them that go to Hampstead.' Valentin produced his official card and said very rapidly: 'Call up two of your men to come with me in pursuit,' and crossed the road with such contagious energy that the ponderous policeman was moved to almost agile obedience. In a minute and a half the French detective was joined on the opposite pavement by an inspector and a man in plain clothes. 'Well, sir,' began the former, with smiling importance, 'and what may –?'

Valentin pointed suddenly with his cane. 'I'll tell you on the top of that omnibus,' he said, and was darting and dodging across the tangle of the traffic. When all three sank panting on the top seats of the yellow vehicle, the inspector said: 'We could go four times as quick in a taxi.' 'Quite true,' replied their leader placidly, 'if we only had an idea of where we were going.' 'Well, where are you going?' asked the other, staring.

Valentin smoked frowningly for a few seconds; then, removing his cigarette, he said: 'If you know what a man's doing, get in front of him; but if you want to guess what he's doing, keep behind him. Stray when he strays; stop when he stops; travel as slowly as he. Then you may see what he saw and may act as he acted. All we can do is to keep our eyes skinned for a queer thing.' 'What sort of queer thing do you mean?' asked the inspector. 'Any sort of queer thing,' answered Valentin, and relapsed into obstinate silence.*

* *The Blue Cross.*

HELP ME, LORD, on those days when I'm working with people who aren't necessarily pulling in my direction! Assist me, I pray, not to relapse into 'obstinate silence' if my colleagues haven't quite seen things my way, or if there has been a breakdown in communications. Grant me – and them – patience. Oh, and thank you, Lord Jesus, that this prayer meets with your understanding and empathy, for you too worked for a living in your father's carpentry shop. What a lovely God you must be – the Christ of the human road, indeed.

6 JANUARY

We are worn out, there is no rest for us (Lamentations 5:5 *NASB*)

The yellow omnibus crawled up the northern roads for what seemed like hours on end; [Valentin] would not explain further, and perhaps his assistants felt a silent and growing desire for lunch, for the hours crept long past the normal luncheon hour, and the long roads of the North London suburbs seemed to shoot out into length after length like an infernal telescope.

It was one of those journeys on which a man perpetually feels that now at last he must have come to the end of the universe, and then finds he has only come to the beginning of Tufnell Park.

London died away in draggled taverns and dreary scrubs, and then was unaccountably born again in blazing high streets and blatant hotels. It was like passing through thirteen separate vulgar cities all just touching each other. But though the winter twilight was already threatening the road ahead of them, the Parisian detective still sat silent and watchful, eyeing the frontage of the streets that slid by on either side.*

LIFE IS A JOURNEY, Lord, and in the normal run of things, long is the road, so I pray for anyone I know who is finding their personal pilgrimage heavy-going and arduous at the moment, for one reason or another. Meet with them on their pathway and encourage them. Lift their spirits by your presence.

* *The Blue Cross.*

7 JANUARY

Let this mind be in you, which was also in Christ Jesus (Philippians 2:5 *KJV*)

'This is a very painful matter, Father Brown,' said Adams. 'The truth is, those diamonds we all saw this afternoon seem to have vanished from my friend's tail-coat pocket. And as you –' 'As I,' supplemented Father Brown, with a broad grin, 'was sitting just behind him – '

'Nothing of the sort shall be suggested,' said Colonel Adams, with a firm look . . . which rather implied that some such thing *had* been suggested. 'I only ask you to give me the assistance that any gentleman might give.' 'Which is turning out his pockets,' said Father Brown, and proceeded to do so, displaying seven and sixpence, a return ticket, a small silver crucifix, a small breviary, and a stick of chocolate. The colonel looked at him long and then said, 'Do you know, I should like to see the inside of your head more than the inside of your pockets. '

'If you want the inside of my head you can have it,' said Brown rather wearily. 'What it's worth you can say afterwards.'*

HEAVENLY FATHER, IT would be wonderful if my friends and family were as interested in the inside of my head – my mind, my psyche, what makes me tick – as Colonel Adams was in Father Brown's, especially if that was on account of Jesus Christ within. Holy Spirit, come as the guest of my soul, I pray, so that those who notice my way of thinking may also notice your indwelling presence. Grant me that privilege.

* *The Flying Stars.*

8 JANUARY

I beheld all the work of God, that a man cannot find out the work that is done under the sun: because though a man labour to seek it out, yet he shall not find it; yea farther; though a wise man think to know it, yet shall he not be able to find it (Ecclesiastes 8:17 *KJV*)

Father Brown was made of two men.

There was a man of action, who was as modest as a primrose and as punctual as a clock; who went his small round of duties and never dreamed of altering it.

There was also a man of reflection, who was much simpler but much stronger, who could not easily be stopped; whose thought was always (in the only intelligent sense of the words) free thought.

He could not help, even unconsciously, asking himself all the questions that there were to be asked, and answering as many of them as he could; all that went on like his breathing or circulation.*

HOW THESE WORDS resonate with me, Heavenly Father! Whenever I contemplate myself, or my behaviour, I sometimes think there are at least two people making up my whole! It seems I can be a mass of contradictions at times. Yet, I am not several people, but simply the person you have created, and gifted with almost as many facets as you award to diamonds. I may not ever really be able to understand myself, yet you know me full well, and you love me too.

* *The Salad of Colonel Cray.*

9 JANUARY

Beloved, do not believe every spirit, but test the spirits to see whether they are from God, for many false prophets have gone out into the world (1 John 4:1 *ESV*)

Flambeau and his friend the priest were sitting in the Temple Gardens about sunset; and their neighbourhood or some such accidental influence had turned their talk to matters of legal process. From the problem of the licence in cross-examination, their talk strayed to Roman and mediaeval torture, to the examining magistrate in France and the Third Degree in America.

'I've been reading,' said Flambeau, 'of this new psychometric method they talk about so much, especially in America. You know what I mean; they put a pulsometer on a man's wrist and judge by how his heart goes at the pronunciation of certain words. What do you think of it?'

'I think it very interesting,' replied Father Brown; 'it reminds me of that interesting idea in the Dark Ages that blood would flow from a corpse if the murderer touched it.'

'Do you really mean,' demanded his friend, 'that you think the two methods equally valuable?'

'I think them equally valueless,' replied Brown. 'Blood flows, fast or slow, in dead folk or living, for so many more million reasons than we can ever know. Blood will have to flow very funnily; blood will have to flow up the Matterhorn, before I will take it as a sign that I am to shed it.'

'The method,' remarked the other, 'has been guaranteed by some of the greatest American men of science.'

'What sentimentalists men of science are!' exclaimed Father Brown, 'and how much more sentimental must American men of science be! Who but a Yankee would think of proving anything from heart-throbs? Why, they must be as sentimental as a man who thinks a woman is in love with him if she blushes.'*

* *The Mistake of the Machine.*

A SPIRIT OF discernment, Lord! I pray to have one! Let me never ignore sentiment, or dismiss it, but let me never be taken in by it, either, like a gullible fool. Likewise, that which appears to carry a certain logic, but does nothing of the sort, really; shield me from its bogus claims. Hem me in with spiritual wisdom that comes directly from heaven, and does not depend upon earthly proof for its veracity, but simply stands alone, steadfast in the face of every passing novelty.

10 JANUARY

The LORD God called to the man and said to him, 'Where are you?' (Genesis 3:9 *ESV*)

Between the silver ribbon of morning and the green glittering ribbon of sea, the boat touched Harwich and let loose a swarm of folk like flies, among whom the man we must follow was by no means conspicuous – nor wished to be. There was nothing notable about him, except a slight contrast between the holiday gaiety of his clothes and the official gravity of his face. His clothes included a slight, pale grey jacket, a white waistcoat, and a silver straw hat with a grey-blue ribbon. His lean face was dark by contrast, and ended in a curt black beard that looked Spanish and suggested an Elizabethan ruff. He was smoking a cigarette with the seriousness of an idler. There was nothing about him to indicate the fact that the grey jacket covered a loaded revolver, that the white waistcoat covered a police card, or that the straw hat covered one of the most powerful intellects in Europe. For this was Valentin himself, the head of the Paris Police and the most famous investigator of the world; and he was coming from Brussels to London to make the greatest arrest of the century.

Flambeau was in England. The police of three countries had tracked the great criminal at last from Ghent to Brussels, from Brussels to the Hook of Holland; and it was conjectured that he would take some advantage of the unfamiliarity and confusion of the Eucharistic Congress, then taking place in London. Probably he would travel as some minor clerk or secretary connected with it; but, of course, Valentin could not be certain; nobody could be certain about Flambeau . . .

Almost every morning the daily paper announced that he had escaped the consequences of one extraordinary crime by committing another . . .

Hence the great Valentin, when he set out to find Flambeau, was perfectly aware that his adventures would not end when he had found him. But how was he to find him? On this the great Valentin's ideas were still in process of settlement.*

* *The Blue Cross.*

RELENTLESS AND SEARCHING God, you sought me, you found me, and you saved me. You are indeed the Divine Detective, utterly inexhaustible in the grace and energy that seeks the lost. Thank you for finding me. Thank you for steadfastly refusing to abandon that pursuit. Thank you for your every tireless soul-saving idea.

11 JANUARY

The LORD does not look at the things people look at. People look at the outward appearance, but the LORD looks at the heart (1 Samuel 16:7 *NIV)*

About the people on the boat [Valentin] had already satisfied himself; and the people picked up at Harwich or on the journey limited themselves with certainty to six. There was a short railway official travelling up to the terminus, three fairly short market gardeners picked up two stations afterwards, one very short widow lady going up from a small Essex town, and a very short Roman Catholic priest going up from a small Essex village.

When it came to the last case, Valentin gave it up and almost laughed. The little priest was so much the essence of those Eastern flats; he had a face as round and dull as a Norfolk dumpling; he had eyes as empty as the North Sea; he had several brown paper parcels, which he was quite incapable of collecting. The Eucharistic Congress had doubtless sucked out of their local stagnation many such creatures, blind and helpless, like moles disinterred.

Valentin was a sceptic in the severe style of France, and could have no love for priests. But he could have pity for them, and this one might have provoked pity in anybody. He had a large, shabby umbrella, which constantly fell on the floor. He did not seem to know which was the right end of his return ticket.

He explained with a moon-calf simplicity to everybody in the carriage that he had to be careful, because he had something made of real silver 'with blue stones' in one of his brown-paper parcels. His quaint blending of Essex flatness with saintly simplicity continuously amused the Frenchman till the priest arrived (somehow) at Tottenham with all his parcels, and came back for his umbrella. When he did the last, Valentin even had the good nature to warn him not to take care of the silver by telling everybody about it.*

* *The Blue Cross.*

LOVING GOD, YOU make a point of deliberately looking beyond the surface, and what a blessing that is! You see far beyond the visible as you study the hearts of your children, rich and poor alike, tidy or scruffy, impressive or repulsive. Teach me that skill, I pray, that I may not be so easily swayed by what my eyes tell me. Help me to imitate you by moving beyond that initial analysis, and by doing so in love.

12 JANUARY

Everything must be done so that the church may be built up
(1 Corinthians 14:26 *NIV*)

The little priest, Brown, had arrived while they were talking, and had waited, with characteristic shyness, till they had finished. Then he said awkwardly: 'I say, I'm sorry to interrupt. But I was sent to tell you the news!' 'News?' repeated Simon, and stared at him rather painfully through his glasses. 'Yes, I'm sorry,' said Father Brown mildly. 'There's been another murder, you know.' Both men on the seat sprang up, leaving it rocking. 'And, what's stranger still,' continued the priest, with his dull eye on the rhododendrons, 'it's the same disgusting sort; it's another beheading. They found the second head actually bleeding into the river.'

Commandant O'Brien followed the others towards the inquest, feeling decidedly sick. As a soldier, he loathed all this secretive carnage; where were these extravagant amputations going to stop? First one head was hacked off, and then another; in this case (he told himself bitterly) it was not true that two heads were better than one . . .

The second head, which had been fished from among the river reeds that morning, lay streaming and dripping beside it; Valentin's men were still seeking to recover the rest of this second corpse, which was supposed to be afloat. Father Brown, who did not seem to share O'Brien's sensibilities in the least, went up to the second head and examined it with his blinking care. It was little more than a mop of wet white hair, fringed with silver fire in the red and level morning light; the face, which seemed of an ugly, empurpled and perhaps criminal type, had been much battered against trees or stones as it tossed in the water . . .

'There's no doubt it's Brayne,' said the priest quietly. 'He had exactly that chip in the left ear.' The detective, who had been regarding the priest with steady and glittering eyes, opened his clenched mouth and said sharply: 'You seem to know a lot about him, Father Brown.' 'I do,' said the little man simply. 'I've been about with him for some weeks. He was thinking of joining our church.' The star of the fanatic sprang into Valentin's eyes; he strode towards the priest with clenched hands. 'And, perhaps,' he cried, with a blasting sneer, 'perhaps he was also thinking of leaving all his money to your church.' 'Perhaps he was,' said Brown stolidly; 'it is possible.' 'In that case,' cried Valentin, with a dreadful smile, 'you may indeed know a great deal about him. About his life and about his –'Commandant O'Brien laid a hand on Valentin's arm. 'Drop that slanderous rubbish, Valentin,' he said, 'or there may be more swords yet.'*

LORD OF THE Church, my prayers today are with anyone contemplating going to church for the first time, or the first time in a while, and maybe even (re)joining. There is a possibility, Heavenly Father, that their intention might be met with cynicism or ridicule. Help them, therefore, as they think about church attendance. Keep them strong. Surround them with people who will encourage, protect, pray and support.

* *The Secret Garden.*

13 JANUARY

Out of the heart proceed evil thoughts (Matthew 15:19 *KJV*)

The borderland of the brain, where all the monsters are made, moved horribly in the Gaelic O'Brien. He felt the chaotic presence of all the horse-men and fish-women that man's unnatural fancy has forgotten.

A voice older than his first fathers seemed saying in his ear: 'Keep out of the monstrous garden where grows the tree with double fruit. Avoid the evil garden where died the man with two heads.' Yet, while these shameful symbolic shapes passed across the ancient mirror of his Irish soul, his Frenchified intellect was quite alert, and was watching the odd priest as closely and incredulously as all the rest.*

HAVE MERCY, HEAVENLY Father, on any who are tormented today, with delusions and terrifying figments of imagination. Have mercy on those in the grip of mental illness. Impart peace and courage.

* *The Secret Garden.*

14 JANUARY

They picked up the pieces and filled twelve baskets with scraps left by the people who had eaten from the five barley loaves (John 6:13 *NLT*)

'Twigs,' said the priest gloomily, and turned to the window which looked on the scene of death.

'No one saw the point of the twigs. Why should they lie on that lawn (look at it) so far away from any tree? They were not snapped off; they were chopped off. The murderer occupied his enemy with some tricks with the sabre, showing how he could cut a branch in mid-air, or what not. Then, while his enemy bent down to see the result, a silent slash, and the head fell.'

'Well,' said the doctor slowly, 'that seems plausible enough.'*

TWIGS! HOW EASY it is, Lord, to inadvertently overlook that which appears not to matter; to pay scant attention to something – or, if I'm being perfectly honest, someone. Forgive me, I pray, for those times I have done that, albeit without meaning to. Help me to pick up on the moral of today's Bible text, and to keep an eye out for those who might otherwise be discarded; the scraps left behind.

* *The Secret Garden.*

15 JANUARY

Clothe yourselves, all of you, with humility toward one another (1 Peter 5:5 *ESV*)

In answer to a curt but civil summons, the door opened inwards and there shambled into the room a shapeless little figure, which seemed to find its own hat and umbrella as unmanageable as a mass of luggage.

The umbrella was a black and prosaic bundle long past repair; the hat was a broad-curved black hat, clerical but not common in England; the man was the very embodiment of all that is homely and helpless.

The doctor regarded the newcomer with a restrained astonishment, not unlike that he would have shown if some huge but obviously harmless sea-beast had crawled into his room. The newcomer regarded the doctor with that beaming but breathless geniality which characterizes a corpulent charwoman who has just managed to stuff herself into an omnibus.

It is a rich confusion of social self-congratulation and bodily disarray. His hat tumbled to the carpet, his heavy umbrella slipped between his knees with a thud; he reached after the one and ducked after the other, but with an unimpaired smile on his round face spoke simultaneously as follows:

'My name is Brown. Pray excuse me.'*

WHAT A LOVELY word-picture, Lord Jesus, of a devout priest who is humble and lowly; an example of ego-less humility. Grant me such a basic disposition, I pray, that I may live gently, without thoughts of status.

* *The Absence of Mr Glass.*

16 JANUARY

He who is trustworthy in spirit keeps a thing covered (Proverbs 11:13 *ESV*)

Brown opened the envelope and read the following words:

'Dear Father Brown –

Vicisti, Galilæe! Otherwise, damn your eyes, which are very penetrating ones. Can it be possible that there is something in all that stuff of yours after all?

'I am a man who has ever since boyhood believed in Nature and in all natural functions and instincts, whether men called them moral or immoral. Long before I became a doctor, when I was a schoolboy keeping mice and spiders, I believed that to be a good animal is the best thing in the world.

But just now I am shaken; I have believed in Nature; but it seems as if Nature could betray a man. Can there be anything in your bosh? I am really getting morbid.'

Father Brown carefully folded up the letter and put it in his breast pocket.*

THANK YOU, LORD, for priests, ministers, family members and friends in whom I may safely confide. Blessed are the unshockable! I pray for those to whom confidential matters are entrusted, that you would grant them wisdom, and that they would carry private confidences safely, but lightly, not in any way that would burden them. Thank you for the trustworthy. Thank you for those who refuse to judge. Bless them as they too fold things away close to their heart.

* *The Wrong Shape.*

17 JANUARY

Love the Lord your God with all your . . . mind (Luke 10:27 *NIV*)

Aristide Valentin was unfathomably French; and the French intelligence is intelligence specially and solely.

He was not 'a thinking machine'; for that is a brainless phrase of modern fatalism and materialism. A machine only is a machine because it cannot think. But he was a thinking man, and a plain man at the same time.

All his wonderful successes, that looked like conjuring, had been gained by plodding logic, by clear and commonplace French thought. The French electrify the world not by starting any paradox, they electrify it by carrying out a truism. They carry a truism so far – as in the French Revolution.

But exactly because Valentin understood reason, he understood the limits of reason. Only a man who knows nothing of motors talks of motoring without petrol; only a man who knows nothing of reason talks of reasoning without strong, undisputed first principles.*

HEAVENLY FATHER, WHATEVER sort of intelligence mine may or not be, it is the one you have gifted to me. Thank you for it. Help me, I ask, to apply my intellect to knowing, and loving, you more. My prayers today are also with pastors and Bible teachers who strive to impart doctrine and Christian truth. Bless their efforts, and honour their commitment to that special vocation.

* *The Blue Cross.*

18 JANUARY

The eye that saw him will not see him again; his place will look on him no more (Job 20:9 *NIV*)

Angus . . . called out with some nervousness: 'Where is the policeman?'

'I beg your pardon,' said Father Brown; 'that is my fault. I just sent him down the road to investigate something – that I just thought worth investigating.'

'Well, we want him back pretty soon,' said Angus abruptly, for the wretched man upstairs has not only been murdered, but wiped out.'

'How?' asked the priest.

'Father,' said Flambeau, after a pause, 'upon my soul I believe it is more in your department than mine. No friend or foe has entered the house, but Smythe is gone, as if stolen by the fairies. If that is not supernatural, I – '*

LORD OF ALL there is, seen and unseen, grant me sufficient humility to admit that I know but a fraction (if that) of your ways. In reality, I have but the faintest comprehension of what exists in universes way beyond my understanding, never mind the ways in which you choose to operate. Nevertheless, let that admission be the springboard for my faith, building on what I do know in order to learn more and more about your nature, your plans, and your love.

* *The Invisible Man.*

19 JANUARY

Thine ears shall hear a word behind thee, saying, This is the way, walk ye in it, when ye turn to the right hand, and when ye turn to the left (Isaiah 30:21 *KJV*)

Flambeau had been missed at Harwich; and if he was in London at all, he might be anything from a tall tramp on Wimbledon Common to a tall toast-master at the Hotel Metropole. In such a naked state of nescience, Valentin had a view and a method of his own. In such cases he reckoned on the unforeseen. In such cases, when he could not follow the train of the reasonable, he coldly and carefully followed the train of the unreasonable. Instead of going to the right places – banks, police stations, rendezvous – he systematically went to the wrong places; knocked at every empty house, turned down every cul de sac, went up every lane blocked with rubbish, went round every crescent that led him uselessly out of the way.

He defended this crazy course quite logically. He said that if one had a clue this was the worst way; but if one had no clue at all it was the best, because there was just the chance that any oddity that caught the eye of the pursuer might be the same that had caught the eye of the pursued.

Somewhere a man must begin, and it had better be just where another man might stop. Something about that flight of steps up to the shop, something about the quietude and quaintness of the restaurant, roused all the detective's rare romantic fancy and made him resolve to strike at random. He went up the steps, and sitting down at a table by the window, asked for a cup of black coffee. It was half-way through the morning, and he had not breakfasted; the slight litter of other breakfasts stood about on the table to remind him of his hunger; and adding a poached egg to his order, he proceeded musingly to shake some white sugar into his coffee, thinking all the time about Flambeau.

He remembered how Flambeau had escaped, once by a pair of nail scissors, and once by a house on fire; once by having to pay for an unstamped letter, and once by getting people to look through a telescope at a comet that might destroy the world. He thought his detective brain as good as the criminal's, which was true. But he fully realised the disadvantage. 'The criminal is the creative artist; the detective only the critic,' he said with a sour smile, and lifted his coffee cup to his lips slowly, and put it down very quickly. He had put salt in it.*

GRACIOUS HOLY SPIRIT, you kindly offer to guide us in our decision making – thank you – but we are sometimes quite hard of hearing, for one reason or another. Help us, Lord, to discern your directions, then to trust and obey. I pray for anyone at any kind of crossroads in their life who is seeking to know which way to take. Fulfil your promise of today's Bible text, I ask.

* *The Blue Cross.*

20 JANUARY

God so loved the world (John 3:16 *NIV*)

When Father Brown first stepped off an Atlantic liner on to American soil, he discovered as many other Englishman has done, that he was a much more important person than he had ever supposed.

His short figure, his short-sighted and undistinguished countenance, his rather rusty-black clerical clothes, could pass through any crowd in his own country without being noticed as anything unusual, except perhaps unusually insignificant. But America has a genius for the encouragement of fame; and his appearance in one or two curious criminal problems, together with his long association with Flambeau, the ex-criminal and detective, had consolidated a reputation in America out of what was little more than a rumour in England.

His round face was blank with surprise when he found himself held up on the quay by a group of journalists, as by a gang of brigands, who asked him questions about all the subjects on which he was least likely to regard himself as an authority, such as the details of female dress and the criminal statistics of the country that he had only that moment clapped his eyes on.

Perhaps it was the contrast with the black embattled solidarity of this group that made more vivid another figure that stood apart from it, equally black against the burning white daylight of that brilliant place and season, but entirely solitary; a tall, rather yellow-faced man in great goggles, who arrested him with a gesture when the journalists had finished . . .

Some apology may be made for Father Brown; for he himself would have been sincerely apologetic. It must be remembered that he had never seen America before, and more especially that he had never seen that sort of tortoise-shell spectacles before; for the fashion at this time had not spread to England.

His first sensation was that of gazing at some goggling sea-monster with a faint suggestion of a diver's helmet. Otherwise the man was exquisitely dressed; and to Brown, in his innocence, the spectacles seemed the queerest disfigurement for a dandy. It was as if a dandy had adorned himself with a wooden leg as an extra touch of elegance.*

GOD WHO LOVES the world, you are an international deity, and my prayerful thoughts today turn towards those who are a long way from home for the Kingdom's sake. I think of missionaries and their families, who have crossed oceans, time zones and borders in obedience to your call. Bless them, I pray, especially when everything is unfamiliar, unsettling and disorientating, and when homesickness kicks in. Bless too, their relatives who have stayed put, and who miss them daily.

* *The Arrow of Heaven.*

21 JANUARY

Be still, and know that I am God (Psalm 46:10 *NIV*)

Father Brown was dragged in a somewhat dazed condition towards a car at some little distance, in which a young man with tufts of untidy yellow hair and a rather harassed and haggard expression, hailed him from afar . . .

Before he knew where he was he was stowed in the car and travelling with considerable speed through and beyond the city. He was unused to the impetuous practicality of such American action, and felt about as bewildered as if a chariot drawn by dragons had carried him away into fairyland.*

LORD JESUS, YOU who never rode in a car or flew in an aeroplane, but knew only the three-mile-an-hour pace of walking, donkey-riding and fishing boat excursions, I confess that the pace of modern life sometimes gets the better of me: traffic, deadlines, schedules, and even the speed at which I find myself walking. I gulp down drinks instead of savouring the quenching of a thirst, and I all-too-often hurry meals that should be enjoyed. When I too feel bewildered and hauled along by the dragons of urgency, remind me, I pray, to slow down, and to calm down.

* *The Arrow of Heaven.*

22 JANUARY

When Joshua had grown old, the Lord said to him, 'You are now very old, and there are still very large areas of land to be taken over' (Joshua 13:1 *NIV*)

Flambeau, once the most famous criminal in France and later a very private detective in England, had long retired from both professions . . .

After a life of romantic escapes and tricks of evasion, he had ended at what some might consider an appropriate address: in a castle in Spain. The castle, however, was solid though relatively small; and the black vineyard and green stripes of kitchen garden covered a respectable square on the brown hillside.

For Flambeau, after all his violent adventures, still possessed what is possessed by so many Latins, what is absent (for instance) in so many Americans, the energy to retire. It can be seen in many a large hotel-proprietor whose one ambition is to be a small peasant. It can be seen in many a French provincial shopkeeper, who pauses at the moment when he might develop into a detestable millionaire and buy a street of shops, to fall back quietly and comfortably on domesticity and dominoes.

Flambeau had casually and almost abruptly fallen in love with a Spanish Lady, married and brought up a large family on a Spanish estate, without displaying any apparent desire to stray again beyond its borders.*

WHAT A CONUNDRUM, Lord – knowing when to put one's feet up and call it a day! In your Kingdom, Lord, there is always still work to be done, or 'land to be taken'. There are still prayers to be prayed, books to be read or written, loved ones to be cherished, people to be influenced, and lessons to be learnt. Help me, I pray, to know when to stop and when to keep going; when to pursue one last project or ambition and when to 'fall back quietly'. I pray too for those already retired, that they would find you at the heart of those years, ready to bless, guide and help.

* *The Secret of Father Brown.*

23 JANUARY

Love does no wrong to a neighbour (Romans 13:10 *ESV*)

The black dot gradually increased in size without very much altering in the shape; for it continued, roughly speaking, to be both round and black . . .

These clothes, however clerical, had about them something at once commonplace and yet almost jaunty in comparison with the cassock or soutane, and marked the wearer as a man from the north-western islands, as clearly as if he had been labelled Clapham Junction.

He carried a short thick umbrella with a knob like a club, at the sight of which his Latin friend almost shed tears of sentiment; for it had figured in many adventures that they shared long ago. For this was the Frenchman's English friend, Father Brown, paying a long-desired but long-delayed visit. They had corresponded constantly, but they had not met for years.

Father Brown was soon established in the family circle, which was quite large enough to give the general sense of company or a community. He was introduced to the big wooden images of the Three Kings, of painted and gilded wood, who bring the gifts to the children at Christmas; for Spain is a country where the affairs of the children bulk large in the life of the home. He was introduced to the dog and the cat and the live-stock on the farm. But he was also, as it happened, introduced to one neighbour who, like himself, had brought into that valley the garb and manners of distant lands.

It was on the third night of the priest's stay at the little chateau that he beheld a stately stranger who paid his respects to the Spanish household with bows that no Spanish grandee could emulate. He was a tall, thin grey-haired and very handsome gentleman, and his hands, cuffs and cuff-links had something overpowering in their polish. But his long face had nothing of that languor which is associated with long cuffs and manicuring in the caricatures of our own country . . .

This was, indeed, no less a person than Mr Grandison Chace, of Boston, an American traveller who had halted for a time in his American travels by taking a lease of the adjoining estate; a somewhat similar castle on a somewhat similar hill. He delighted in his old castle, and he regarded his friendly neighbour as a local antiquity of the same type. For Flambeau managed . . . really to look retired in the sense of rooted. He might have grown there with his own vine and fig-tree for ages.*

AH, LORD! THOSE you have placed around me; friends and neighbours! Believing that I live where you want me to live, amongst those you wish me to live amongst, grant me the grace to be a good neighbour. More to the point, to be a good ambassador for Christ. Give me daily wisdom, tact and sensitivity.

* *The Secret of Father Brown.*

24 JANUARY

My brothers and sisters, believers in our glorious Lord Jesus Christ must not show favouritism (James 2:1 *NIV*)

At the twist of a path in the hills, where two poplars stood up like pyramids dwarfing the tiny village of Potter's Pond, a mere huddle of houses, there once walked a man in a costume of a very conspicuous cut and colour, wearing a vivid magenta coat and a white hat tilted upon black ambrosial curls . . .

It was only about a week afterwards that his body was found a quarter of a mile away, broken upon the steep rockeries of a terraced garden leading up to a gaunt and shuttered house called The Grange. Just before he had vanished, he had been accidentally overheard apparently quarrelling with some bystanders, and especially abusing their village as 'a wretched little hamlet'; and it was supposed that he had aroused some extreme passions of local patriotism and eventually been their victim. At least the local doctor testified that the skull had suffered a crushing blow. . . .

A year or two afterwards the question was re-opened . . . which led a certain Dr Mulborough, called by his intimates Mulberry in apt allusion to something rich and fruity about his dark rotundity and rather empurpled visage, travelling by train down to Potter's Pond, with a friend whom he had often consulted upon problems of the kind . . .

He had a shrewd eye and was really a man of very remarkable sense; which he considered that he showed in consulting a little priest named Brown . . .

The little priest was sitting opposite to him, with the air of a patient baby absorbing instruction; and the doctor was explaining at length the real reasons for the journey. 'I cannot agree with the gentleman in the magenta coat that Potter's Pond is only a wretched little hamlet. But it is certainly a very remote and secluded village; so that it seems quite outlandish, like a village of a hundred years ago. The spinsters are really spinsters – damn it, you could almost imagine you saw them spin. The ladies are not just ladies. They are gentlewomen; and their chemist is not a chemist, but an apothecary; pronounced potecary. They do just admit the existence of an ordinary doctor like myself to assist the apothecary. But I am considered rather a juvenile innovation, because I am only fifty-seven years old and have only been in the county for twenty-eight years. The solicitor looks as if he had known it for twenty-eight thousand years. Then there is the old Admiral, who is just like a Dickens illustration; with a house full of cutlasses and cuttle-fish and equipped with a telescope.'*

HOW INTERESTING IT is, Lord, that what one person regards as perfectly normal, another might consider eccentric; a style of dressing, maybe, or even of furnishing one's house. Each to their own! Please teach me that just because things aren't necessarily as I would like them, and don't reflect my preferences, they are not by any means invalid, or of lesser worth. Furthermore, educate my heart in the value and beauty of diversity, I pray.

* *The Vampire of the Village.*

25 JANUARY

Ye shall be unto me a kingdom of priests (Exodus 19:6 *KJV*)

'And then, of course [said the doctor], there is the proper sort of clergyman; Tory and High Church in a dusty fashion dating from Archbishop Laud; more of an old woman than any of the old women.

He's a white-haired studious old bird, more easily shocked than the spinsters. Indeed, the gentlewomen, though Puritan in their principles, are sometimes pretty plain in their speech; as the real Puritans were. Once or twice I have known old Miss Carstairs-Carew use expressions as lively as anything in the Bible. The dear old clergyman is assiduous in reading the Bible; but I almost fancy he shuts his eyes when he comes to those words.

Well, you know I'm not particularly modern. I don't enjoy this jazzing and joy-riding of the Bright Young Things -'

'The Bright Young Things don't enjoy it,' said Father Brown. 'That is the real tragedy.'*

REMIND ME, LORD, to support my minister(s). I sometimes think they must have the most thankless calling imaginable, yet, also, one that is loaded with privileges. May I only ever be a blessing, and never a thorn in the side. I pray for those considering the vocation of priesthood, or ordained ministry in any other guise. Guide their thinking and lead them in their decision-making.

* *The Vampire of the Village.*

26 JANUARY

You should mind your own business (1 Thessalonians 4:11 *NIV*)

'I've come about that business of the MacNabs. I have heard, you often help people out of such troubles. Pray excuse me if I am wrong' . . .

'I hardly understand you,' replied the scientist, with a cold intensity of manner. 'I fear you have mistaken the chambers. I am Dr Hood, and my work is almost entirely literary and educational. It is true that I have sometimes been consulted by the police in cases of peculiar difficulty and importance, but –' 'Oh, this is of the greatest importance,' broke in the little man called Brown. 'Why, her mother won't let them get engaged.' And he leaned back in his chair in radiant rationality. The brows of Dr Hood were drawn down darkly, but the eyes under them were bright with something that might be anger or might be amusement. 'And still,' he said, 'I do not quite understand.' 'You see, they want to get married,' said the man with the clerical hat. 'Maggie MacNab and young Todhunter want to get married. Now, what can be more important than that?'

The great Orion Hood's scientific triumphs had deprived him of many things--some said of his health, others of his God; but they had not wholly despoiled him of his sense of the absurd. At the last plea of the ingenuous priest a chuckle broke out of him from inside, and he threw himself into an arm-chair in an ironical attitude of the consulting physician. 'Mr Brown,' he said gravely, 'it is quite fourteen and a half years since I was personally asked to test a personal problem: then it was the case of an attempt to poison the French President at a Lord Mayor's Banquet. It is now, I understand, a question of whether some friend of yours called Maggie is a suitable fiancée for some friend of hers called Todhunter. Well, Mr Brown, I am a sportsman. I will take it on. I will give the MacNab family my best advice, as good as I gave the French Republic and the King of England – no, better: fourteen years better. I have nothing else to do this afternoon. Tell me your story' . . .

'There is a very honest but rather sharp-tempered member of my flock, a widow called MacNab. She has one daughter, and she lets lodgings, and between her and the daughter, and between her and the lodgers – well, I dare say there is a great deal to be said on both sides. At present she has only one lodger, the young man called Todhunter; but he has given more trouble than all the rest, for he wants to marry the young woman of the house.' 'And the young woman of the house,' asked Dr Hood, with huge and silent amusement, 'what does she want?' 'Why, she wants to marry him,' cried Father Brown, sitting up eagerly. 'That is just the awful complication.' 'It is indeed a hideous enigma,' said Dr Hood.*

OH LORD, FROM well-meaning busybodies, preserve us. From the temptation to pry and poke our noses in to other people's business, deliver us.

* *The Absence of Mr Glass.*

27 JANUARY

Without wood a fire goes out; without a gossip a quarrel dies down (Proverbs 26:20 *NIV*)

'This young James Todhunter,' continued the cleric, 'is a very decent man so far as I know; but then nobody knows very much. He is a bright, brownish little fellow, agile like a monkey, clean-shaven like an actor, and obliging like a born courtier. He seems to have quite a pocketful of money, but nobody knows what his trade is. Mrs MacNab, therefore (being of a pessimistic turn), is quite sure it is something dreadful, and probably connected with dynamite. The dynamite must be of a shy and noiseless sort, for the poor fellow only shuts himself up for several hours of the day and studies something behind a locked door. He declares his privacy is temporary and justified, and promises to explain all before the wedding. That is all anyone knows for certain, but Mrs MacNab will tell you a great deal more than even she is certain of. You know how the tales grow like grass on such a patch of ignorance as that.'*

PRESERVE ME, LORD, from the Mrs MacNabs of this world. Keep me from being one.

* *The Absence of Mr. Glass.*

28 JANUARY

Search me, O God, and know my heart: try me, and know my thoughts (Psalm 139:23 *KJV*)

There was something hardly human about the colonel's wolfish pursuit of pleasure, and his chronic resolution not to go home till morning had a touch of the hideous clarity of insomnia.

He was a tall, fine animal, elderly, but with hair startlingly yellow. He would have looked merely blond and leonine, but his eyes were sunk so deep in his face that they looked black. They were a little too close together. He had very long yellow moustaches: on each side of them a fold or furrow from nostril to jaw, so that a sneer seemed to cut into his face. Over his evening clothes he wore a curious pale yellow coat that looked more like a very light dressing gown than an overcoat, and on the back of his head was stuck an extraordinary broad-brimmed hat of a bright green colour, evidently some oriental curiosity caught up at random. He was proud of appearing in such incongruous attires – proud of the fact that he always made them look congruous.

His brother the curate had also the yellow hair and the elegance, but he was buttoned up to the chin in black, and his face was clean-shaven, cultivated and a little nervous. He seemed to live for nothing but his religion; but there were some who said (notably the blacksmith, who was a Presbyterian) that it was a love of Gothic architecture rather than of God, and that his haunting of the church like a ghost was only another and purer turn of the almost morbid thirst for beauty which had sent his brother raging after women and wine.*

EXAMINE MY MOTIVES, Lord, with the searchlight of your Spirit. Enable me to see, or to realise, not only what I do, but why I do it. Sweep away any dubious motivation, perhaps especially if it masquerades as something holy or righteous. Create in me a heart that can withstand scrutiny; one that need not fear speculation.

* *The Hammer of God.*

29 JANUARY

When I consider your heavens, the work of your fingers, the moon and the stars, which you have set in place, what is mankind that you are mindful of them, human beings that you care for them? (Psalm 8:3, 4 *NIV*)

Father Brown was speaking:

'Reason and justice grip the remotest and the loneliest star. Look at those stars. Don't they look as if they were single diamonds and sapphires?

Well, you can imagine any mad botany or geology you please. Think of forests of adamant with leaves of brilliants. Think the moon is a blue moon, a single elephantine sapphire.

But don't fancy that all that frantic astronomy would make that smallest difference to the reason and justice of conduct. On plains of opal, under cliffs cut out of pearl, you would still find a notice-board, "Thou shalt not steal." ' . . .

When at last [Valentin] did speak, he said simply, his head bowed and his hands on his knees:

'Well, I still think that other worlds may perhaps rise higher than our reason. The mystery of heaven is unfathomable, and I for one can only bow my head.'*

SOMETIMES, ALMIGHTY GOD, bowing in your presence is all I can do. This is one of those times, as my heart silently echoes the words of the psalmist.

* *The Blue Cross.*

30 JANUARY

Speaking the truth in love (Ephesians 4:15 *NIV*)

[Father Brown said], 'I want you to give [the jewels] back, Flambeau, and I want you to give up this life. There is still youth and honour and humour in you; don't fancy they will last in that trade. Men may keep a sort of level of good, but no man has ever been able to keep on one level of evil. That road goes down and down.

The kind man drinks and turns cruel; the frank man kills and lies about it. Many a man I've known started like you to be an honest outlaw, a merry robber of the rich, and ended stamped with slime . . .

I know the woods look very free behind you, Flambeau; I know that in a flash you could melt into them like a monkey. But some day you will be an old grey monkey, Flambeau. You will sit up in your free forest cold at heart and close to death, and the tree-tops will be very bare . . .

Your downward steps have begun. You used to boast of doing nothing mean, but you are doing something mean.'*

THE GIFT OF seeing the good in others, Heavenly Father, when some might only notice the bad – cultivate that in me, I pray. The gift of speaking words dripping with mercy, when sometimes the overriding crescendo of opinion is in favour of retribution – cultivate that too. The gift of holy courage – grant me that one, Lord.

* *The Flying Stars.*

31 JANUARY

Jesus answered, 'I am the way and the truth and the life' (John 14:6 *NIV*)

They had come up on the grassy scalp of the hill, one of the few bald spots that stood clear of the crashing and roaring pine forest.

A mean enclosure, partly timber and partly wire, rattled in the tempest to tell them the border of the graveyard. But by the time Inspector Craven had come to the corner of the grave, and Flambeau had pointed his spade downwards and leaned on it, they were both almost as shaken as the shaky wood and wire.

At the foot of the grave grew tall thistles, grey and silver in their decay. Once or twice, when a ball of thistledown broke under the breeze and flew past him, Craven jumped slightly as if it had been an arrow.

Flambeau drove the blade of his spade through the whistling grass into the wet clay below. Then he seemed to stop and lean on it as on a staff.

'Go on,' said the priest very gently. 'We are only trying to find the truth. What are you afraid of?'

'I am afraid of finding it,' said Flambeau.*

LORD, WE HUMAN beings are curious creatures; sometimes, for some peculiar reason, preferring lies to truth. Given that you are the personification of truth, Lord Jesus, that seems a strange predisposition, yet it is ours. I pray today for anyone known to me who is, like Flambeau, afraid of finding truth. Look with pity and not with blame, Lord, and hear my prayers for them. Melt such fears.

* *The Honour of Israel Gow.*

1 FEBRUARY

Above all, keep loving one another earnestly, since love covers a multitude of sins (1 Peter 4:8 *ESV*)

'There are tales of two voices heard talking in the room; though, when the door is opened, Todhunter is always found alone. There are tales of a mysterious tall man in a silk hat, who once came out of the sea mists and apparently out of the sea, stepping softly across the sandy fields and through the small back garden at twilight, till he was heard talking to the lodger at his open window. The colloquy seemed to end in a quarrel. Todhunter dashed down his window with violence, and the man in the high hat melted into the sea-fog again. The story is told by the family with the fiercest mystification; but I really think Mrs MacNab prefers her own original tale: that the other man (or whatever it is) crawls out every night from the big box in the corner, which is kept locked all day. You see, therefore, how this sealed door of Todhunter's is treated as the gate of all the fancies and monstrosities of the "Thousand and One Nights." And yet there is this little fellow in his respectable black jacket, as punctual and innocent as a parlour clock. He pays his rent to the tick; he is practically a teetotaller; he is tirelessly kind with the younger children, and can keep them amused for a day on end; and, last and most urgent of all, he has made himself equally popular with the eldest daughter, who is ready to go to church with him to-morrow.'*

GRACIOUS GOD, IF ever I am listing the characteristics of my friends, then help that list to be biased in favour of kindness. May I learn to be generous in my compliments; not in some artificial way, but simply in a way that prioritises positives long before it notices negatives.

* *The Absence of Mr Glass.*

2 FEBRUARY

We must quickly carry out the tasks assigned us by the one who sent us. The night is coming, and then no one can work (John 9:4 *NLT*)

Before [Dr Hood] could conclude his sentence, another more impatient summons sounded from without; someone with swishing skirts was marshalled hurriedly down the corridor, and the door opened on a young girl, decently dressed but disordered and red-hot with haste. She had sea-blown blonde hair, and would have been entirely beautiful if her cheek-bones had not been, in the Scotch manner, a little high in relief as well as in colour. Her apology was almost as abrupt as a command. 'I'm sorry to interrupt you, sir,' she said, 'but I had to follow Father Brown at once; it's nothing less than life or death.'

Father Brown began to get to his feet in some disorder. 'What, what has happened, Maggie?' he said. 'James [Todhunter] has been murdered, for all I can make out,' answered the girl, still breathing hard from her rush. 'That man Glass has been with him again; I heard them talking through the door quite plain. Two separate voices: for James speaks low, with a burr, and the other voice was high and quavery.' 'That man Glass?' repeated the priest in some perplexity. 'I know his name is Glass,' answered the girl, in great impatience. 'I heard it through the door. They were quarrelling – about money, I think – for I heard James say again and again, 'That's right, Mr Glass,' or 'No, Mr Glass,' and then 'Two or three, Mr Glass.' But we're talking too much; you must come at once, and there may be time yet.'*

HEAVENLY FATHER, DO we (I) talk too much, where there is work to be done? Forgive us (me) if that if the case; any number of church committees, endless planning meetings, etc. Push your people, Lord, towards a bit more action and a little less procrastination, while the light lingers.

* *The Absence of Mr Glass.*

3 FEBRUARY

Amend your ways and your deeds and obey the voice of the Lord your God; and the Lord will change His mind about the misfortune which He has pronounced against you (Jeremiah 26:13 *NASB*)

'But time for what?' asked Dr Hood, who had been studying the young lady with marked interest. What is there about Mr Glass and his money troubles that should impel such urgency?' 'I tried to break down the door and couldn't,' answered the girl shortly. 'Then I ran round to the back-yard, and managed to climb on to the window-sill that looks into the room. It was all dim, and seemed to be empty, but I swear I saw James lying huddled up in a corner, as if he were drugged or strangled.'

'This is very serious,' said Father Brown, gathering his errant hat and umbrella and standing up; 'in point of fact I was just putting your case before this gentleman, and his view – '

'Has been largely altered,' said the scientist gravely, 'I do not think this young lady is so Celtic as I had supposed. As I have nothing else to do, I will put on my hat and stroll down the town with you. In a few minutes all three were approaching the dreary tail of the MacNabs' street: the girl with the stern and breathless stride of the mountaineer, the criminologist with a lounging grace (which was not without a certain leopard-like swiftness), and the priest at an energetic trot entirely devoid of distinction.*

LORD, GRANT ME sufficient humility and grace to change my mind – publicly, if necessary – if and when I come to realise I am mistaken. Help me to be willing to amend my views if it appears I am in the wrong, rather than stick rigidly to an idea that is patently incorrect.

* *The Absence of Mr Glass.*

4 FEBRUARY

Truly I tell you, if you have faith as small as a mustard seed, you can say to this mountain, 'Move from here to there,' and it will move. Nothing will be impossible for you (Matthew 17:20 *NIV*)

Father Brown, touching other people, was as sensitive as a barometer; but today he seemed about as sensitive as a rhinoceros. By no social law, rigid or implied, could he be supposed to linger round the lunch . . . but he lingered, covering his position with torrents of amusing but quite needless conversation. He was the more puzzling because he did not seem to want any lunch. As one after another of the most exquisitely balanced kedgerees of curries, accompanied with their appropriate vintages, were laid before the other two, he only repeated that it was one of his fast-days, and munched a piece of bread and sipped and then left untasted a tumbler of cold water. His talk, however, was exuberant. 'I'll tell you what I'll do for you,' he cried; 'I'll mix you a salad! I can't eat it, but I'll mix it like an angel! You've got a lettuce there' . . . .

And to the amazement of the two men he took a pepper-pot out of his waistcoat pocket and put it on the table . . .

'You're an astounding card,' [Colonel Cray] said, staring. 'I shall come and hear your sermons if they're as amusing as your manners.' His voice changed a little, and he leaned back in his chair. 'Oh, there are sermons in a cruet-stand, too,' said Father Brown, quite cravenly. 'Have you heard of faith like a grain of mustard-seed; or charity that anoints with oil?'*

LORD JESUS, YOU so often taught by way of telling stories; imparting deep truths with everyday illustrations. How clearly – and how keenly! – you shared Kingdom insights using ordinary objects. Maybe, Lord, we have confused the issue at times? If so, we ask your forgiveness. Keep me alert, I pray, to appropriate opportunities for witnessing well. Likewise, keep the Church's message clear, and at least as attractive as Colonel Cray found Father Brown's company.

* *The Salad of Colonel Cray.*

5 FEBRUARY

I am certain that God, who began the good work within you, will continue his work until it is finally finished on the day when Christ Jesus returns (Philippians 1:6 *NIV*)

Both by calling and conviction Father Brown knew better than most of us, that every man is dignified when he is dead. But even he felt a pang of incongruity when he was knocked up at daybreak and told that Sir Aaron Armstrong had been murdered. There was something absurd and unseemly about secret violence in connection with so entirely entertaining and popular a figure.

For Sir Aaron Armstrong was entertaining to the point of being comic; and popular in such a manner as to be almost legendary. It was like hearing that Sunny Jim had hanged himself; or that Mr Pickwick had died in Hanwell. For though Sir Aaron was a philanthropist, and thus dealt with the darker side of our society, he prided himself on dealing with it in the brightest possible style. His political and social speeches were cataracts of anecdotes and 'loud laughter'; his bodily health was of a bursting sort; his ethics were all optimism; and he dealt with the Drink problem (his favourite topic) with that immortal or even monotonous gaiety which is so often a mark of the prosperous total abstainer.

The established story of his conversion was familiar on the more puritanic platforms and pulpits, how he had been, when only a boy, drawn away from Scotch theology to Scotch whisky, and how he had risen out of both and become (as he modestly put it) what he was. Yet his wide white beard, cherubic face, and sparkling spectacles, at the numberless dinners and congresses where they appeared, made it hard to believe, somehow, that he had ever been anything so morbid as either a dram-drinker or a Calvinist. He was, one felt, the most seriously merry of all the sons of men.*

* *The Three Tools of Death.*

GOD OF MY conversion, help me always to resist the strange temptation to exaggerate or embellish my personal testimony. Rather, let me be gratefully and humbly content with the work of grace you have done in my life; a work you have promised to continue. I may not have a dramatic story to tell, but, nevertheless, I have one plea, that Jesus died for me, and that is all-sufficient.

6 FEBRUARY

Do everything without grumbling or arguing, so that you may become blameless and pure, 'children of God without fault in a warped and crooked generation.' Then you will shine among them like stars in the sky (Philippians 2:14, 15 *NIV*)

'If you've got ten minutes, I wish you'd follow that man with the false nose.' Flambeau looked up in surprise; but the girl with the red hair also looked up, and with something that was stronger than astonishment. She was simply and even loosely dressed in light brown sacking stuff; but she was a lady, and even, on a second glance, a rather needlessly haughty one. 'The man with the false nose!' repeated Flambeau. 'Who's he?' 'I haven't a notion,' answered Father Brown. 'I want you to find out; I ask it as a favour. He went down there' – and he jerked his thumb over his shoulder in one of his undistinguished gestures – 'and can't have passed three lamp-posts yet. I only want to know the direction.'

Flambeau gazed at his friend for some time, with an expression between perplexity and amusement; and then, rising from the table; squeezed his huge form out of the little door of the dwarf tavern, and melted into the twilight. Father Brown took a small book out of his pocket and began to read steadily; he betrayed no consciousness of the fact that the red-haired lady had left her own table and sat down opposite him. At last she leaned over and said in a low, strong voice: 'Why do you say that? How do you know it's false?' . . .

She looked back at him for some time with a heated face, in which there hung a red shadow of anger; then, despite her anxieties, humour broke out of her eyes and the corners of her mouth . . . After a pause she added: 'I had the honour to ask you why you thought the man's nose was false.'

'The wax always spots like that just a little in this weather,' answered Father Brown with entire simplicity. 'But it's such a crooked nose,' remonstrated the red-haired girl. The priest smiled in his turn. 'I don't say it's the sort of nose one would wear out of mere foppery,' he admitted. 'This man, I think, wears it because his real nose is so much nicer.' 'But why?' she insisted. 'What is the nursery-rhyme?' observed Brown absent-mindedly. 'There was a crooked man and he went a crooked mile. That man, I fancy, has gone a very crooked road – by following his nose.'*

AN AMUSING LITTLE conversation, Lord, but it leads me to pray for your help in living as a Christian in what remains a 'crooked generation' – however that crookedness actually manifests itself; deception, pretence, fraud, dishonesty, and so on. Grant me daily strength to live a life pleasing to you. I am weak, but you are strong.

* *The Head of Caesar.*

7 FEBRUARY

A champion named Goliath, who was from Gath, came out of the Philistine camp. His height was six cubits and a span. He had a bronze helmet on his head and wore a coat of scale armour of bronze weighing five thousand shekels; on his legs he wore bronze greaves, and a bronze javelin was slung on his back. His spear shaft was like a weaver's rod, and its iron point weighed six hundred shekels. His shield bearer went ahead of him (1 Samuel 17:4-7 *NIV*)

There was one thing which Flambeau, with all his dexterity of disguise, could not cover, and that was his singular height. If Valentin's quick eye had caught a tall apple-woman, a tall grenadier, or even a tolerably tall duchess, he might have arrested them on the spot. But all along the train there was nobody that could be a disguised Flambeau, any more than a cat could be a disguised giraffe.*

GOD OF MY protection, there is no disguising the fact that in this world, I will encounter giants from time to time. They might well be real – intimidating circumstances that loom above me, for example, and which threaten my peace of mind – or they might sometimes be figments of my imagination; imaginary threats that have little basis in reality. Help me, I pray, to differentiate one from the other, and to remember to call upon you if and when life itself threatens to engulf me.

* *The Blue Cross.*

8 FEBRUARY

They said to him, 'We have come down to bind you so that we may give you into the hands of the Philistines' (Judges 15:12 *NASB*)

[The doctor and the priest] passed through the narrow passage in the front of the house until they came to the lodger's door at the back, and there Dr Hood, with the trick of an old detective, put his shoulder sharply to the panel and burst in the door.

It opened on a scene of silent catastrophe. No one seeing it, even for a flash, could doubt that the room had been the theatre of some thrilling collision between two, or perhaps more, persons. Play-cards lay littered across the table or fluttered about the floor as if a game had been interrupted. Two wine glasses stood ready for wine on a side-table, but a third lay smashed in a star of crystal upon the carpet. A few feet from it lay what looked like a long knife or short sword, straight, but with an ornamental and pictured handle; its dull blade just caught a grey glint from the dreary window behind, and which showed the black trees against the leaden level of the sea.

Towards the opposite corner of the room was rolled a gentleman's silk top, as if it had just been knocked off his head; so much so, indeed, that one almost looked to see it still rolling. And in the corner behind it, thrown like a sack of potatoes, but corded like a railway trunk, lay Mr James Todhunter, with a scarf across his mouth, and six or seven ropes knotted round his elbows and ankles. His brown eyes were alive and shifted alertly.*

LOVING GOD, MY thoughts and prayers turn towards those who are held captive in one way or another. I don't necessarily mean captive to sin, but prisoners of war, for example, or victims of human trafficking, or slaves imprisoned against their will; those who are at the mercy of their captors, day in and day out. Bless those agencies and forces who work on their behalf, searching them out and campaigning for their release. Help their efforts on behalf of the helpless.

* *The Absence of Mr Glass.*

9 FEBRUARY

Elisha went up to Bethel. As he was walking along the road, some boys came out of the town and jeered at him. 'Get out of here, baldy!' they said. 'Get out of here, baldy!' (2 Kings 2:23 *NIV*)

'Mr Glass's hat,' said the doctor, returning with it and peering into the inside with a pocket lens. 'How to explain the absence of Mr Glass and the presence of Mr Glass's hat? For Mr Glass is not a careless man with his clothes. This hat is of a stylish shape and systematically brushed and burnished, though not very new. An old dandy, I should think.'

'But, good heavens!' called out Miss MacNab, 'aren't you going to untie the man first?'

'I say "old" with intention, though not with certainty,' continued the expositor; 'my reason for it might seem a little far-fetched. The hair of human beings falls out in varying degrees, but almost always falls out slightly, and with the lens I should see the tiny hairs in a hat recently worn. It has none, which leads me to guess that Mr Glass is bald. Now when this is taken with the high-pitched and querulous voice which Miss MacNab described so vividly . . . when we take the hairless head together with the tone common in senile anger, I should think we may deduce some advance in years. Nevertheless, he was probably vigorous, and he was almost certainly tall. I might rely in some degree on the story of his previous appearance at the window, as a tall man in a silk hat, but I think I have more exact indication. This wine-glass has been smashed all over the place, but one of its splinters lies on the high bracket beside the mantelpiece. No such fragment could have fallen there if the vessel had been smashed in the hand of a comparatively short man like Mr Todhunter.'

'By the way,' said Father Brown, 'might it not be well to untie Mr Todhunter?'*

* *The Absence of Mr Glass.*

DISTINCTIVE PHYSICAL CHARACTERISTICS, Creator God! I think of people who are desperately unhappy with their body image, Lord. Perhaps they don't like being bald, or they are unhappy about their weight, or they really dislike their appearance for one reason or other. Maybe they are ridiculed for the way they look. I pray for those whose self-image is so poor, and whose self-esteem is correspondingly low, that they entertain thoughts of self-harm or even suicide. In your mercy, Holy Spirit, come to them as Counsellor.

10 FEBRUARY

These who have turned the world upside down (Acts 17:6 NKJV)

As [Valentin] was walking in the streets and squares beyond Victoria, he paused suddenly and stood. It was a quaint, quiet square, very typical of London, full of accidental stillness. The tall, flat houses round looked at once prosperous and uninhabited; the square of shrubbery in the centre looked as deserted as a green Pacific inlet.

One of the four sides was much higher than the rest, like a daïs; and the line of this side was broken by one of London's admirable accidents – a restaurant that looked as if it had strayed from Soho. It was an unreasonably attractive object, with dwarf plants in pots and long, striped blinds of yellow and white. It stood specially high above the street, and in the usual patchwork way of London, a flight of steps from the street ran up to meet the front door almost as a fire-escape might run up to a first-floor window. Valentin stood and smoked in front of the yellow-white blinds and considered them long . . .

He was a thinking man, and a plain man at the same time. All his wonderful successes, that looked like conjuring, had been gained by plodding logic, by clear and commonplace French thought. The French electrify the world not by starting any paradox, they electrify it by carrying out a truism.*

LORD JESUS, IF I am to play any part at all in turning this world upside down, or electrifying it for the gospel's sake, then perhaps my best option is to:

a) Carefully consider my immediate surroundings and circumstances, thinking them through, and

b) To serve and witness with sanctified plodding logic.

Help me on both fronts, I pray.

* *The Blue Cross.*

11 FEBRUARY

If you have been merciful, God will be merciful when he judges you (James 2:13 *NLT*)

Their host [Valentin] had telephoned that he was detained for ten minutes. He was, in truth, making some last arrangements about executions and such ugly things; and though these duties were rootedly repulsive to him, he always performed them with precision. Ruthless in the pursuit of criminals, he was very mild about their punishment.

Since he had been supreme over French – and largely over European – police methods, his great influence had been honourably used for the mitigation of sentences and the purification of prisons. He was one of the great humanitarian French freethinkers.*

HEAVENLY FATHER, I may not be involved in decisions of life and death, and I may not be supreme over anything in particular, but I pray, nonetheless, that my influence will be one that is honourable; that my thinking and the performance of my duties may be hallmarked by merciful humanitarianism. So help me, God.

* *The Secret Garden.*

12 FEBRUARY

What a blessing it will be to attend a banquet in the Kingdom of God! (Luke 14:15 *NLT*)

[Valentin] saw all the other pillars of the little party: he saw Lord Galloway, the English Ambassador – a choleric old man with a russet face like an apple, wearing the blue ribbon of the Garter. He saw Lady Galloway, slim and thread-like, with silver hair and a face sensitive and superior. He saw her daughter, Lady Margaret Graham, a pale and pretty girl with an elfish face and copper-coloured hair. He saw the Duchess of Mont St Michel, black-eyed and opulent, and with her two daughters, black-eyed and opulent also. He saw Dr Simon, a typical French scientist, with glasses, a pointed brown beard, and a forehead barred with those parallel wrinkles which are the penalty of superciliousness, since they come through constantly elevating the eyebrows. He saw Father Brown of Cobhole, in Essex, whom he had recently met in England. He saw – perhaps with more interest than any of those – a tall man in uniform, who had bowed to the Galloways without receiving any very hearty acknowledgement, and who now advanced alone to pay his respects to his hosts. This was Commandant O'Brien, of the French Foreign Legion.*

THAT'S QUITE SOME guest list there, Lord! How I thank you, therefore, that I am on standing invitation to your banquet. What tremendous grace that invitation represents. How wonderful it is, Lord Jesus, that you warmly invite all and sundry to share in your heavenly feast. What an honour! Let me savour that thought today, in grateful anticipation of all that is yet to come.

* *The Secret Garden.*

13 FEBRUARY

Welcome one another as Christ has welcomed you (Romans 15:7 *ESV*)

The Vernon Hotel, at which The Twelve True Fishermen held their annual dinners, was an institution such as can only exist in an oligarchical society which has almost gone mad on good manners. It was that topsy-turvy product – an 'exclusive' commercial enterprise. That is, it was a thing which paid, not by attracting people, but actually by turning people away.

In the heart of a plutocracy tradesmen become cunning enough to be more fastidious than their customers. They positively create difficulties so that their wealthy and weary clients may spend money and diplomacy in overcoming them. If there were a fashionable hotel in London which no man could enter who was under six foot, society would meekly make up parties of six-foot men to dine in it. If there were an expensive restaurant which by a mere caprice of its proprietor was only open on Thursday afternoon, it would be crowded on Thursday afternoon.*

THIS REMINDS ME, Lord, that yours is an inclusive and welcoming Kingdom. For sure, there are Terms & Conditions, but they are all entirely predicated upon lavish grace and mercy. Help me, therefore, to reflect such inclusivity in my behaviour. Help my church to do the same, especially in the light of today's Bible text. Teach me your ways of love and acceptance.

* *The Queer Feet.*

14 FEBRUARY

The other disciples followed in the boat, towing the net full of fish, for they were not far from shore, about a hundred yards. When they landed, they saw a fire of burning coals there with fish on it, and some bread. Jesus said to them, 'Bring some of the fish you have just caught.' So Simon Peter climbed back into the boat and dragged the net ashore. It was full of large fish, 153, but even with so many the net was not torn. Jesus said to them, 'Come and have breakfast.' None of the disciples dared ask him, 'Who are you?' They knew it was the Lord. Jesus came, took the bread and gave it to them, and did the same with the fish (John 21:8-13 *NIV*)

The club of The Twelve True Fishermen would not have consented to dine anywhere but in such a place, for it insisted on luxurious privacy; and would have been quite upset by the mere thought that any other club was even dining in the same building.

On the occasion of their annual dinner the Fishermen were in the habit of exposing all their treasures, as if they were in a private house, especially the celebrated set of fish knives and forks which were, as it were, the insignia of the society, each being exquisitely wrought in silver in the form of a fish, and each loaded at the hilt with one large pearl. They were always laid out for the fish course, and the fish course was always the most magnificent in that magnificent repast.

The society had a vast number of ceremonies and observances, but it had no history and no object; that was where it was so very aristocratic. You did not have to be anything in order to be one of the Twelve Fishers; unless you were already a certain sort of person, you never even heard of them. It had been in existence twelve years. Its president was Mr Audley. Its vice-president was the Duke of Chester.*

* *The Queer Feet.*

WHAT AN IMMENSE privilege it is, Lord Jesus, to belong to a group whose president is God incarnate! What a privilege it is, Lord Jesus, to have been so graciously welcomed into a group whose membership is by no means limited to twelve. What a privilege it is, Lord Jesus, to have been warmly invited into a group not organised around luxurious privacy, but humility, grace and sacrificial love. What a privilege it is, Lord Jesus, that you are only too willing to consent to dine with the likes of me – a fish supper on the beach, if necessary!

15 FEBRUARY

Like one from whom people hide their faces he was despised, and we held him in low esteem (Isaiah 53:3 *NIV*)

One of the waiters [at the Vernon Hotel], an Italian, had been struck down with a paralytic stroke . . .

His Jewish employer, marvelling mildly at such superstitions, had consented to send for the nearest Popish priest. With what the waiter confessed to Father Brown we are not concerned, for the excellent reason that the cleric kept it to himself; but apparently it involved him in writing out a note or statement for the conveying of some message or the righting of some wrong.

Father Brown, therefore, with a meek impudence which he would have shown equally in Buckingham Palace, asked to be provided with a room and writing materials. Mr Lever was torn in two. He was a kind man, and had also that bad imitation of kindness, the dislike of any difficulty or scene. At the same time the presence of one unusual stranger in his hotel that evening was like a speck of dirt on something just cleaned. There was never any borderland or ante-room in the Vernon Hotel, no people waiting in the hall, no customers coming in on chance. There were fifteen waiters. There were twelve guests. It would be as startling to find a new guest in the hotel that night as to find a new brother taking breakfast or tea in one's own family.

Moreover, the priest's appearance was second-rate and his clothes muddy; a mere glimpse of him afar off might precipitate a crisis in the club.*

LORD JESUS, WE esteemed you not. You know all about being unwanted and treated as little more than a speck of dirt, when all you came to do was love and give and bless and help. Forgive us, Lord. Help us henceforth always to regard you as the beloved guest of the soul.

* *The Queer Feet.*

16 FEBRUARY

When the woman saw that the tree was good for food, and that it was pleasant to the eyes, and a tree to be desired to make one wise, she took of the fruit thereof, and did eat, and gave also unto her husband with her; and he did eat (Genesis 3:6 *KJV*)

'The most beautiful crime I ever committed,' Flambeau would say in his highly moral old age, 'was also, by a singular coincidence, my last. It was committed at Christmas. As an artist I had always attempted to provide crimes suitable to the special season or landscapes in which I found myself, choosing this or that terrace or garden for a catastrophe, as if for a statuary group. Thus squires should be swindled in long rooms panelled with oak . . . Thus, in England, if I wished to relieve a dean of his riches (which is not so easy as you might suppose), I wish to frame him, if I make myself clear, in the green lawns and grey towers of some cathedral town. Similarly, in France, when I had got money out of a rich and wicked peasant (which is almost impossible), it gratified me to get his indignant head relieved against a grey line of clipped poplars . . .'

'Well, my last crime was a Christmas crime, a cheery, cosy, English middle-class crime; a crime of Charles Dickens. I did it in a good old middle-class house near Putney, a house with a crescent of carriage drive, a house with a stable by the side of it, a house with the name on the two outer gates, a house with a monkey tree. Enough, you know the species. I really think my imitation of Dickens's style was dexterous and literary. It seems almost a pity I repented the same evening.'*

LORD, IF I MAY be perfectly candid with you, I cannot deny the allure of sin. Descriptions of wrongdoing like this one, for example, resonate with excitement and daring – humour, even. Such is the shining nature of temptation! Grant me, therefore, a heart that knows the difference between right and wrong, however attractive sinful options might seem. I pray too for those who today find themselves tempted. Draw alongside us all in our weaker moments.

* *The Flying Stars.*

17 FEBRUARY

Do not hastily bring into court (Proverbs 25:8 *ESV*)

'We have thus something like a picture of the man, or at least of the type: tall, elderly, fashionable, but somewhat frayed, certainly fond of play and strong waters, and perhaps rather too fond of them. Mr Glass is a gentleman not unknown on the fringes of society.'

'Look here,' cried the young woman, 'if you don't let me pass to untie him I'll run outside and scream for the police.' 'If should not advise *you*, Miss MacNab,' said Dr Hood gravely, 'to be in any hurry to fetch the police. Father Brown, I seriously ask you to compose your flock, for their sakes not for mine . . .'

'The faded finery, the profligate habits, and the shrill irritation of Mr Glass are the unmistakable marks of the kind of man who blackmails' . . .

'Are you going to take those ropes off?' asked the girl stubbornly.

Dr Hood replaced the silk hat carefully on the side table, and went across to the captive. He studied him intently, even moving him a little and half-turning him round by the shoulders, but he only answered: 'No; I think these ropes will do very well until your friends the police bring the handcuffs.'*

REMIND ME, HOLY Spirit, not to jump to conclusions, but to be more like Dr Hood, even if circumstances appear to lead me in a particular direction. Grant me discernment, wisdom, charity and patience, and help me not to jump the gun in formulating an opinion. If I am not in possession of all the facts, Lord, then I am in no position to come to a conclusion – yet that is so easily done!

* *The Absence of Mr Glass.*

18 FEBRUARY

You shall not spread a false report. You shall not join hands with a wicked man to be a malicious witness (Exodus 23:1 *ESV*)

Sir Leopold Fischer was leaning against the mantelpiece and heaving with all the importance of panic.

'This is a very painful matter, Father Brown,' said [Colonel] Adams. 'The truth is, those diamonds we all saw this afternoon seem to have vanished from my friend's tail-coat pocket. And as you – '

'As I,' supplemented Father Brown, with a broad grin, was sitting just behind him – '

'Nothing of the sort shall be suggested,' said Colonel Adams, with a firm look at Fischer, which rather implied that some such thing *had* been suggested. 'I only ask you to give me the assistance that any gentleman might give.'

'Which is turning out his pockets,' said Father Brown, and proceeded to do so, displaying seven and sixpence, a return ticket, a small silver crucifix, a small breviary, and a stick of chocolate.*

LORD JESUS, YOU know all about false reports and malicious witnesses; you were their victim. My prayer today is threefold: help me always to think the best of people, not participating in gossip or rumour, and help me to live honestly and openly. Help me now, too, even as I pray, to empty my pockets, as it were, of anything that shouldn't be there, so that henceforth I needn't object to their emptying.

* *The Flying Stars.*

19 FEBRUARY

Respect those who labour among you and are over you in the Lord and admonish you . . . esteem them very highly in love because of their work (1 Thessalonians 5:12, 13 *ESV*)

'A Radical does not mean a man who lives on radishes,' remarked Crook, with some impatience; 'and a Conservative does not mean a man who preserves jam. Neither, I assure you, does a Socialist mean a man who desires a social evening with the chimney-sweep. A Socialist means a man who wants all the chimneys swept and all the chimney-sweeps paid for it.'

'But who won't allow you,' put in the priest in a low voice, 'to own your own soot.'

Crook looked at him with an eye of interest and even respect. 'Does one want to own soot?' he asked.

'One might,' answered Brown, with speculation in his eye. 'I've heard that gardeners use it. And I once made six children happy at Christmas when the conjuror didn't come, entirely with soot . . . '*

WHAT A FASCINATING example of good priesthood we have here, Lord! A cleric who quietly puts a word in for the workers and perhaps even for the downtrodden (yet does so with good humour and charm), and a man of the cloth who is at ease with entertaining children – no small quality. I pray for my minister(s) today; so often called upon to be all things to all people. Bless those who lead my church.

* *The Flying Stars.*

20 FEBRUARY

If the trumpet does not sound a clear call, who will get ready for battle? (1 Corinthians 14:8 *NIV*)

The first two courses of the dinner of The Twelve Fishermen had proceeded with placid success. I do not possess a copy of the menu; and if I did it would not convey anything to anybody. It was written in a sort of super-French employed by cooks, but quite unintelligible to Frenchmen.

There was a tradition in the club that the *hors d'oeuvres* should be various and manifold to the point of madness. They were taken seriously because they were avowedly useless extras, like the whole dinner and the whole club.*

OF WHAT USE is an unintelligible menu? By the same token, Lord, of how much use is a church whose message is conveyed in such a way that no-one outside the established 'club' can make head nor tail of it? Lead us not into Christianese jargon, Lord, and deliver us from verbiage if it is largely irrelevant. For your Kingdom's sake.

* *The Queer Feet.*

21 FEBRUARY

How good and pleasant it is when God's people live together in unity! It is like precious oil poured on the head, running down on the beard, running down on Aaron's beard, down on the collar of his robe. It is as if the dew of Hermon were falling on Mount Zion. For there the LORD bestows his blessing, even life forevermore (Psalm 133 NIV)

There was also the tradition that the soup course should be light and unpretending – a sort of simple and austere vigil for the feast of fish that was to come.

The talk was that strange, slight talk which governs the British Empire, which governs it in secret, and yet would scarcely enlighten an ordinary Englishman even if he could overhear it. Cabinet Ministers on both sides were alluded to by their Christian names with a sort of bored benignity. The Radical Chancellor of the Exchequer, whom the whole Tory party was supposed to be cursing for his extortions, was praised for his minor poetry, or his saddle in the hunting-field. The Tory leader, whom all Liberals were supposed to hate as a tyrant, was discussed and, on the whole, praised – as a Liberal. It seemed somehow that politicians were very important. And yet, anything seemed important about them except their politics.*

QUITE A PLEASANT picture here, Lord – and an amusing one too! Traditions that serve their purpose and what appears to be a cordial atmosphere of friendship and goodwill. Not without its weaknesses, but not, either, such a bad picture of what Christian fellowship might be like; seeing the best in others, that is, and rubbing along in harmony. That'll do, for starters.

* *The Queer Feet.*

22 FEBRUARY

Not that we dare to classify or compare ourselves with some of those who are commending themselves. But when they measure themselves by one another and compare themselves with one another, they are without understanding (2 Corinthians 10:12 *NIV*)

Mr Audley, the chairman, was an amiable, elderly man who still wore Gladstone collars; he was a kind of symbol of all that phantasmal and yet fixed society. He had never done anything – not even anything wrong. He was not fast; he was not even particularly rich. He was simply in the thing; and there was an end of it. No party could ignore him, and if he had wished to be in the Cabinet he certainly would have been put there. The Duke of Chester, the vice-president, was a young and rising politician. That is to say, he was a pleasant youth, with flat, fair hair and a freckled face, with moderate intelligence and enormous estates. In public his appearances were always successful and his principle was simple enough. When he thought of a joke he made it, and was called brilliant. When he could not think of a joke he said that this was no time for trifling, and was called able. In private, in a club of his own class, he was simply quite pleasantly frank and silly, like a schoolboy. Mr Audley, never having been in politics, treated them a little more seriously . . .

He had a roll of grey hair over the back of his collar like certain old-fashioned statesmen, and seen from behind he looked like the man the empire wants. Seen from the front he looked like a mild, self-indulgent bachelor, with rooms in the Albany – which he was.*

THANK YOU, GOD, for making me, me; how I am and who I am. A work in progress, that's for sure, but nevertheless, myself in Christ. Save me, I pray, from the tyranny of comparison, the thief of joy.

* *The Queer Feet.*

23 FEBRUARY

A cord of three strands is not quickly broken (Ecclesiastes 4:12 *NIV*)

[Angus] was a tall, burly, red-haired young man, with a resolute face but a listless manner . . .

He walked through the confectioner's shop into the back room, which was a sort of pastry-cook restaurant, merely raising his hat to the young lady who was serving there. She was a dark, elegant, alert girl in black, with a high colour and very quick, dark eyes; and after the ordinary interval she followed him into the inner room to take his order.

His order was evidently a usual one. 'I want, please,' he said with precision, 'one halfpenny bun and a small cup of black coffee.' An instant before the girl could turn away he added, 'Also, I want you to marry me.' The young lady of the shop stiffened suddenly, and said: 'Those are jokes I don't allow.'

The red-haired young man lifted his grey eyes of an unexpected gravity. 'Really and truly,' he said, 'it's as serious – as serious as the halfpenny bun. It is expensive, like the bun; one pays for it. It is indigestible, like the bun. It hurts.' The dark young lady had never taken her dark eyes off him, but seemed to be studying him with almost tragic exactitude. At the end of her scrutiny she had something like the shadow of a smile, and she sat down in a chair.

'Don't you think,' observed Angus, absently, 'that it's rather cruel to eat these halfpenny buns? They might grow up into penny buns. I shall give up these brutal sports when we are married.'*

HEAVENLY FATHER WHOSE name is Love, draw alongside all those today who are contemplating marriage; those who are planning to propose, whether that be over a halfpenny bun or in some other way, and those who will be on the receiving end of such requests. Grant them wisdom, even in the heat of the moment and the giddiness of the situation, as they contemplate such an

* *The Invisible Man.*

important step. Bless especially, I pray, those who long to spend the rest of their lives together, but whose circumstances are not easy; financial difficulties, for example, or parental opposition. Guide them all through. Be, as it were, the third strand in their relationship.

24 FEBRUARY

Be as shrewd as snakes and as innocent as doves (Matthew 10:16 *NIV*)

'You see' [said Father Brown], 'I suspected you when we first met. It's the little bulge up the sleeve where you people have the spiked bracelet.'

'How in Tartarus,' cried Flambeau, 'did you ever hear of the spike bracelet?'

'Oh, one's little flock, you know!' said Father Brown, arching his eyebrows rather blankly. 'When I was a curate in Hartlepool, there were three of them with spiked bracelets . . .

I'm afraid I watched you, you know.'*

LORD, TEACH ME how to be snake-like and dove-like, as the need arises; alert to evil and nobody's fool, yet gentle and harmless too. It's such an unusual combination that I can't hope to learn it without your help.

* *The Blue Cross.*

25 FEBRUARY

He had no beauty or majesty to attract us to him, nothing in his appearance that we should desire him (Isaiah 53:2 *NIV*)

Valentin was expecting, for special reasons, a man of world-wide fame, whose friendship he had secured during some of his great detective tours and triumphs in the United States. He was expecting Julius K. Brayne, that multi-millionaire whose colossal and even crushing endowments of small religions have occasioned so much easy sport and easier solemnity for the American and English papers.

Nobody could quite make out whether Mr Brayne was an atheist or a Mormon, or a Christian Scientist; but he was ready to pour money into any intellectual vessel, so long as it was an untried vessel. One of his hobbies was to wait for the American Shakespeare – a hobby more patient than angling . . .

He liked anything that he thought 'progressive.' He thought Valentin 'progressive,' thereby doing him a grave injustice.

The solid appearance of Julius K. Brayne in the room was as decisive as a dinner bell. He had this great quality, which very few of us can claim, that his presence was as big as his absence. He was a huge fellow, as fat as he was tall, clad in complete evening black, without so much relief as a watch-chain or a ring. His hair was white and well brushed back . . . his face was red, fierce and cherubic, with one dark tuft under the lower lip that threw up that otherwise infantile visage with an effect theatrical and even Mephistophelean.*

LORD JESUS, *YOU came to us as God made flesh, yet (deliberately?) without any particular beauty or striking appearance. My prayers today, Lord, are for those whose culture is entirely defined by looks and clothes and fashions and hairstyles; people for whom peer pressure in such ways is a daily burden. I think especially of teenagers who are pressurised into conforming. Teach us all your example, and help them to see that there is so much more to life than simply looking good.*

* *The Secret Garden.*

26 FEBRUARY

My thoughts are not your thoughts, neither are your ways my ways,' declares the Lord. 'As the heavens are higher than the earth, so are my ways higher than your ways and my thoughts than your thoughts' (Isaiah 55:8, 9 *NIV*)

'But the ropes?' inquired the priest, whose eyes had remained open with a rather vacant admiration. 'Ah, the ropes,' said the expert with a singular intonation. 'Miss MacNab very much wanted to know why I did not set Mr Todhunter free from his ropes. Well, I will tell her. I did not do it because Mr Todhunter can set himself free from them at any minute he chooses.' 'What?' cried the audience on quite different notes of astonishment.

'I have looked at all the knots on Mr Todhunter,' reiterated Hood quietly. 'I happen to know something about knots; they are quite a branch of criminal science. Every one of these knots he has made himself and could loosen himself; not one of them would have been made by an enemy really trying to pinion him. The whole of this affair of the ropes is a clever fake, to make us think him the victim of the struggle instead of the wretched Glass, whose corpse may be hidden in the garden or stuffed up the chimney.'*

GOD OF WISDOM, teach my heart the value of trusting you even when I think I know the answers. Teach me to leave space in my thinking for that which I may not have realised. You are the expert, and I am not!

* *The Absence of Mr Glass.*

27 FEBRUARY

'Is not this the carpenter, the son of Mary and brother of James and Joses and Judas and Simon? And are not his sisters here with us?' And they took offence at him (Mark 6:3 *ESV*)

The face of the little Catholic priest, which was commonly complacent and even comic, had suddenly become knotted with a curious frown. It was not the blank curiosity of his first innocence. It was rather that creative curiosity which comes when a man has the beginnings of an idea. 'Say it again, please,' he said in a simple, bothered manner; 'do you mean that Todhunter can tie himself up all alone and untie himself all alone?'

'That is what I mean,' said the doctor.

'Jerusalem!' ejaculated Brown suddenly; 'I wonder if it could possibly be that!'

He scuttled across the room rather like a rabbit, and peered with quite a new impulsiveness into the partially-covered face of the captive. Then he turned his own rather fatuous face to the company. 'Yes, that's it!' he cried in a certain excitement. 'Can't you see it in the man's face? Why, look at his eyes!'

Both the professor and the girl followed the direction of his glance. And though the broad black scarf completely masked the lower half of Todhunter's visage, they did grow conscious of something struggling and intense about the upper part of it. 'His eyes do look queer,' cried the young woman, strongly moved. 'You brutes; I believe it's hurting him!' 'Not that, I think,' said Dr Hood; 'the eyes have a certain singular expression. But I should interpret those transverse wrinkles as expressing rather such slight psychological abnormality – '

'Oh, bosh!' cried Father Brown; 'can't you see he's laughing?' 'Laughing!' repeated the doctor, with a start; 'but what on earth can he be laughing at?' 'Well, replied the Reverend Brown apologetically, 'not to put too fine a point on it, I think he is laughing at you. And indeed, I'm a little inclined to laugh at myself, now I know about it.' 'Now you know about what?' asked Hood, in some exasperation. 'Now I know,' replied the priest, 'the profession of Mr Todhunter.'*

* *The Absence of Mr Glass.*

HOW EASILY, LORD, we look down upon certain so-called 'lowly' professions, whilst looking up, as it were, at careers that seem, in our eyes, to carry more status. How quickly we form such judgments! Forgive us, and help us to remember that you yourself, Lord Jesus, came as a carpenter's son. Help me to see the person, long before I see the profession, and to treat all forms of honest, dignified, decent employment with due respect.

28 FEBRUARY

Daniel answered the king and said, 'No wise men, enchanters, magicians, or astrologers can show to the king the mystery that the king has asked, but there is a God in heaven who reveals mysteries' (Daniel 2:27, 28 *ESV*)

Everyone agreed that the bazaar at Mallowood Abbey (by kind permission of Lady Mounteagle) was a great success; there were roundabouts and swings and side-shows, which the people greatly enjoyed; I would also mention the Charity, which was the excellent object of the proceedings, if any of them could tell me what it was.

However, it is only with a few of them that we are here concerned; and especially with three of them, a lady and two gentlemen, who passed between two of the principal tents or pavilions, their voices high in argument. On their right was the tent of the Master of the Mountain, that world-famous fortune-teller by crystals and chiromancy; a rich purple tent, all over which were traced, in black and gold, the sprawling outlines of Adriatic gods waving any number of arms like octopods. Perhaps they symbolized the readiness of divine help to be had within; perhaps they merely implied that the ideal of being a pious palmist would have as many hands as possible. On the other side stood the plainer tent of Phroso the Phrenologist; more austerely decorated with diagrams of the heads of Socrates and Shakespeare, which were apparently of a lumpy sort. But these were presently merely in black and white, with numbers and notes, as became the rigid dignity of a purely rationalistic science. The purple tent had an opening like a black cavern, and all was fittingly silent within. But Phroso the Phrenologist . . . was standing outside his own temple, and talking, at the top of his voice, to nobody in particular, explaining that the head of any passer-by would doubtless proved, on examination, to be every bit as knobby as Shakespeare's. Indeed, the moment the lady appeared between the tents, the vigilant Phroso leapt on her and offered, with a pantomime of old-world courtesy, to feel her bumps.

She refused with civility that was rather like rudeness; but she must be excused, because she was in the middle of an argument. She also had to be excused, or at any rate was excused, because she was Lady Mounteagle.*

* *The Red Moon of Meru.*

O LORD, IN a veritable circus of spiritual options and superstitions by the dozen, my prayers today reach out to seekers after truth. When so many choices dazzle and beguile, may they find their way safely to you, the God of heaven.

1 MARCH

He who oppresses the poor taunts his Maker, but he who is gracious to the needy honours Him (Proverbs 14:31 *NASB*)

A waiter came swiftly along the room, and then stopped dead. His stoppage was as silent as his tread; but all those vague and kindly gentlemen were so used to the utter smoothness of the unseen machinery which surrounded and supported their lives, that a waiter doing anything unexpected was a start and a jar. They felt as you and I would feel if the inanimate world disobeyed – if a chair ran away from us.

The waiter stood staring a few seconds, while there deepened on every face at table a strange shame which is wholly the product of our time. It is the combination of modern humanitarianism with the horrible modern abyss between the souls of the rich and poor. A genuine historic aristocrat would have thrown things at the waiter, beginning with empty bottles, and very probably ending with money. A genuine democrat would have asked him, with a comrade-like clearness of speech, what the devil he was doing. But these modern plutocrats could not bear a poor man near to them, either as a slave or as a friend. That something had gone wrong with the servants was merely a dull, hot embarrassment. They did not want to be brutal, and they dreaded the need to be benevolent. They wanted the thing, whatever it was, to be over. It was over. The waiter, after standing for some seconds rigid, like a cataleptic, turned round and ran madly out of the room.*

HOW SHOCKING, AND how sad, this is, Lord, that the poor should be shunned. Yet, how typical of the global situation even in today's modern times. Show me what I can do to make amends, I pray, even in my small corner.

* *The Queer Feet.*

2 MARCH

Do not believe every spirit, but test the spirits to see whether they are from God, because many false prophets have gone out into the world (1 John 4:1 *NIV*)

Lady Mounteagle seemed to catch sight of somebody she wanted; a black stumpy figure standing at a booth where children were throwing hoops at hideous table ornaments. She darted across and cried:

'Father Brown, I've been looking for you. I want to ask you something. Do you believe in fortune-telling?'

The person addressed looked rather helplessly at the little hoop in his hand and said at last: 'I wonder in which sense you're using the word "believe." Of course, if it's all a fraud – '

'Oh, but the Master of the Mountain isn't a bit of a fraud,' she cried. 'He isn't a common conjurer or a fortune-teller at all. It's really a great honour for him to condescend to tell fortunes at my parties; for he's a great religious leader in his own country; a Prophet and a Seer. And even his fortune-telling isn't vulgar stuff about coming into a fortune. He tells you great spiritual truths about yourself, about your ideals.'

'Quite so,' said Father Brown. 'That's what I object to. I was just going to say that if it's all a fraud, I don't mind it so much. It can't be much more of a fraud than most things at fancy bazaars; and there, in a way, it's a sort of practical joke. But if it's a religion and reveals spiritual truths – then it's all as false as hell and I wouldn't touch it with a barge-pole.'*

STRAIGHT TALKING FROM Father Brown, *Lord! Grant me sensitivity and courage in my witnessing for Jesus; not to discourage robust dialogue, but not, either, to shy away from sharing honest convictions. Holy Spirit, guide my thinking and my talking.*

* *The Red Moon of Meru.*

3 MARCH

If you only love the lovable, do you expect a pat on the back? Run-of-the-mill sinners do that. If you only help those who help you, do you expect a medal? Garden-variety sinners do that (Luke 6:32, 33 *The Message*)

Father Brown was wandering through a picture gallery with an expression that suggested he had not come there to look at the pictures. Indeed, he did not want to look at the pictures, though he liked pictures well enough. Not that there was anything immoral or improper about those highly modern pictorial designs. He would indeed be of an inflammable temperament who was stirred to any of the more pagan passions by the display of interrupted spirals, inverted cones and broken cylinders with which the art of the future inspired or menaced mankind.

The truth is that Father Brown was looking for a young friend who had appointed that somewhat incongruous meeting-place, being herself of a futuristic turn. The young friend was also a relative; one of the few relatives that he had. Her name was Elizabeth Fane, simplified into Betty, and she was the child of a sister who had married into a race of refined but impoverished squires. As the squire was dead as well as impoverished, Father Brown stood in the relation of a protector as well as a priest, and in some sense a guardian as well as an uncle. At the moment, however, he was blinking about at the groups in the gallery without catching sight of the familiar brown hair and bright face of his niece. Nevertheless, he saw some people he knew and a number of people he did not know, including some that, as a mere matter of taste, he did not much want to know.*

O LORD! 'PEOPLE he did not much want to know'. How familiar is that feeling – when I have an appointment or a catch-up coffee with someone I'd really rather not be with, truth be told! People who bore me, or annoy me, or just somehow rub me up the wrong

* *The Worst Crime in the World.*

way, yet whom I can't easily avoid or shake off. Forgive the paucity of love that sometimes exists within my heart, and help me, I pray, to do something about it. (Or at least, help me to want you to help me to do something about it!)

4 MARCH

Lift up thine eyes now the way toward the north (Ezekiel 8:5 *KJV*)

A stormy evening of olive and silver was closing in, as Father Brown, wrapped in a grey Scotch plaid, came to the end of a grey Scotch valley and beheld the strange castle of Glengyle. It stopped one end of the glen or hollow like a blind alley; and it looked like the end of the world. Rising in steep roofs and spires of seagreen slate in the manner of the old French-Scottish châteaux, it reminded an Englishman of the sinister steeple-hats of witches in fairy tales; and the pine woods that rocked round the green turrets looked, by comparison, as black as numberless flocks of ravens.

This note of a dreamy, almost a sleepy devilry, was no mere fancy from the landscape. For there did rest on the place one of those clouds of pride and madness and mysterious sorrow which lie more heavily on the noble houses of Scotland than on any other of the children of men. For Scotland has a double dose of the poison called heredity; the sense of blood in the aristocrat, and the sense of doom in the Calvinist.*

Today's prayer is kindly supplied by the author's mother-in-law, Major Ena Latham. Ena was born and bred in Perthshire, in the heart of Scotland, and nowadays lives there in retirement after a lifetime of service in Africa as a Salvation Army missionary officer.

'I TO THE hills will lift my eyes.' Heavenly Father, as I see the beautiful Scottish mountains surrounding my home, my heart is always filled with a sense of your power, and wonder at your creation. There is also the thrill of realising that my Creator God cares for me and those I love. Lord, I thank you for this day; a day of privilege to walk with you and to enjoy your company; a day to tell you all that is on my heart. Thank you for listening to my thoughts and prayers. As I mention fun experiences as well as the things I am anxious about, help me to remember above all else that you love me and that I, and those I love, are in your care. Amen.

* *The Honour of Israel Gow.*

5 MARCH

Can you fathom the mysteries of God? Can you probe the limits of the Almighty? (Job 11:7 *NIV*)

For many centuries there had never been a decent lord in Glengyle Castle; and with the Victorian era one would have thought that all eccentricities were exhausted. The last Glengyle, however, satisfied his tribal tradition by doing the only thing that was left for him to do; he disappeared. I do not mean that he went abroad; by all accounts he was still in the castle, if he was anywhere. But though his name was in the church register and the big red Peerage, nobody ever saw him under the sun.

If anyone saw him it was a solitary man-servant, something between a groom and a gardener. He was so deaf that the more business-like assumed him to be dumb; while the more penetrating declared him to be half-witted. A gaunt, red-haired labourer, with a dogged jaw and chin, but quite blue black eyes, he went by the name of Israel Gow, and was the one silent servant on that deserted estate. But the energy with which he dug potatoes, and the regularity with which he disappeared into the kitchen gave people an impression that he was providing for the meals of a superior, and that the strange earl was still concealed in the castle. If society needed any further proof that he was there, the servant persistently asserted that he was not at home.*

LIFE IS FULL of mystery, Lord. Why are we here? How did God begin? What happens when we die? Why do people suffer? How can we understand the Holy Trinity? Job asks rhetorical questions, Lord, because none of us can hope to comprehend the inscrutabilities of your being, even if we dig with as much energy as Israel Gow dug for potatoes. Faith, though, is the victory; faith that reminds us that we do not need to understand in order to believe, but that we believe in order to (one day) understand. Let that be our solace and satisfaction.

* *The Honour of Israel Gow.*

6 MARCH

I face daily the pressure of my concern for all the churches
(2 Corinthians 11:28 *NIV*)

'How in blazes do you know all these horrors?' cried Flambeau.

The shadow of a smile crossed the round, simple face of his clerical opponent.

'Has it never struck you that a man who does next to nothing but hear men's real sins is not likely to be wholly unaware of human evil?'*

SOMETHING TO REALLY think about here, Lord – the impact upon a priest or minister of listening to the confessions, cares and woes of their congregation. Help me to be sensitive to that. Grant all such listeners and confidants your protection, so that, with your assistance, all appropriate filters might remain in place.

* *The Blue Cross.*

7 MARCH

They did not see fit to acknowledge God (Romans 1:28 *ESV*)

[Father Brown] turned to the fuming specialist. 'Dr Hood,' he cried enthusiastically, 'you are a great poet! You have called an uncreated being out of the void. How much more godlike that is than if you had only ferreted out the mere facts! Indeed, the mere facts are rather commonplace and comic by comparison.'

'I have no notion what you are talking about,' said Dr Hood rather haughtily; 'my facts are all inevitable, though necessarily incomplete. A place may be permitted to intuition, perhaps (or poetry if you prefer the term), but only because the corresponding details cannot as yet be ascertained. In the absence of Mr Glass –' 'That's it, that's it,' said the little priest, nodding quite eagerly; 'that's the first idea to get fixed; the absence of Mr Glass. He is so extremely absent, I suppose,' he added reflectively, 'that there was never anybody so absent as Mr Glass.' 'Do you mean he is absent from the town?' demanded the doctor. 'I mean he is absent from everywhere,' answered Father Brown; 'he is absent from the Nature of Things, so to speak.'

'Do you seriously mean,' said the specialist with a smile, 'that there is no such person?' The priest made a sign of assent. 'It does seem a pity,' he said.*

ALMIGHTY GOD, IT does seem strange that so many people regard you as being entirely absent or even non-existent. Have mercy, Lord, on those who do not see fit to acknowledge you; warm and soften their hearts with grace. Draw alongside those for whom I pray this day.

* *The Absence of Mr Glass.*

8 MARCH

All these with one accord were devoting themselves to prayer (Acts 1:14 *ESV*)

Orion Hood broke into a contemptuous laugh. 'Well,' he said, 'before we go on to the hundred and one other evidences, let us take the first proof we found; the first fact we fell over when we fell into this room. If there is no Mr Glass, whose hat is this?' 'It is Mr Todhunter's,' replied Father Brown. 'But it doesn't fit him,' cried Hood impatiently. 'He couldn't possibly wear it!' Father Brown shook his head with ineffable mildness. 'I never said he could wear it,' he answered. 'I said it was his hat. Or, if you insist on a shade of difference, a hat that is his.' 'And what is the shade of difference?' asked the criminologist with a slight sneer. 'My good sir,' cried the mild little man, with his first movement akin to impatience, 'if you will walk down the street to the nearest hatter's shop, you will see that there is, in common speech, a difference between a man's hat and the hats that are his'. . . .

'Well, what in the name of Bedlam do you mean?' 'Mr Todhunter,' explained Father Brown placidly, 'is learning to be a professional conjurer, as well as juggler, ventriloquist, and expert in the rope trick. The conjuring explains the hat. It is without traces of hair, not because it is worn by the prematurely bald Mr Glass, but because it has never been worn by anybody . . . being only at the stage of practice, he smashed one glass against the ceiling. . . He was also practising the trick of a release from ropes'. . .

'But what about the two voices?' asked Maggie, staring. 'Have you never heard a ventriloquist?' asked Father Brown. 'Don't you know they speak first in their natural voice, and then answer themselves in just that shrill, squeaky, unnatural voice that you heard?'. . .

'But there is just one part of Mr Glass you have not succeeded in explaining away, and that is his name. Miss MacNab distinctly heard him so addressed by Mr Todhunter.' The Rev. Mr Brown broke into a rather childish giggle. 'Well, that,' he said, that's the silliest part of the whole silly story. When our juggling friend here threw up the three glasses in turn, he counted them aloud as he caught them, and also commented aloud when he failed to catch them. What he really said was: 'One, two and three – missed a glass; one, two – missed a glass.' And so on.' There was a sound of stillness in the room, and then everyone with one accord burst out laughing.*

HOW WONDERFUL IT is, Lord, when, perhaps after times of confusion and misunderstanding – frustration, even – your people move forward together in one accord. Lead us through such times, I pray, so that together we may explore our disagreements and progress towards unity of spirit. Bind us together!

* *The Absence of Mr Glass.*

9 MARCH

[One of the criminals] was saying, 'Jesus, remember me when You come into Your kingdom!' And He said to him, 'Truly I say to you, today you will be with Me in Paradise' (Luke 23:42, 43 *NASB*)

The crowd of diners and attendants that tumbled helter-skelter down the passages divided into two groups. Most of the Fishermen followed the proprietor to the front room . . .

As they did so they passed the dim alcove or cavern of the cloak-room, and saw a short, black-coated figure, presumably an attendant, standing a little way back in the shadow of it. 'Hallo there!' called out the duke. 'Have you seen anyone pass?' The short figure did not answer the question directly, but merely said: 'Perhaps I have got what you are looking for, gentlemen.' They paused, wavering and wondering, while he quietly went to the back of the cloak-room, and came back with both hands full of shining silver, which he laid out on the counter as calmly as a salesman. It took the form of a dozen quaintly shaped forks and knives.

'You – you –' began the colonel, quite thrown off his balance at last. Then he peered into the dim little room and saw two things first: first, that the short, black-clad man was dressed like a clergyman; and, second, that the window of the room behind him was burst, as if someone had passed violently through. 'Valuable things to deposit in a cloak-room, aren't they?' remarked the clergyman, with cheerful composure. 'Did – did you steal those things?' stammered Mr Audley, with staring eyes. 'If I did,' said the cleric pleasantly, 'at least I am bringing them back again.' 'But you didn't,' said Colonel Pound, still staring at the broken window. 'To make a clean breast of it, I didn't,' said the other, with some humour. And he seated himself quite gravely on a stool. 'But you know who did,' said the colonel.

'I don't know his real name,' said the priest placidly; 'but I know something of his fighting weight, and a great deal about his spiritual difficulties. I formed the physical estimate when he was trying to throttle me, and the moral estimate when he repented.' 'Oh, I say – repented!' cried young Chester, with a sort of crow of laughter. Father Brown got to his feet, putting his hands behind him.

'Odd, isn't it,' he said, 'that a thief and a vagabond should repent, when so many who are rich and secure remain hard and frivolous, and without fruit for God or man? But there, if you will excuse me, you trespass a little upon my province.'*

ROOM FOR REPENTANT thieves and last-minute decision-makers! Yours really is a Kingdom of extravagant grace, Lord Jesus! I pray that you will touch hearts that are hardened, and even if it takes a lifetime, you will somehow usher the keepers of those hearts into Paradise. Only you can do that, Christ of Calvary.

* *The Queer Feet.*

10 MARCH

Cast all your anxiety on him because he cares for you (1 Peter 5:7 *NIV*)

Father Brown . . . sprung stiffly to his feet, and was holding his temples tight like a man in sudden and violent pain.

'Stop, stop, stop!' he cried: 'stop talking for a minute, for I see half. Will God give me strength? Will my brain make the one jump and see all? Heaven help me! I used to be fairly good at thinking. I could paraphrase any page in Aquinas once. Will my head split – or will it see? I see half – I only see half.' He buried his head in his hands, and stood in a sort of rigid torture of thought or prayer . . .

When Father Brown's hands fell they showed a face quite fresh and serious, like a child's. He heaved a huge sigh.*

GOD OF GRACE and understanding, my prayers today are for those whose heads are buried in their hands, and whose temples are tight with worry and concern. We've all been there, Lord, at one time or another, and I pray for those who are so worried that they don't know where to turn. May they find the lovely truth of today's Bible verse gently embracing and permeating their situations.

* *The Secret Garden.*

11 MARCH

For the word of the cross is folly to those who are perishing, but to us who are being saved it is the power of God (1 Corinthians 1:18 *ESV*)

'The murderer,' went on Brown quietly, 'hacked off the enemy's head and flung the sword far over the wall. But he was too clever to fling the sword only. He flung the *head* over the wall also. Then he had only to clap on another head to the corpse, and (as he insisted on a private inquest) you all imagined a totally new man.'

'Clap on another head!' said O'Brien, staring. 'What other head? Heads don't grown on garden bushes, do they?'

'No,' said Father Brown huskily, and looking at his boots; 'there is only one place where they grow. They grow in the basket of the guillotine, beside which the Chief of Police, Aristide Valentin, was standing not an hour before the murder. Oh, my friends, hear me a minute before you tear me in pieces. Valentin is an honest man, if being mad for an arguable cause is honesty. But did you ever see in that cold, grey eye of his that he is mad? He would do anything, *anything,* to break what he calls the superstition of the Cross. He has fought for it and starved for it, and now he has murdered for it. Brayne's crazy millions had hitherto been scattered among so many sects that they did little to alter the balance of things. But Valentin heard a whisper that Brayne, like so many scatter-brained sceptics, was drifting to us; and that was quite a different thing. Brayne would pour supplies into the impoverished and pugnacious Church of France.'*

LORD OF THE Church, I pray for those who are facing relentless opposition, hatred and fanatical persecution, simply because of their adherence to the Cross of Christ. I pray for believers who face the daily prospect of frightening harassment, deliberate obstruction and even murder and martyrdom when they refuse to deny their Saviour. Grant them enabling grace, moment by moment.

* *The Secret Garden.*

12 MARCH

I will seek the lost, bring back the scattered (Ezekiel 34:16 *NASB*)

When you enter (as you never will) the Vernon Hotel, you pass down a short passage decorated with a few dingy but important pictures, and you come to the main vestibule and lounge which opens on your right into passages leading to the public rooms, and on your left to a similar passage pointing to the kitchens and offices of the hotel. Immediately on your left hand is the corner of a glass office, which abuts upon the lounge – a house within a house, so to speak, like the old hotel bar which probably once occupied its place.

In this office sat the representative of the proprietor (nobody in this place ever appeared in person if he could help it), and just beyond the office, on the way to the servants' quarters, was the gentlemen's cloak-room, the last boundary of the gentlemen's domain. But between the office and the cloak-room was a small private room without other outlet, sometimes used by the proprietor for delicate and important matters, such as lending a duke a thousand pounds, or declining to lend him sixpence. It is a mark of the magnificent tolerance of Mr Lever that he permitted this holy place to be for about half an hour profaned by a mere priest, scribbling away on a piece of paper.*

WHAT A MAZE of a place, Lord! Passages leading to passages and rooms leading to rooms! So easy to become confused and disorientated . . . All the more reason, then, for your people, somewhat like Father Brown, to be present and available for anyone who has lost their way. Just where you need us to be today, Heavenly Father, please make sure we are in the right places as your ambassadors. Lead us.

* *The Queer Feet.*

13 MARCH

Be silent before me (Isaiah 41:1 *NIV*)

The time of darkness and dinner was drawing on; his own forgotten little room was without a light, and perhaps the gathering gloom, as occasionally happens, sharpened the sense of sound. As Father Brown wrote the last and least essential part of his document, he caught himself writing to the rhythm of a recurrent noise outside, just as one sometimes thinks to the tune of a railway train. When he became conscious of the thing he found what it was: only the ordinary patter of feet passing the door, which in an hotel was no very unlikely matter. Nevertheless, he stared at the darkened ceiling, and listened to the sound. After he had listened for a few seconds dreamily, he got to his feet and listened intently, with his head a little on one side. Then he sat down again and buried his brow in his hands, now not merely listening, but listening and thinking also.*

LET THIS BE me, Lord; listening and thinking. Let this be me in prayer. Let this be me, often; alone with myself, yet never alone, for I am ever with you. Instruct my heart in the ways of silent thought, and of sitting down with you.

* *The Queer Feet.*

14 MARCH

Establish my footsteps in Your word (Psalm 119:133 *NASB*)

The footsteps outside at any given moment were such as one might hear in any hotel; and yet, taken as a whole, there was something very strange about them. There were no other footsteps. It was always a very silent house, for the few familiar guests went at once to their own apartments, and the well-trained waiters were told to be almost invisible until they were wanted. One could not conceive any place where there was less reason to apprehend anything irregular. But these footsteps were so odd that one could not decide to call them regular or irregular. Father Brown followed them with his finger on the edge of the table, like a man trying to learn a tune on the piano.*

HEAVENLY FATHER, IN a world that offers multiple pathways, and which is full of mysteries, how immensely reassuring it is to realise the possibility of establishing my footsteps in that which is ultra-reliable; your word and your will. Help me, I pray, to tune in to both, and for that to be my security.

* *The Queer Feet.*

15 MARCH

Look at the birds of the air, for they neither sow nor reap nor gather into barns; yet your heavenly Father feeds them. Are you not of more value than they? Which of you by worrying can add one cubit to his stature? (Matthew 6:26, 27 NKJV)

The front doors of the house with the stable opened on the garden with the monkey tree, and a young girl came out with bread to feed the birds on the afternoon of Boxing Day. She had a pretty face, with brave brown eyes; but her figure was beyond conjecture, for she was so wrapped up in brown furs that it was hard to say which was hair and which was fur. But for the attractive face she might have been a small toddling bear.

The winter afternoon was reddening towards evening, and already a ruby light was rolled over the bloomless beds, filling them, as it were, with the ghosts of dead roses. On one side of the house stood the table, on the other an alley or cloister of laurels led to the larger garden behind. The young lady, having scattered bread for the birds (for the fourth or fifth time that day, because the dog ate it), passed unobtrusively down the lane of laurels and into a glimmering plantation of evergreen behind. Here she gave an exclamation of wonder, real or ritual, and looking up at the high garden wall above her, beheld it fantastically bestridden by a somewhat fantastic figure.

'Oh, don't jump, Mr Crook,' she called out in some alarm; 'it's much too high.'*

WHAT A CURIOUS juxtaposition this is, Lord. On one hand, there is a tranquil, perfectly ordinary little scene of birds being fed in a garden, yet on the other, there is the scenario of an apparent suicide attempt. Such is the way of humankind, Lord; normality and tragedy sometimes co-existing; the mundane alongside the horribly sad. All the more reason, then, given the unpredictability

* *The Flying Stars.*

and frailty of any of our lives, for us to take today's Bible text to heart. Deeply impress its comforting truth upon our circumstances as we walk with you this day.

16 MARCH

The LORD God said, 'It is not good for the man to be alone. I will make a helper suitable for him' (Genesis 2:18 *NIV*)

The individual riding the party wall like an aerial horse was a tall, angular young man, with dark hair sticking up like a hair brush, intelligent and even distinguished lineaments, but a sallow and almost alien complexion. This showed the more plainly because he wore an aggressive red tie, the only part of his costume of which he seemed to take any care. Perhaps it was just a symbol. He took no notice of the girl's alarmed adjuration, but leapt like a grasshopper to the ground beside her, where he might very well have broken his legs.

'I think I was meant to be a burglar,' he said placidly, 'and I have no doubt I should have been if I hadn't happened to be born in that nice house next door. I can't see any harm in it, anyhow.'

'How can you say such things?' she remonstrated.

'Well,' said the young man, 'if you're born on the wrong side of the wall, I can't see that it's wrong to climb over.'

'I never know what you will say or do next,' she said.

'I don't often know myself,' replied Mr Crook; 'but then I am on the right side of the wall now.'

'And which is the right side of the wall?' asked the young lady, smiling.

'Whichever side you are on,' said the young man named Crook.*

GOD OF LOVE and romance, God of fledgling friendships and relationships, my prayers today are with those looking for life-partners. Bless and guide their searching!

* *The Flying Stars.*

17 MARCH

Do your best to get here before winter (2 Timothy 4:21 *NIV*)

'This is my friend, Father Brown,' said Flambeau. 'I've often wanted you to meet him. Splendid weather, this; a little cold for Southerners like me.'

'Yes, I think it will keep clear,' said Angus, sitting down on a violet-striped Eastern ottoman.

'No,' said the priest quietly; 'it has begun to snow.'

And indeed, as he spoke, the first few flakes . . . began to drift across the darkening window-pane.

Well,' said Angus heavily. 'I'm afraid I've come on business, and rather jumpy business at that. The fact is, Flambeau, within a stone's throw of your house is a fellow who badly wants your help; he's perpetually being haunted and threatened by an invisible enemy – a scoundrel whom nobody has ever seen.'*

GRACIOUS FATHER, I pray for those whose days are, for one reason or another, darkening and cold. I pray for those who feel haunted and threatened by enemies real or imagined. I pray for those whose terrors of the mind are frightening and disturbing. Grant them your peace, Lord.

* *The Invisible Man.*

18 MARCH

When a stranger sojourns with you in your land, you shall not do him wrong. You shall treat the stranger who sojourns with you as the native among you, and you shall love him as yourself, for you were strangers in the land of Egypt (Leviticus 19:33, 34 ESV)

One morning the provost and the minister (for the Glengyles were Presbyterian) were summoned to the castle. There they found that the gardener, groom and cook had added to his many professions that of undertaker, and had nailed up his master in a coffin. With how much or how little further inquiry this odd fact was passed, did not as yet very plainly appear; for the thing had never been legally investigated . . .

By then the body of Lord Glengyle (if it was the body) had lain for some time in the little churchyard on the hill.

As Father Brown passed through the dim garden and came under the shadow of the château, the clouds were thick and the whole air damp and thundery. Against the last stripe of the green-gold sunset he saw a black human silhouette; a man in a chimney-pot hat, with a big spade over his shoulder. The combination was queerly suggestive of a sexton; but when Brown remembered the deaf servant who dug potatoes, he thought it natural enough. He knew something of the Scotch peasant; he knew the respectability which might well feel it necessary to wear 'blacks' for an official inquiry; he knew also the economy that would not lose an hour's digging for that. Even the man's start and suspicious stare as the priest went by were consonant enough with the vigilance and jealousy of such a type.*

SENSITIVE ISSUES OF culture and tradition, Lord! Thank you for those representatives of yours who tread carefully and with respect, even (especially) when matters are not always straightforward or easy to understand. Such are the delicate complexities of cross-cultural ministry, and I pray for those engaged in witnessing for Christ against a backdrop of important local sensitivities. Grant them your wisdom and holy tact!

* *The Honour of Israel Gow.*

19 MARCH

My fruit is better than gold, even fine gold, and my yield than choice silver (Proverbs 8:19 *ESV*)

'That old local rhyme [said Father Brown] about the house of Glengyle –

"As green sap to the summer trees
Is red gold to the Ogilvies" –

was literal as well as metaphorical. It did not merely mean that the Glengyles sought for wealth; it was also true that they literally gathered gold; they had a huge collection of ornaments and utensils in that metal. They were, in fact, misers whose mania took that turn.'*

GRANT ME WISDOM, Lord, when it comes to my own priorities. Teach me what matters, and what is really important in this life. Walk with me, I pray, through a personal audit of my ambitions.

* *The Honour of Israel Gow.*

20 MARCH

Build houses and live in them; plant gardens and eat their produce (Jeremiah 29:5 *ESV*)

It is a long, low house, running parallel with the road, painted mostly white and pale green, with a veranda and sun-blinds, and porches capped with those quaint sort of cupolas like wooden umbrellas that one sees in some old-fashioned houses. In fact, it is an old-fashioned house, very English and very suburban in the good old wealthy Clapham sense. And yet the house has a look of having been built chiefly for the hot weather. Looking at its white paint and sun-blinds one thinks vaguely of pugarees and even of palm trees. I cannot trace the feeling to its root; perhaps the place was built by an Anglo-Indian.

Anyone passing this house, I say, would be namelessly fascinated by it; would feel that it was a place about which some story was to be told.*

TODAY, HEAVENLY FATHER, I want to say thank you for my house – my home. Thank you for a roof over my head; a place to call my own. Thank you for the safety and security it represents, and for the memories its walls hold. And, Lord, as I thank you, I pray for those who don't have a house of their own. Help them, Lord, and bless those churches and organisations who endeavour to improve their situation.

* *The Wrong Shape.*

21 MARCH

Make yourself an ark of cypress wood; make rooms in it and coat it with pitch inside and out. This is how you are to build it: The ark is to be three hundred cubits long, fifty cubits wide and thirty cubits high. Make a roof for it, leaving below the roof an opening one cubit high all around. Put a door in the side of the ark and make lower, middle and upper decks
(Genesis 6:14-16 *NIV*)

Anyone passing the house on the Thursday before Whit-Sunday at about half-past four p.m. would have seen the front door open, and Father Brown, of the small church of St Mungo, come out smoking a large pipe in company with a very tall French friend of his called Flambeau, who was smoking a very small cigarette. These persons may or may not be of interest to the reader, but the truth is that they were not the only interesting things that were displayed when the front door of the white-and-green house was opened . . .

The whole house was built upon the plan of a T, but a T with a very long cross piece and a very short tail piece. The long cross was the frontage that ran along in the face of the street, with the front door in the middle; it was two stories high, and contained nearly all the important rooms. The short tail piece, which ran out at the back immediately opposite the front door, was one story high, and consisted only of two long rooms, the one leading into the other.*

HEAVENLY FATHER, AS Noah came to realise, you are a God of specifics. Detail matters to you! How reassuring it is, therefore, to know that the details of my life have not escaped your attention, nor will they. Thank you for the degree of interest you take in my wellbeing. Thank you for being an interested God.

* *The Wrong Shape.*

22 MARCH

He told them: 'Take nothing for the journey – no staff, no bag, no bread, no money, no extra shirt' (Luke 9:3 *NIV*)

When Flambeau took his month's holiday from his office in Westminster he took it on a small sailing-boat, so small that it passed much of its time as a rowing-boat. He took it, moreover, on little rivers in the Eastern counties, rivers so small that the boat looked like a magic boat sailing on land through meadows and cornfields. The vessel was just comfortable for two people; there was room only for necessities, and Flambeau had stocked it with such things as his special philosophy considered necessary. They reduced themselves, apparently, to four essentials: tins of salmon, if he should want to eat; loaded revolvers, if he should want to fight; a bottle of brandy, presumably in case he should faint; and a priest, presumably in case he should die. With this light luggage he crawled down the little Norfolk rivers, intending to reach the Broads at last, but meanwhile delighting in the overhanging gardens and meadows, the mirrored mansions or villages, lingering to fish in the pools and corners, and in some sense hugging the shore.*

TEACH ME, LORD of my journey, the worth and beauty of travelling lightly, for it is a form of trust. Teach me to shed any kind of unnecessary baggage that is weighing me down. I pray for anyone who is finding their pilgrimage heavy-going and not plain sailing; meet them along the way.

* *The Sins of Prince Saradine.*

23 MARCH

I long to see you, that I may impart to you some spiritual gift to strengthen you (Romans 1:11 *ESV*)

Like a true philosopher, Flambeau had no aim in his holiday; but, like a true philosopher, he had an excuse. He had a sort of half purpose, which he took just so seriously that its success would crown the holiday, but just so lightly that its failure would not spoil it. Years ago, when he had been a king of thieves and the most famous figure in Paris, he had often received wild communications of approval, denunciation or even love; but one had, somehow, stuck in his memory. It consisted simply of a visiting-card, in an envelope with an English postmark. On the back of the card was written in French and in green ink: 'If you ever retire and become respectable, come and see me. I want to meet you, for I have met all the other great men of my time . . .'

On the front of the card was engraved in the formal fashion, 'Prince Saradine, Reed House, Reed Island, Norfolk.'*

IS THERE ANYONE I should be making the effort to see, Lord? Or someone I should write to?

* *The Sins of Prince Saradine.*

24 MARCH

From the rising of the sun to its setting, the name of the LORD is to be praised! (Psalm 113:3 *ESV*)

The little village of Bohun Becon was perched on a hill so steep that the tall spire of its church seemed only like the peak of a small mountain. At the foot of the church stood a smithy, generally red with fires and always littered with hammers and scraps of iron; opposite to this, over a rude cross of cobbled paths, was 'The Blue Boar,' the only inn of the place.

It was upon this crossway, in the lifting of a leaden and silver daybreak, that two brothers met in the street and spoke; though one was beginning the day and the other finishing it. The Rev. and Hon. Wilfred Bohun was very devout, and was making his way to some austere exercises of prayer or contemplation at dawn. Colonel the Hon. Norman Bohun, his elder brother, was by no means devout, and was sitting in evening-dress on the bench outside 'The Blue Boar,' drinking what the philosophic observer was free to regard either as his last glass on Tuesday or his first on Wednesday. The colonel was not particular.*

LORD OF ALL my days and all my hours, I pray for the devout, that you would keep them so, and I pray for those who are by no means devout, that you would persuade them to be so. In your mercy, bless the prayerful and reach out to the prayer-less.

* *The Hammer of God.*

25 MARCH

When your days are over and you rest with your ancestors, I will raise up your offspring to succeed you, your own flesh and blood, and I will establish his kingdom (2 Samuel 7:12 *NIV*)

The Bohuns were one of the very few aristocratic families really dating from the Middle Ages, and their pennon* had actually seen Palestine. But it is a great mistake to suppose that such houses stand high in chivalric traditions. Few except the poor preserve traditions. Aristocrats live not in traditions but in fashions. The Bohuns had been Mohocks† under Queen Anne and Mashers‡ under Queen Victoria. But, like more than one of the really ancient houses, they had rotted in the last two centuries into mere drunkards and dandy degenerates, till there had even come a whisper of insanity.§

ALPHA AND OMEGA, your royal household will endure for ever, with you at the majestic helm. You are everlasting God, and on this day in history, I worship you. Receive my homage, for it is the very least you are due.

* Heraldic flag.

† Gangs of violent (usually well-born) criminals that terrorised London, often as paid mercenaries.

‡ Men who would dress as women in order to lull women into a false sense of security, before committing acts of sexual harassment.

§ *The Hammer of God.*

26 MARCH

Beware not to lift up your eyes to heaven and see the sun and the moon and the stars, all the host of heaven, and be drawn away and worship them and serve them (Deuteronomy 4:19 *NASB*)

The two men crossed Westminster Bridge. One man was very tall and the other very short; they might even have been fantastically compared to the arrogant clock-tower of Parliament and the humbler humped shoulders of the Abbey, for the short man was in clerical dress. The official description of the tall man was M. Hercule Flambeau [now working as a] private detective, and he was going to his new offices in a new pile of flats facing the Abbey entrance. The official description of the short man was the Rev. J. Brown, attached to St Francis Xavier's Church, Camberwell, and he was coming from a Camberwell death-bed to see the new offices of his friend.

The building was American in its sky-scraping altitude, and American also in the oiled elaboration of its machinery of telephones and lifts. But it was barely finished and still understaffed: only three tenants had moved in; the office just above Flambeau was occupied, as also was the office just below him; the two floors above that and the three floors below were entirely bare. But the first glance at the new tower of flats caught something much more arresting. Save for a few relics of scaffolding, the one glaring object was erected outside the office just above Flambeau's. It was an enormous gilt effigy of the human eye, surrounded with rays of gold, and taking up as much room as two or three office windows.

'What on earth is that?' asked Father Brown, and stood still. 'Oh, a new religion,' said Flambeau, laughing; 'one of those new religions that forgive your sins by saying you never had any . . . I have two lady typewriters underneath me, and this enthusiastic old humbug on top. He calls himself the New Priest of Apollo, and he worships the sun.'*

* *The Eye of Apollo.*

GOD OF TRUTH and light, draw close to those who are seeking spiritual truth, but looking in the wrong directions. Bless and help those who are sincerely wrong, that by your Spirit's gracious guidance they will be drawn to your loving reality.

27 MARCH

If we claim to be without sin, we deceive ourselves and the truth is not in us (1 John 1:8 *NIV*)

'The sun was the cruellest of all the gods,' [said Father Brown] 'but what does that monstrous eye mean?'

'As I understand it, it is a theory of theirs,' answered Flambeau, 'that a man can endure anything if his mind is quite steady. Their two great symbols are the sun and the open eye; for they say that if a man were really healthy he could stare at the sun.'

'If a man were really healthy,' said Father Brown, 'he would not bother to stare at it.'

'Well, that's all I can tell you about the new religion,' went on Flambeau carelessly. 'It claims, of course, that it can cure all physical diseases.'

'Can it cure the one spiritual disease?' asked Father Brown, with a serious curiosity.

'And what is the one spiritual disease?' asked Flambeau, smiling.

'Oh, thinking one is quite well,' said his friend.*

WHAT A SICKNESS, Lord – sin itself. Yet, what a Saviour! Humankind's chronic condition cured by Christ himself.

* *The Eye of Apollo.*

28 MARCH

False prophets also arose among the people, just as there will be false teachers among you, who will secretly bring in destructive heresies (2 Peter 2:1 *ESV*)

The man who called himself Kalon was a magnificent creature, worthy, in a physical sense, to be the pontiff of Apollo. He was nearly as tall even as Flambeau, and very much better looking, with a golden beard, strong blue eyes, and a mane flung back like a lion's. In structure he was the blonde beast of Nietzsche, but all this animal beauty was heightened, brightened and softened by genuine intellect and spirituality.

If he looked like one of the great Saxon kings, he looked like one of the kings that were also saints. And this despite the cockney incongruity of his surroundings; the fact that he had an office half-way up a building in Victoria Street; that the clerk (a commonplace youth in cuffs and collars) sat in the outer room, between him and the corridor; that his name was on a brass plate, and the gilt emblem of his creed hung above his street, like the advertisement of an oculist.

All this vulgarity could not take away from the man called Kalon the vivid oppression and inspiration that came from his soul and body. When all was said, a man in the presence of this quack did feel in the presence of a great man. Even in the loose jacket-suit of linen that he wore as a workshop dress in his office he was a fascinating and formidable figure; and when robed in the white vestments and crowned with the golden circlet, in which he daily saluted the sun, he really looked so splendid that the laughter of the street people sometimes died suddenly on their lips.*

COMICAL AND AMUSING in its own way, Lord – a bit of a joke at the expense of an eccentric character, maybe. Not quite so funny, though, when cults and sects are led by people capable of manipulation and a charm that is often sinister; those who seek to

* *The Eye of Apollo.*

control and even brainwash. I pray, Lord, for those who are victims of such deception; those whose spiritual experience has become ensnared in webs of falsehood. I ask your blessing on Christians who seek to bring freedom.

29 MARCH

I will build my church, and the gates of hell shall not prevail against it (Matthew 16:18 *NIV*)

The thousand arms of the forest were grey, and its million fingers silver. In a sky of dark green-blue-like slate the stars were bleak and brilliant like splintered ice. All that thickly wooded and sparsely tenanted countryside was stiff with a bitter and brittle frost.

The black hollows between the trunks of the trees looked like bottomless, black caverns of that heartless Scandinavian hell, a hell of incalculable cold. Even the square stone tower of the church looked northern to the point of heathenry, as if it were some barbaric tower among the sea rocks of Iceland. It was a queer night for anyone to explore a churchyard. But, on the other hand, perhaps it was worth exploring.

It rose abruptly out of the ashen wastes of forest in a sort of hump or shoulder of green turf that looked grey in the starlight. Most of the graves were on a slant, and the path leading up to the church was as steep as a staircase. On the top of the hill, in the one flat and prominent place, was the monument for which the place was famous. It contrasted strangely with the featureless graves all round, for it was the work of one of the greatest sculptors of modern Europe; and yet his fame was at once forgotten in the fame of the man whose image he had made. It showed, by touches of the small silver pencil of starlight, the massive metal figure of a soldier recumbent, the strong hands sealed in an everlasting worship, the great head pillowed upon a gun . . . by his right lay a sword, of which the tip was broken off; on the left side lay a Bible.*

IN MANY WAYS, Lord, this account is deeply symbolic. Your Church, that is, standing firm in the midst of what appears to be something of a hellish scene. How wonderful it is to know, Heavenly Father, that yours is the Church Triumphant; surrounded at times by evil and scenarios that would encourage us to lose hope, yet holding fast and refusing to give in. Help those of us who belong, to remember that, especially when perhaps all seems lost.

* *The Sign of the Broken Sword.*

30 MARCH

The disciples came to him and asked, 'Why do you speak to the people in parables?' He replied, 'Because the knowledge of the secrets of the kingdom of heaven has been given to you, but not to them . . . For this people's heart has become calloused; they hardly hear with their ears, and they have closed their eyes. Otherwise, they might see with their eyes, hear with their ears, understand with their hearts and turn, and I would heal them (Matthew 13:10-15 *NIV*)

> 'Where does a wise man hide a pebble?' . . .
> The tall man answered in a low voice:
> 'On the beach.'
> The small man nodded, and after a short silence said:
> 'Where does a wise man hide a leaf?'
> And the other answered:
> 'In the forest.'*

PROTECT MY HEART, Lord, from callouses. I do not ask to know all the secrets of your Kingdom; simply that you help me on a need-to-know basis. Grant me understanding as you see fit, for whatever I need to comprehend, moment-by-moment. Grant me, too, contentment in the face of that which you choose not to reveal to me.

* *The Sign of the Broken Sword.*

31 MARCH

Beware, the Lord is about to take firm hold of you and hurl you away, you mighty man (Isaiah 22:17 *NIV*)

'You're pretty sure, I suppose,' remarked the young man, 'that he really did kill his master?' 'Yes, my son; I'm pretty sure,' replied Gilder drily; 'for the trifling reasons that he has gone off with twenty thousand pounds in papers that were in his master's desk. No; the only thing worth calling a difficulty is how he killed him. The skull seems broken as with some big weapon, but there's no weapon at all lying about, and the murderer would have found it awkward to carry it away, unless the weapon was too small to be noticed.' 'Perhaps the weapon was too big to be noticed,' said the priest with an odd little giggle.

Gilder looked round at his wild remark, and rather sternly asked Brown what he meant. 'Silly way of putting it, I know,' said Father Brown apologetically. 'Sounds like a fairy tale. But poor Armstrong was killed with a giant club, a great green club, too big to be seen, and which we call the earth. He was broken against this green bank we are standing on.'

'How do you mean?' asked the detective quickly. Father Brown turned his moon face up to the narrow façade of the house and blinked hopelessly up. Following his eyes, they saw that right at the top of the otherwise blind back quarter of the building, an attic window stood open. 'Don't you see,' he explained, pointing a little awkwardly like a child, 'he was thrown down from there?'*

LORD GOD, TODAY'S Bible verse makes for uncomfortable reading. It is not the easy, go-to material of daily devotions, for it speaks of your wrath and vengeance in the face of sin. Nevertheless, I pray that you will speak to me through it, so that my heart may learn holy awe. Let that be an integral part of my relationship with you, Lord.

* *The Three Tools of Death.*

1 APRIL

Then they spit in his face and struck him with their fists. Others slapped him (Matthew 26:67 *NIV*)

His huge shoulder heaved and he sent an iron fist smash into Magnus's bland Mongolian visage, laying him on the lawn as flat as a starfish.

Two or three of the police instantly put their hands on Royce; but to the rest it seemed as if all reason had broken up and the universe were turning into a brainless harlequinade.

'None of that, Mr Royce,' Gilder had called out authoritatively. 'I shall arrest you for assault.'*

LORD JESUS, HOW dreadful it is to think that an iron fist was smashed into your face. How shocking to imagine that scene. And then I remember that you took those blows for my sake – for me – with no police officer to come to your rescue. Such was the stunning extent of your love. You are my God.

* *The Three Tools of Death.*

2 APRIL

Refrain from anger and turn from wrath; do not fret – it leads only to evil (Psalm 37:8 *NIV*)

The eyes of the tradesman stood out of his head like a snail's; he really seemed for an instant likely to fling himself upon the stranger. At last he stammered angrily: 'I don't know what you 'ave to do with it, but if you're one of their friends, you can tell 'em from me that I'll knock their silly 'eads off, parsons or no parsons, if they upset my apples again.'

'Indeed?' asked the detective, with great sympathy. 'Did they upset your apples?'

'One of 'em did,' said the heated shopman; 'rolled 'em all over the street. I'd 'ave caught the fool but for havin' to pick 'em up.'

'Which way did these parsons go?' asked Valentin.

'Up that second road on the left-hand side, and then across the square,' said the other promptly.

'Thanks,' said Valentin, and vanished like a fairy.*

EASIER SAID THAN done, Lord – keeping one's emotions in check! Help me, I pray, when I am upset, at that crucial tipping point, to retain my self-control. It's unlikely I'll manage to do so without your assistance, so please remember this prayer!

* *The Blue Cross.*

3 APRIL

The prudent gives thought to his steps (Proverbs 14:15 *ESV*)

When Valentin arrived he was already dressed in black clothes and the red rosette – an elegant figure, his dark beard already streaked with grey. He went straight through the house to his study, which opened on the grounds behind. The garden door of it was open, and after he had carefully locked his box in its official place, he stood for a few seconds at the open door looking out upon the garden. A sharp moon was fighting with the flying rags and tatters of a storm, and Valentin regarded it with a wistfulness unusual in such scientific natures as his. Perhaps such scientific natures have some psychic prevision of the most tremendous problem of their lives. From any such occult mood, at least, he quickly recovered, for he knew he was late and his guests had already begun to arrive.*

GRANT ME TIMES of wistfulness, Heavenly Father, especially when my life is fighting with storms; times to pause and reflect, and to allow my soul to catch up with the rest of me. Teach me the value of wistful reflection.

* *The Secret Garden.*

4 APRIL

Now Mary stood outside the tomb crying. As she wept, she bent over to look into the tomb and saw two angels in white, seated where Jesus' body had been, one at the head and the other at the foot. They asked her, 'Woman, why are you crying?' 'They have taken my Lord away,' she said, 'and I don't know where they have put him.' At this, she turned around and saw Jesus standing there, but she did not realize that it was Jesus. He asked her, 'Woman, why are you crying? Who is it you are looking for?' Thinking he was the gardener, she said, 'Sir, if you have carried him away, tell me where you have put him, and I will get him.' Jesus said to her, 'Mary.' She turned toward him and cried out in Aramaic, 'Rabboni!' (which means 'Teacher') (John 20:11 *NIV*)

'Is there any more news, Ivan?' asked Dr Simon, as the chief of police strode out of the room.

'Only one more thing, I think, sir,' said Ivan, wrinkling up his grey old face; 'but that's important, too, in its way. There's that old buffer you found on the lawn,' and he pointed without pretence of reverence at the big black body with the yellow head. 'We've found out who he is, anyhow.'

'Indeed!' cried the astonished doctor: 'and who is he?'

'His name was Arnold Becker,' said the under-detective, 'though he went by many aliases. He was a wandering sort of scamp, and is known to have been in America.'*

A CASE OF correct identity, Lord – unlike Mary's situation, in which she mistook you for a gardener. How very gracious you are, Lord Jesus, not to have been offended or hurt by Mary's mistake; thinking God to be the hired help! Teach me that spiritual art, I pray: blessed are the unoffended!

* *The Secret Garden.*

5 APRIL

Thy way is in the sea, and thy path in the great waters, and thy footsteps are not known (Psalm 77:19 KJV)

As [Father Brown] began to think steadily, the very blackness of his cell seemed to make his thoughts more vivid; he began to see as in a kind of vision the fantastic feet capering along the corridor in unnatural or symbolic attitudes.

Was it a heathen religious dance? Or some entirely new kind of scientific exercise?

Father Brown began to ask himself with more exactness what the steps suggested. Taking the slow step first; it certainly was not the step of the proprietor. Men of his type walk with a rapid waddle, or they sit still. It could not be any servant or messenger waiting for directions. It did not sound like it.

The poorer orders (in an oligarchy) sometimes lurch about when they are slightly drunk, but generally, and especially in gorgeous scenes, they stand or sit in constrained attitudes. No; that heavy yet springy step, with a kind of careless emphasis, not specially noisy, yet not caring what noise it made, belonged to only one of the animals of this earth. It was a gentleman of western Europe, and probably one who had never worked for his living.*

LORD, TO BE perfectly honest, it is sometimes difficult to discern your footsteps. It is not always easy to follow you, or straightforward. You are of course God, and it is entirely up to you where you choose to plant your footsteps, but I pray for grace in following, that you would lead me in your ways, despite what is often my ignorance.

* *The Queer Feet.*

6 APRIL

The fruit of the Spirit is . . . kindness (Galatians 5:22 *NIV*)

As they went together through the laurels towards the front garden a motor horn sounded thrice, coming nearer and nearer, and a car of splendid speed, great elegance, and a pale green colour swept up to the front doors like a bird and stood throbbing.

'Hullo, hullo!' said the young man with the red tie; 'here's somebody born on the right side, anyhow. I didn't know, Miss Adams, that your Santa Claus was so modern as this.'

'Oh, that's my godfather, Sir Leopold Fischer. He always comes on Boxing Day.'

Then, after an innocent pause, which unconsciously betrayed some lack of enthusiasm, Ruby Adams added:

'He is very kind.'*

HEAVENLY FATHER, MAYBE it is easy to underestimate the quality of kindness, or simply to regard it as a mere nicety or common courtesy. Yet, your word today reminds me that it is nothing less than one of your Spirit's gifts to humanity. That boosts its importance somewhat! May it be said of me that I am very kind.

* *The Flying Stars.*

7 APRIL

Forget the former things; do not dwell on the past (Isaiah 43:18 *NIV*)

Angus emptied his coffee-cup and regarded her with mild and patient eyes. Her own mouth took a slight twist of laughter as she resumed:

'I suppose you've seen on the hoardings all about this "Smythe's Silent Service"? Or you must be the only person that hasn't. Oh, I don't know much about it, it's some clockwork invention for doing all the housework by machinery. You know the sort of thing: "Press a button – A Butler who Never Drinks." "Turn a handle – Ten Housemaids who Never Flirt." You must have seen the advertisements. Well, whatever these machines are, they are making pots of money; and they are making it all for the little imp whom I knew down in Ludbury. I can't help feeling pleased the poor little chap has fallen on his feet; but the plain fact is, I'm in terror of his turning up any minute and telling me he's carved his way in the world – as he certainly has.'*

HOW UNCOMFORTABLE THE past can be, Lord – traumatic and disturbing, even. Regrets, mistakes, shameful secrets, failed relationships, sins and all kinds of issues that might haunt us long after they actually appeared in our lives or took place. Help us, Lord of the years, not to live in terror like the woman in the story, but to hand everything over to you. In return, Lord, meet us at that moment of exchange and grant us your peace.

* *The Invisible Man.*

8 APRIL

He will baptize you with the Holy Spirit and fire (Luke 3:16 *NIV*)

This very dapper but dwarfish figure, with the spike of black beard carried insolently forward, the clever unrestful eyes, the neat but very nervous fingers, could be none other than the man just described to him: Isidore Smythe, who made dolls out of banana skins and match-boxes; Isidore Smythe, who made millions out of undrinking butlers and unflirting housemaids of metal.

For a moment the two men, instinctively understanding each other's air of possession, looked at each other with that curious cold generosity which is the soul of rivalry.*

WHAT EXACTLY IS cold generosity, Lord? Isn't that an oxymoron? You gave everything you had for me, Lord Jesus – your very life – with a generosity that blazed with holy fire. In that light, I simply cannot grasp the concept of cold generosity. God forbid such an idea should ever creep into my soul.

* *The Invisible Man.*

9 APRIL

The pleasantness of a friend springs from their heartfelt advice (Proverbs 27:9 *NIV*)

Laura Hope got to her feet suddenly. 'My friend,' she said: 'I think you are a witch. Yes, you are quite right. I have not seen a line of the other man's writing; and I have no more notion than the dead of what or where he is. But it is of him that I am frightened. It is he who is all about my path. It is he who has half driven me mad. Indeed, I think he has driven me mad; for I have felt him where he could not have been, and I have heard his voice when he could not have spoken.'

'Well, my dear,' said the young man, cheerfully, 'if he were Satan himself, he is done for now you have told somebody. One goes mad all alone, old girl.'*

THANK YOU, HEAVENLY Father, for caring friends who will sit alongside me in my days or worry, even when I think I am being driven mad. Thank you for the relief such friendships bring. Thank you for those who listen without judging; for those who sympathise and empathise. Such friends are worth their weight in gold. I pray to be like that to those who need a listening ear.

* *The Invisible Man.*

10 APRIL

And he said unto them, 'I beheld Satan as lightning fall from heaven' (Luke 10:18 *KJV*)

The path up the hill to the churchyard was crooked but short; only under the stress of wind it seemed laborious and long. Far as the eye could see, farther and farther as they mounted the slope, were seas beyond seas of pines, now all aslope one way under the wind. And that universal gesture seemed as vain as it was vast, as vain as if that wind were whistling about some unpeopled and purposeless planet. Through all that infinite growth of grey-blue forests sang, shrill and high, that ancient sorrow that is in the heart of all heathen things. One could fancy that the voices from the underworld of unfathomable foliage were cries of the lost and wandering pagan gods: gods who had gone roaming in that irrational forest, and who will never find their way back to heaven.*

WHAT ASTONISHING THEOLOGY, Heavenly Father! A fallen angel, Satan, falling from heaven, as part of a cosmic spiritual battle. It seems like science fiction, Lord, yet it is anything but; the voices of the underworld are all-too real. Show me what I realise and understand about spiritual warfare, I pray, that I might all the more find my security in Christ, who is Lord of all.

* *The Honour of Israel Gow.*

11 APRIL

In the past God spoke to our ancestors through the prophets at many times and in various ways, but in these last days he has spoken to us by his Son (Hebrews 1:1, 2 *NIV*)

'You see,' said Father Brown in a low but easy tone, 'Scotch people before Scotland existed were a curious lot. In fact, they're a curious lot still. But in the prehistoric times I fancy they really worshipped demons. That,' he added genially, 'is why they jumped at the Puritan theology.'*

LORD, I HAVE no idea whether or not prehistoric people worshipped demons! What I do know, though, is that you have loved humankind through century after century; from prehistoric times into modern days. What astonishing, inexhaustible love this must be! What truly great faithfulness! What a God you must be.

* *The Honour of Israel Gow.*

12 APRIL

He has filled them with skill to do all kinds of work as engravers, designers, embroiderers in blue, purple and scarlet yarn and fine linen, and weavers – all of them skilled workers and designers (Exodus 35:35 *NIV*)

Leonard Quinton, the poet . . . was a man who drank and bathed in colours, who indulged his lust for colour somewhat to the neglect of form – even of good form. This it was that had turned his genius so wholly to eastern art and imagery; to those bewildering carpets or blinding embroideries in which all the colours seems to have fallen into a fortunate chaos, having nothing to typify or to teach.

He had attempted, not perhaps with complete artistic success, but with acknowledged imagination and invention, to compose epics and love stories reflecting the riot of violent and even cruel colour; tales of tropical heavens of burning gold or blood-red copper; of eastern heroes who rode with twelve-turbaned mitres upon elephants painted purple or peacock green; of gigantic jewels . . . which burned with ancient and strange-hued fires.*

VIVACIOUS GOD OF colour and immense style, how graciously and how generously you inspire poets, artists, skilled workers and designers to represent your burning heart of variety in all manner of vibrant ways. And yet, somehow, quite astonishingly, we have often succeeded in portraying you to a watching world as a deity who is as dull as can be, and a boring killjoy. Forgive us, Lord, and teach us afresh to find ways of portraying you as you really are – life itself!

* *The Wrong Shape.*

13 APRIL

The Spirit of the Lord is on me, because he has anointed me to proclaim good news to the poor. He has sent me to proclaim freedom for the prisoners and recovery of sight for the blind, to set the oppressed free (Luke 4:18 *NIV*)

[Leonard Quinton] dealt much in eastern heavens, rather worse than most western hells; in eastern monarchs, whom we might possibly call maniacs; and in eastern jewels which a Bond Street jeweller . . . might possibly not regard as genuine. Quinton was a genius, if a morbid one; and even his morbidity appeared more in his life than in his work.

In temperament he was weak and waspish, and his health had suffered heavily from oriental experiments with opium. His wife – a handsome, hard-working, and, indeed, over-worked woman – objected to the opium, but objected much more to a live Indian hermit in white and yellow robes, whom her husband insisted on entertaining for months together, a Virgil to guide his spirit through the heavens and the hells of the east.

It was out of this artistic household that Father Brown and his friend stepped on to the door-step; and to judge from their faces, they stepped out of it with much relief. Flambeau had known Quinton in wild student days in Paris, and they had renewed the acquaintance for a week-end; but apart from Flambeau's more responsible developments of late, he did not get on well with the poet now. Choking oneself with opium and writing little erotic verses on vellum was not his notion of how a gentleman should go to the devil.*

GOD OF GRACE and God of power, I pray for addicts today, and for those who reach out to try to help them. I pray for those enslaved by addictive substances, whose lives are in chains. In your mercy, bring deliverance, as only you can. Set them free, I pray, by all means at your disposal.

* *The Wrong Shape.*

14 APRIL

I will be merciful to their unrighteousness, and their sins and their lawless deeds I will remember no more (Hebrews 8:12 *NKJV*)

[Prince Saradine] had been a brilliant and fashionable figure in southern Italy. In his youth, it was said, he had eloped with a married woman of high rank; the escapade was scarcely startling in his social world, but it had come to men's minds because of an additional tragedy: the alleged suicide of the insulted husband, who appeared to have flung himself over a precipice in Sicily.

The prince then lived in Vienna for a time, but his more recent years seemed to have been passed in perpetual and restless travel. But when Flambeau, like the prince himself, had left European celebrity and settled in England, it occurred to him that he might pay a surprise visit to this eminent exile in the Norfolk Broads. Whether he should find the place he had no idea; and, indeed, it was sufficiently small and forgotten. But, as things fell out, he found it much sooner than he expected.*

HERE WE HAVE it, Lord; two men moving towards the evening of life, looking back over their years and realising that sin is written indelibly into the parchment of their stories. And thus, Lord, it is with all of us – except, that is, for the fact that your spilt blood has washed away every single stain. Help us to know that, I pray, and to believe it, and to lean hard into it, for it is our only hope of eternal rest. Look upon us sinners and release us from the perpetual restlessness of sins unforgiven.

* *The Sins of Prince Saradine.*

15 APRIL

You will keep in perfect peace those whose minds are steadfast, because they trust in you (Isaiah 26:3 *NIV*)

[Flambeau and Father Brown] had moored their boat one night under a bank veiled in high grasses and short pollarded trees. Sleep, after heavy sculling, had come to them early, and by a corresponding accident they awoke before it was light. To speak more strictly, they awoke before it was daylight; for a large lemon moon was only just setting in the forest of high grass above their heads, and the sky was of a vivid violet-blue, nocturnal but bright.

Both men had simultaneously a reminiscence of childhood, of the elfin and adventurous time when tall weeds close over us like woods. Standing up thus against the large low moon the daisies really seemed to be giant daisies, the dandelions to be giant dandelions. Somehow it reminded them of the dado of a nursery wall-paper. The drop of the river-bed sufficed to sink them under the roots of all shrubs and make them gaze upwards at the grass.

'By Jove!' said Flambeau; 'it's like being in fairyland.' Father Brown sat bolt upright in the boat and crossed himself. His movement was so abrupt that his friend asked him, with a mild stare, what was the matter.

'The people who wrote the medieval ballads,' answered the priest, 'knew more about fairies than you do. It isn't only nice things that happen in fairyland.' 'Oh, bosh!' said Flambeau. 'Only nice things could happen under such an innocent moon. I am for pushing on now and seeing what does really come. We may die and rot before we ever see again such a moon or such a wood.'

'All right,' said Father Brown. 'I never said it was always wrong to enter fairyland. I only said it was always dangerous.'*

* *The Sins of Prince Saradine.*

HOW POWERFUL, HOW frightening, and how controlling, superstition can be, Lord! Likewise, the imagination, which can dream up and imagine all kinds of fears and dangers. I guess that's natural, Lord, and all part and parcel of the way we are created. Help me, though, I pray, to keep a straight head when it comes to that which is true, and real, and that which is imaginary. My prayers today are with those whose minds are in the grip of superstitious fear.

16 APRIL

A man named Ananias, together with his wife Sapphira, also sold a piece of property. With his wife's full knowledge he kept back part of the money for himself, but brought the rest and put it at the apostles' feet. Then Peter said, 'Ananias, how is it that Satan has so filled your heart that you have lied to the Holy Spirit and have kept for yourself some of the money you received for the land? Didn't it belong to you before it was sold? And after it was sold, wasn't the money at your disposal? What made you think of doing such a thing? You have not lied just to human beings but to God.' When Ananias heard this, he fell down and died. And great fear seized all who heard what had happened. Then some young men came forward, wrapped up his body, and carried him out and buried him. About three hours later his wife came in, not knowing what had happened. Peter asked her, 'Tell me, is this the price you and Ananias got for the land?' 'Yes,' she said, 'that is the price.' Peter said to her, 'How could you conspire to test the Spirit of the Lord? Listen! The feet of the men who buried your husband are at the door, and they will carry you out also.' At that moment she fell down at his feet and died. Then the young men came in and, finding her dead, carried her out and buried her beside her husband (Acts 5:1-10 *NIV*)

Though the blacksmith was a Puritan and none of his people, [The Rev. and Hon.] Wilfred Bohun had heard some scandals about a beautiful and rather celebrated wife. He flung a suspicious look across the shed, and [Colonel the Hon. Norman Bohun, his elder brother] stood up laughing to speak to him.

'Good morning, Wilfred,' he said. 'Like a good landlord I am watching sleeplessly over my people. I am going to call on the blacksmith.' Wilfred looked at the ground and said: 'The blacksmith is out. He is over at Greenford.' 'I know,' answered the other with silent laughter; 'that is why I am calling on him.'

'Norman,' said the cleric, with his eye on a pebble in the road, 'are you ever afraid of thunderbolts?' 'What do you mean?' asked the colonel. 'Is your hobby meteorology?' 'I mean,' said Wilfred, without looking up, 'do you ever think that God might strike you in the street?' 'I beg your pardon,' said the colonel; 'I see your hobby is folk-lore.' 'I know your hobby is blasphemy,' retorted the religious man, stung in the one live place of his nature. 'But if you do not fear God, you have good reason to fear man.' The elder raised his eyebrows politely. 'Fear man?' he said.

'Barnes the blacksmith is the biggest and strongest man for forty miles round,' said the clergyman sternly. 'I know you are no coward or weakling, but he could throw you over the wall.'*

FOOD FOR THOUGHT, Heavenly Father:

1. *A brave and honest priest.*
2. *A side of your character that sometimes we prefer to ignore.*
3. *The reassurance that, in your Kingdom, right will prevail.*
4. *A challenge to live uprightly, with your help.*

* *The Hammer of God.*

17 APRIL

This is none other but the house of God, and this is the gate of heaven (Genesis 28:17 *KJV*)

[The colonel] took off the queer round hat covered with green, showing that it was lined within with steel. Wilfred recognised it indeed as a light Japanese or Chinese helmet torn down from a trophy that hung in the old family hall.

'It was the first hat to hand,' explained the brother airily; 'always the nearest hat – and the nearest woman.'

'The blacksmith is away at Greenford,' said Wilfred quietly; 'the time of his return is unsettled.'

And with that he turned and went into the church with bowed head, crossing himself like one who wishes to be quit of an unclean spirit. He was anxious to forget such grossness in the cool twilight of his tall Gothic cloisters.*

WHAT A PRIVILEGE and a blessing it can be, Lord, to sit quietly in an old church when the pressures of the day have sullied my thinking or wearied my soul. I realise, of course, that even the most beautiful church is only a building, when all is said and done, but I thank you for sacred spaces, nonetheless. Thank you for walls that have absorbed the prayers of the centuries, and for the fact that I may add mine.

* *The Hammer of God.*

18 APRIL

Because the Sovereign LORD helps me, I will not be disgraced. Therefore have I set my face like flint (Isaiah 50:7 *NIV*)

[Flambeau] was a lucid Southerner, incapable of conceiving himself as anything but a Catholic or an atheist; and new religions of a bright and pallid sort were not much in his line. But humanity was always in his line, especially when it was good-looking; moreover, the ladies downstairs were characters in their way.

The office was kept by two sisters, both slight and dark, one of them tall and striking. She had a dark, eager and aquiline profile, and was one of those women whom one always thinks of in profile, as of the clean-cut edge of some weapon. She seemed to cleave her way through life. She had eyes of startling brilliancy, but it was the brilliancy of steel rather than of diamonds; and her straight, slim figure was a shade too stiff for its grace.

Her younger sister was like her shortened shadow, a little greyer, paler, and more insignificant. They both wore a business-like black, with little masculine cuffs and collars. There are thousands of such curt, strenuous ladies in the offices of London.*

THERE ARE THOSE times, Lord, when I need to set my face like flint. I can't pretend to want to do that, but I pray, nonetheless, that if and when such moments arrive, and I need to stand my ground, that you would strengthen me. Flint is hard, Lord, but so is life, sometimes. Grant me strength for my day.

* *The Eye of Apollo.*

19 APRIL

Jacob set up a pillar in the place where he talked with him, even a pillar of stone (Genesis 35:14 *KJV*)

The big man fumbled in his pocket, and soon a scratch and a flare painted gold the whole flat side of the monument. On it was cut in black letters the well-known words which so many Americans had reverently read: 'Sacred to the Memory of General Sir Arthur St Clare, Hero and Martyr, who Always Vanquished his Enemies and Always Spared Them, and Was Treacherously Slain by Them At Last. May God in Whom he Trusted both Reward and Revenge him' . . .

'I know nothing about English generals, Father Brown,' answered the large man, laughing, 'though a little about English policemen. I only know that you have dragged me a precious long dance to all the shrines of this fellow, whoever he is. One would think he got buried in six different places. I've seen a memorial to General St Clare in Westminster Abbey; I've seen a ramping equestrian statue of General St Clare on the Embankment; I've seen a medallion of General St Clare in the street he was born in; and another in the street he lived in; and now you drag me after dark to his coffin in the village churchyard. I am beginning to be a bit tired of his magnificent personality, especially as I don't in the least know who he was.'*

FAITHFUL AND EVERLASTING God, teach me to construct memorials in my heart, in my memory, or in my prayer journal, detailing those times when you have talked with me, as you talked with Jacob. They might not be monuments of stone, but they will encourage me in my pilgrimage, as I look back and recount your goodness.

* *The Sign of the Broken Sword.*

20 APRIL

Do your best to present yourself to God as one approved, a worker who has no need to be ashamed, rightly handling the word of truth (2 Timothy 2:15 *ESV*)

'Now, what everybody knows is short and plain enough. It is also entirely wrong' [said Father Brown].

'Right you are,' said the big man called Flambeau cheerfully. 'Let's begin at the wrong end. Let's begin with what everybody knows, which isn't true.'

'If not wholly untrue, it is at least very inadequate,' continued Brown; 'for in point of fact, all that the public knows amounts precisely to this: The public knows that Arthur St Clare was a great and successful English general. It knows that after splendid yet careful campaigns both in India and Africa he was in command against Brazil when the great Brazilian patriot Olivier issued his ultimatum. It knows that on that occasion St Clare with a very small force attacked Olivier with a very large one, and was captured after heroic resistance. And it knows that after his capture, and to the abhorrence of the civilised world, St Clare was hanged on the nearest tree. He was found swinging there after the Brazilians had retired, with his broken sword hung round his neck.'*

THE IMPORTANCE OF checking one's facts, Lord! The importance, too, of not following the crowd, and of realising that just because something is believed to be true by a majority, that isn't necessarily the case. As I read my Bible, Lord, and as I listen to (or preach) sermons week-by-week, for example, help me to fact-check; not ever in a cynical or critical way, and certainly not in hopes of eagerly spotting others' mistakes, but simply so that mine is not a 'face value faith'. Matters of belief and doctrine are too important for that, and they deserve my excavation.

* *The Sign of the Broken Sword.*

21 APRIL

And when his family heard it, they went out to seize him, for they were saying, 'He is out of his mind' (Mark 3:21 *ESV*)

Flambeau lifted his head, but lowered his voice. 'General Sir Arthur St Clare,' he said, 'came of a family in which madness was hereditary; and his whole aim was to keep this from his daughter, and even, if possible, from his future son-in-law. Rightly or wrongly, he thought the final collapse was close, and resolved on suicide. Yet ordinary suicide would blazon the very idea he dreaded. As the campaign approached the clouds came thicker on his brain; and at last in a mad moment he sacrificed his public duty to his private. He rushed rashly into battle, hoping to fall by the first shot. When he found that he had only attained capture and discredit, the sealed bomb in his brain burst, and he broke his own sword and hanged himself.'

He stared firmly at the grey facade of forest in front of him, with the one black gap in it, like the mouth of the grave, into which their path plunged. Perhaps something menacing in the road thus suddenly swallowed reinforced his vivid vision of the tragedy, for he shuddered.

'A horrid story,' he said.

'A horrid story,' repeated the priest with bent head. 'But not the real story.'

Then he threw back his head with a sort of despair and cried: 'Oh, I wish it had been.'*

I REALLY DO thank you, Heavenly Father, for the massive shifts and strides that have been made in terms of modern-day mental health awareness and improved care or treatment. My heart goes out to those who are struggling and suffering with issues of mental health, and I lift them to you in prayer. I pray too for medical professionals and those who specialise in psychiatric expertise. Bless them as they do what they can to help.

* *The Sign of the Broken Sword.*

22 APRIL

The bloodthirsty hate the upright (Proverbs 29:10 *KJV*)

[Sir Aaron Armstrong] lived on the rural skirt of Hampstead in a handsome house, high but not broad, a modern and prosaic tower. The narrowest of its narrow sides overhung the steep green bank of a railway, and was shaken by passing trains. Sir Aaron Armstrong, as he boisterously explained, had no nerves. But if the train had often given a shock to the house, that morning the tables were turned, and it was the house that gave a shock to the train.

The engine slowed down and stopped just beyond that point where an angle of the house impinged upon the sharp slope of turf. The arrest of most mechanical things must be slow; but the living cause of this had been very rapid. A man clad completely in black, even (it was remembered) to the dreadful detail of black gloves, appeared on the ridge above the engine, and waved his black hands like some sable windmill. This in itself would hardly have stopped even a lingering train. But there came out of him a cry which was talked of afterwards as something utterly unnatural and new. It was one of those shouts that are horribly distinct even when we cannot hear what is shouted. The word in this case was 'Murder!'*

LORD GOD, THE Bible includes its fair share of murderous activities! So too, human history. Murder most foul, repeated over and over as the ages have passed. And yet, you steadfastly refuse to abandon humanity. What grace this is! Amidst all the carnage and bloodshed, there is your love. Amidst the hatred and violence, there is God. There is God, and there will be God.

* *The Three Tools of Death.*

23 APRIL

Joseph of Arimathea asked Pilate for the body of Jesus. Now Joseph was a disciple of Jesus, but secretly because he feared the Jewish leaders. With Pilate's permission, he came and took the body away. He was accompanied by Nicodemus, the man who earlier had visited Jesus at night. Nicodemus brought a mixture of myrrh and aloes, about seventy-five pounds. Taking Jesus' body, the two of them wrapped it, with the spices, in strips of linen. This was in accordance with Jewish burial customs (John 19:38-40 *NIV*)

The engine-driver swears he would have pulled up just the same if he had heard only the dreadful accent and not the word.

The train once arrested, the most superficial stare could only take in many features of this tragedy. The man in black on the green bank was Sir Aaron Armstrong's man-servant, Magnus. The baronet in his optimism had often laughed at the black gloves of this dismal attendant; but no one was likely to laugh at him just now.

So soon as an inquirer or two had stepped off the line and across the smoky hedge, they saw, rolled down almost to the bottom of the ban, the body of an old man in a yellow dressing-gown with a very vivid scarlet lining. A scrap of rope seemed caught about his leg, entangled presumably in a struggle. There was a smear or so of blood, though very little; but the body was bent or broken into a posture impossible to any living thing.*

CHRIST, MY GOD. Broken and bloodied for me.

* *The Three Tools of Death.*

24 APRIL

Jesus replied, 'Foxes have dens and birds have nests, but the Son of Man has no place to lay his head' (Matthew 8:20 *NIV*)

The consulting-rooms of Dr Orion Hood, the eminent criminologist and specialist in certain moral disorders, lay along the sea-front at Scarborough, in a series of very large and well-lighted French windows, which showed the North Sea like one endless outer wall of blue-green marble. In such a place the sea had something of the monotony of a blue-green dado: for the chambers themselves were ruled throughout by a terrible tidiness not unlike the terrible tidiness of the sea. It must not be supposed that Dr Hood's apartments excluded luxury, or even poetry. These things were there, in their place; but one felt that they were never allowed out of their place. Luxury was there: there stood upon a special table eight or ten boxes of the best cigars; but they were built upon a plan so that the strongest were always nearest the wall and the mildest nearest the window. A Tantalus containing three kinds of spirit, all of a liqueur excellence, stood always on this table of luxury.*

THIS IS GRACE and mercy personified, Lord Jesus; that you should leave the splendour and majesty of heaven in order to live as a homeless, itinerant preacher. Love incarnate! You knew nothing of luxury or comfort, yet you were God here on earth. Thank you, Lord Jesus, for leaving everything behind in order to seek and to save the lost. Thank you for doing this for me.

* *The Absence of Mr Glass.*

25 APRIL

The LORD scattered them abroad from thence upon the face of all the earth (Genesis 11:8 *KJV*)

The great Muscari, most original of the young Tuscan poets, walked swiftly into his favourite restaurant, which overlooked the Mediterranean, was covered by an awning and fenced by little lemon and orange trees, Waiters in white aprons were already laying out on white tables the insignia of an early and elegant lunch; and this seemed to increase a satisfaction that already touched the top of swagger.

Muscari had an eagle nose like Dante; his hair and neckerchief were dark and flowing; he carried a black cloak, and might almost have carried a black mask, so much did he bear with him a sort of Venetian melodrama. He acted as if a troubadour had still a definite social office, like a bishop. He went as near as his century permitted to walking the world literally like Don Juan, with rapier and guitar. For he never travelled without a case of swords, with which he had fought many brilliant duels, or without a corresponding case for his mandolin, with which he had actually serenaded Miss Ethel Harrogate, the highly-conventional daughter of a Yorkshire banker on holiday. Yet he was neither a charlatan nor a child; but a hot, logical Latin who liked a certain thing and was it. His poetry was as straightforward as anyone else's prose. He desired fame or wine or the beauty of women with a torrid directness inconceivable among the cloudy ideals or cloudy promises of the north; to vaguer races his intensity smelt of danger or even crime. Like fire or the sea, he was too simple to be trusted.*

LORD, I AM reluctant to generalise, but it does indeed seem that you have created different races with markedly different traits and temperaments; some nations appear to be calm and collected and methodical (on the whole), while others are somewhat more

* *The Paradise of Thieves.*

fiery and exuberant. All of this leads me to pray, Heavenly Father, for anyone I know living overseas; family and friends alike. In whatever culture they find themselves, living or working, I ask your blessing on them today.

26 APRIL

Is it nothing to you, all you who pass by? (Lamentations 1:12 *NIV*)

The banker and his beautiful English daughter were staying at the hotel attached to Muscari's restaurant; that was why it was his favourite restaurant. A glance flashed round the room told him at once, however, that the English party had not yet descended.

The restaurant was glittering, but still comparatively empty. Two priests were talking at a table in a corner, but Muscari (an ardent Catholic) took no more notice of them than a couple of crows.*

LORD, IT SADDENS me a little that in this day and age, priests and clergy do tend to be ignored, with no-one taking much notice of them or the Church. Forgive my pessimism, but that's how it seems these days; as though faith is somewhat irrelevant to society at large. I pray for change in that direction, Lord; that your Church may once again find its voice and reclaim its rightful place in current affairs and the life of the nation.

* *The Paradise of Thieves.*

27 APRIL

The fool says in his heart, 'There is no God' (Psalm 14:1 *NIV*)

M. Maurice Brun and M. Armand Armagnac were crossing the sunlit Champs Elysées with a kind of vivacious respectability. They were both short, brisk and bold. They both had black beards that did not seem to belong to their faces, after the strange French fashion which makes real hair look like artificial. M. Brun had a dark wedge of beard apparently affixed under his lower lip. M. Armagnac, by way of a change, had two beards; one sticking out from each corner of his emphatic chin. They were both young. They were both atheists, with a depressing fixity of outlook but great mobility of exposition. They were both pupils of the great Dr Hirsch, scientist, publicist and moralist.

M. Brun had become prominent by his proposal that the common expression 'Adieu' should be obliterated from all the French classics, and a slight fine imposed for its use in private life. 'Then,' he said, 'the very name of your imagined God will have echoed for the last time in the ear of man.'*

LORD, WHILST IT is true that atheists don't believe in you, it is equally true that you believe in them! To that end, I pray for any atheists known to me personally. I pray a simple, straightforward, unapologetic prayer: that in your mercy you would somehow draw them to a place of faith.

* *The Duel of Dr Hirsch.*

28 APRIL

What did you go out to see? A man dressed in fine clothes? No, those who wear fine clothes are in kings' palaces (Matthew 11:8 *NIV*)

Sir Wilson Seymour was the kind of man whose importance is known to everybody who knows. The more you mixed with the innermost ring in every polity or profession, the more often you met with Sir Wilson Seymour.

He was the one intelligent man on twenty unintelligent committees – on every sort of subject, from the reform of the Royal Academy to the project of bimetallism for Greater Britain. In the arts especially he was omnipotent. He was so unique that nobody could decide whether he was a great aristocrat who had taken up Art, or a great artist whom the aristocrats had taken up. But you could not meet him for five minutes without realizing that you had really been ruled by him all your life.

His appearance was 'distinguished' in exactly the same sense; it was at once conventional and unique. Fashion could have found no fault with his high silk hat; yet it was unlike anyone else's hat – a little higher, perhaps, and adding something to his natural height. His tall, slender figure had a slight stoop, yet it looked the reverse of feeble. His hair was silver-grey, but he did not look old; it was worn longer than the common yet he did not look effeminate; it was curly but it did not look curled. His carefully pointed beard made him look more manly and militant rather than otherwise, as it does in those old admirals of Velazquez with whose dark portraits his house was hung. His grey gloves were a shade bluer, his silver-knobbed cane a shade longer than scores of such gloves and canes flapped and flourished about the theatres and the restaurants.*

WHAT HAVE I gone out to see today, Lord? In other words, what has caught my attention? Fine clothes and fancy ways? That which is expensive and commonly regarded as impressive? There's nothing at all wrong with smartness and quality, and dignity is a

* *The Man in the Passage.*

fine quality, to be admired, but for all that, I pray that you would keep my eyes fixed on matters of faith. The things of this world have their place, but help me to go out to see that which is of you, and of greater value.

29 APRIL

'I know the plans I have for you,' declares the LORD, 'plans to prosper you and not to harm you, plans to give you hope and a future' (Jeremiah 29:11 *NIV*)

This figure was clad in tweeds of a piebald check, with a pink tie, a sharp collar and protuberant yellow boots. He contrived, in the true tradition of 'Arry at Margate, to look at once startling and commonplace. But as the Cockney apparition drew nearer, Muscari was astounded to observe that the head was distinctly different from the body. It was an Italian head: fuzzy, swarthy and very vivacious, that rose abruptly out of the standing collar like cardboard and the comic pink tie.

In fact it was a head he knew. He recognized it, above all the dire erection of English holiday array, as the face of an old but forgotten friend named Ezza. This youth had been a prodigy at college, and European fame was promised to him when he was barely fifteen, but when he appeared in the world he failed, first publicly as a dramatist and a demagogue, and then privately for years on end as an actor, a traveller, a commission agent or a journalist. Muscari had known him last behind the footlights; he was but too well attuned to the excitements of that profession and it was believed that some moral calamity had swallowed him up.

'Ezza!' cried the poet, rising and shaking hands in a pleasant astonishment. 'Well, I've seen you in many costumes in the green room; but I never expected to see you dressed up as an Englishman. 'This,' answered Ezza gravely: 'is not the costume of an Englishman, but of the Italian of the future.'*

GOD OF OUR highs and lows, I pray for those who feel themselves to be failures. Reach out to them by your Spirit in order to lift them from that identity towards a future. Lord, you specialise in restoration, so I pray that you would impart healing, help and hope.

* *The Paradise of Thieves.*

30 APRIL

I and the Father are one (John 10:30 *ESV*)

'In the sixteenth century [said the man in tweeds] we Tuscans made the morning: we had the newest steel, the newest carving, the newest chemistry. Why should we not now have the newest factories, the newest motors, the newest finance – and the newest clothes?'

'Because they are not worth having,' answered Muscari. 'You cannot make Italians really progressive; they are too intelligent. Men who see the short cut to good living will never go by the new elaborate roads.'

'Well, to me Marconi, or D'Annunzio, is the star of Italy,' said the other. 'That is why I have become a Futurist – and a courier.' *

'A courier!' cried Muscari, laughing. 'Is that the last of your list of trades? And whom are you conducting?' 'Oh, a man of the name of Harrogate, and his family, I believe.' 'Not the banker in this hotel?' inquired the poet, with some eagerness. 'That's the man, answered the courier. 'Does it pay well?' asked the troubadour innocently. 'It will pay me,' said Ezza, with a very enigmatic smile. 'But I am a rather curious sort of courier.'

Then, as if changing the subject, he said abruptly: 'He has a daughter – and a son.' 'The daughter is divine,' affirmed Muscari, 'the father and son are, I suppose, human.'†

THE DIVINE AND human natures! Wonderfully and uniquely combined in Jesus; God with the skin on! Such love. Father and Son as one.

* In this context, a traveller's paid attendant.

† *The Paradise of Thieves.*

1 MAY

You are altogether beautiful, my darling; there is no flaw in you (Song of Songs 4:7 *NIV*)

[Muscari affirmed] 'Harrogate has millions in his safes, and I have – the hole in my pocket. But you daren't say – you can't say – that he's cleverer than I, or even more energetic. He's not clever; he's got eyes like blue buttons; he's not energetic, he moves from chair to chair like a paralytic. He's a conscientious, kindly old blockhead; he's got money simply because he collects money, as a boy collects stamps. You're too strong-minded for business, Ezza. You won't get on. To be clever enough to get all that money, one must be stupid enough to want it.'

'I'm stupid enough for that,' said Ezza gloomily. 'But I should suggest a suspension of your critique for the banker, for here he comes.'

Mr Harrogate, the great financier, did indeed enter the room, but nobody looked at him. He was a massive elderly man with a boiled blue eye and faded grey-sandy moustaches; but for his heavy stoop he might have been a colonel. He carried several unopened letters in his hand. His son Frank was a really fine lad, curly-haired, sun-burnt and strenuous; but nobody looked at him either.

All eyes, as usual, were riveted, for the moment at least, upon Ethel Harrogate, whose golden Greek head and colour of the dawn seemed purposely set above that sapphire sea, like a goddess's. The poet Muscari drew a deep breath as if he were drinking something, as indeed he was.*

LORD, WHAT A peculiar relationship your Church has sometimes had with matters acknowledging physical beauty or sexual attraction, as though they were somehow shameful or even sinful! It's such an odd dynamic at times, and loaded with pretence and all kinds of conflicting emotions. Come and help us, Lord, by your Spirit, to move towards honesty, openness and a much healthier normality.

* *The Paradise of Thieves.*

2 MAY

Ephraim has surrounded me with lies, Israel with deceit
(Hosea 11:12 *NIV*)

'A man telling lies on chance would have told some of the truth . . . Suppose someone sent you to find a house with a green door and a blue blind, with a front garden but no back garden, with a dog but no cat, and where they drank coffee but not tea. You would say if you found no such house that it was all made up. But I say no. I say if you found a house where the door was blue and the blind green, where there was a back garden and no front garden, where cats were common and dogs instantly shot, where tea was drunk in quarts and coffee forbidden – then you would know you had found the house.'*

PART-TRUTHS AND HALF-TRUTHS, Lord! Semantics and word-games! You who came full of grace and truth, teach my heart such ways.

* *The Duel of Dr Hirsch.*

3 MAY

Whoever says he is in the light and hates his brother is still in darkness (1 John 2:9 *ESV*)

Two men appeared simultaneously at the two ends of a sort of passage running along the side of the Apollo Theatre in the Adelphi.

The evening daylight in the streets was large and luminous, opalescent and empty. The passage was comparatively long and dark, so each man could see the other as a mere black silhouette at the other end.

Nevertheless, each man knew the other, even in that inky outline; for they were both men of striking appearance and they hated each other.*

HOW EASY IT is to hate, Lord! And how sad, and how wrong. Please forgive those moments in my life, whether lingering or temporary, when I have hated. Cleanse me from within, as only you are able.

* *The Man in the Passage.*

4 MAY

In quietness and in confidence shall be your strength (Isaiah 30:15 *KJV*)

The covered passage opened at one end on one of the steep streets of the Adelphi, and the other on a terrace overlooking the sunset-coloured river. One side of the passage was a blank wall, for the building it supported was an old unsuccessful theatre restaurant, now shut up. The other side of the passage contained two doors, one at each end. Neither was what was commonly called the stage door; they were a sort of special and private stage doors used by very special performers, and in this case by the star actor and actress in the Shakespearean performance of the day. Persons of that eminence often like to have such private exits and entrances, for meeting friends or avoiding them.

The two men in question were certainly two such friends, men who evidently knew the doors and counted on their opening, for each approached the door at the upper end with coolness and confidence. Not, however, with equal speed; but the man who walked fast was the man from the other end of the tunnel, so they both arrived before the secret stage door almost at the same instant. They saluted each other with civility, and waited a moment before one of them, the sharper walker, who seemed to have the shorter patience, knocked at the door.*

IT'S NO BAD thing to walk along with coolness and confidence, Lord, but if that is merely on the surface, for public show, then it isn't worth anything at all except for keeping up appearances. Grant me, I pray, a quietness and a confidence that emerges from within, and is to do with your love. Let that be my inner strength today, and if it serves as a witness, all the better. Walk along with me, please.

* *The Man in the Passage.*

5 MAY

I was in prison and you came to visit me (Matthew 25:36 *NIV*)

It happened nearly twenty years before, when [Father Brown] was chaplain to his co-religionists in a prison in Chicago – where the Irish population displayed a capacity for both crime and penitence which kept him tolerably busy.

The official second-in-command under the Governor was an ex-detective named Greywood Usher, a cadaverous, careful-spoken Yankee philosopher, occasionally varying a very rigid visage with an odd apologetic grimace. He liked Father Brown in a slightly patronising way; and Father Brown liked him, though he heartily disliked his theories. His theories were extremely complicated and were held with extreme simplicity.*

Our prayer for today is kindly provided by Major Carl Huggins, who at this time of writing serves as a Salvation Army officer in Leicester, England, and whose ministry includes chaplaincy at Her Majesty's Prison Leicester:

LOVING HEAVENLY FATHER, I want to pray for my fellow prison chaplains who face many challenging situations. Give them the wisdom to help and guide the people with whom they come into contact. Give them the protection they need every day. I ask this in the name of our Lord and Saviour, Jesus Christ. Amen.

* *The Mistake of the Machine.*

6 MAY

They do not belong to this world any more than I do (John 17:16 *NLT*)

One evening [Greywood Usher] had sent for the priest, who, according to his custom, took a seat in silence at a table piled and littered with papers, and waited. The official selected from the papers a scrap of newspaper cutting, which he handed across to the cleric, who read it gravely.

It appeared to be an extract from one of the . . . American Society papers:

'Miss Etta Todd is one of our deep-souled New Yorkers, and comes into an income of nearly twelve hundred million dollars.'

'Well,' asked Usher, 'does that interest you?' 'Why, words rather fail me,' answered Father Brown. 'I cannot think at this moment of anything in this world that would interest me less. And . . . I don't quite see why it should interest you either.'*

WELL, LORD, WE haven't much choice but to be in this world, at least for the time being, but as representatives of another world, I pray that we would be something like Father Brown; unfazed by wealth – even great wealth – and all that society holds dear. Why should such things interest us, unless, that is, they are connected to your Kingdom in some way or other.

* *The Mistake of the Machine.*

7 MAY

Enter through the narrow gate. For wide is the gate and broad is the road that leads to destruction, and many enter through it. But small is the gate and narrow the road that leads to life, and only a few find it (Matthew 7:13, 14 *NIV*)

There is somewhere in Brompton or Kensington an interminable avenue of tall houses, rich but largely empty, that looks like a terrace of tombs. The very steps up to the dark front doors seem as steep as the sides of pyramids; and one would hesitate to knock at the door, lest it should be opened by a mummy.

But a yet more depressing feature in the grey façade is its telescopic length and changeless continuity. The pilgrim walking down it begins to think he will never come to a break or a corner; but there is one exception – a very small one, but hailed by the pilgrim almost without a shout. There is a sort of mews between two of the tall mansions, a mere slit like the crack of a door by comparison with the street.*

ONCE AGAIN, HEAVENLY Father, I pray for those known to me who appear not to be interested in the narrow way. As I name them before you in prayer – family, friends, neighbours and colleagues – I carry them, so to speak, to your Throne of Grace. May they too become pilgrims, one day, according to your loving mercy.

* *The Head of Caesar.*

8 MAY

I urge, then, first of all, that petitions, prayers, intercession and thanksgiving be made for all people – for kings and all those in authority, that we may live peaceful and quiet lives in all godliness and holiness (1 Timothy 2:1, 2 *NIV*)

Mr Edward Nutt, the industrious editor of the *Daily Reformer*, sat at his desk, opening letters and marking proofs to the merry tune of a typewriter, worked by a vigorous young lady.

He was a stoutish, fair man, in his shirt-sleeves; his movements were resolute, his mouth firm and his tones final; but his round, rather babyish blue eyes had a bewildered and even wistful look that rather contradicted all this. Nor indeed was the expression altogether misleading. It might truly be said of him, as of many journalists in authority, that his most familiar emotion was one of continuous fear; fear of libel actions, fear of lost advertisements, fear of misprints, fear of the sack.

His life was a series of distracted compromises between the proprietor of the paper (and of him), who was a senile soap-boiler with three ineradicable mistakes in his mind, and the very able staff he had collected to run the paper; some of whom were brilliant and experienced men and (what was even worse) sincere enthusiasts for the political policy of the paper.*

LORD, MY PRAYERS today are for political leaders at local and national level. I may not necessarily agree with their political policies, but I am still obliged to pray for them. I pray especially for them to act out of conviction, and to be motivated by conscience rather than fear. In the political arena, when the electorate can sometimes be incredibly hostile, fear can so often be a deciding factor. Help those who lead, Lord, to lead well and with good heart. Make them daily reformers.

* *The Purple Wig.*

9 MAY

Life does not consist in an abundance of possessions (Luke 12:15 *NIV*)

With a more thoughtful eye [Edward Nutt] ripped open the letter from his more distinguished contributor, which bore the postmark of Devonshire, and ran as follows:

' . . . It seems to me that we make a mistake in attacking aristocracy entirely for its champagne and diamonds. Most men rather admire the nobs for having a good time, but I think we surrender too much when we admit that aristocracy has made even the aristocrats happy. I suggest a series of articles pointing out how dreary, how inhuman, how downright diabolist, is the very smell and atmosphere of some of these great houses . . .'*

HOW TEMPTING IT can be, Lord, to imagine that an abundance of possessions might be the answer to our problems; a bigger car, a country house, champagne and diamonds. Those are all lovely things, but they are just exactly that: things. Thank you that life itself – the enjoyment of life – does not depend upon them. Let me walk in that spirit today.

* *The Purple Wig.*

10 MAY

Do your best to get here before winter (2 Timothy 4:21 *NIV*)

It was one of those chilly and empty afternoons in early winter, when the daylight is silver rather than gold and pewter rather than silver. If it was dreary in a hundred bleak offices and yawning drawing-rooms, it was drearier still along the edges of the flat Essex coast, where the monotony was the more inhuman for being broken at very long intervals by a lamp-post that looked less civilised than a tree, or a tree that looked more ugly than a lamp-post. A light fall of snow had half-melted into a few strips, also looking leaden rather than silver, when it had been fixed again by the seal of frost; no fresh snow had fallen, but a ribbon of the old snow ran along the very margin of the coast, so as to parallel the pale ribbon of the foam.

The line of the sea looked frozen in the very vividness of its violet-blue, like the vein of a frozen finger. For miles and miles, forward and back, there was no breathing soul, save two pedestrians, walking at a brisk pace, though one had much longer legs and took much longer strides than the other.

It did not seem a very appropriate place or time for a holiday, but Father Brown had few holidays, and had to take them when he could, and he always preferred, if possible, to take them in company with his old friend Flambeau, ex-criminal and ex-detective. The priest had had a fancy for visiting his old parish at Cobhole, and was going north-eastward along the coast.*

SEASONS ARE SO very evocative, Heavenly Father. They provoke all kinds of feelings, simply by being as they are. My prayers today are for those who might be passing through some kind of spiritual winter, so to speak, when all seems frozen and ice-hard. My prayer is that, even in a tough climate, faith-wise, they will still be able to see beauty, and even trace your fingerprints in their situation. Draw near.

* *The God of the Gongs.*

11 MAY

Enoch walked with God (Genesis 5:24 *ESV*)

Father Brown was walking home from Mass on a white weird morning when the mists were slowly lifting – one of those mornings when the very element of light appears as something mysterious and new. The scattered trees outlined themselves more and more out of the vapour, as if they were first drawn in grey chalk and then in charcoal. At yet more distant intervals appeared the houses upon the broken fringe of the suburb; their outlines became clearer and clearer until he recognised many in which he had chance acquaintances, and many more the names of whose owners he knew. But all the windows and doors were sealed; none of the people were of the sort that would be up at such a time, or still less on such an errand.*

WHAT A BEAUTIFULLY poignant word-picture we have here, Lord! A believer making his way home from church, having heard, perhaps, something helpful and meaningful from the Bible, or having participated in morning worship that lifted his soul and spoke to his heart. Those are sacred moments, and I thank you for them, including the walk home, which can often be a time for quiet reflection. I pray for all such walks and all such walkers, that before the houses once again appear and life resumes its usual rhythm, you would bless those times of contemplation.

* *The Salad of Colonel Cray.*

12 MAY

Stay awake, for you do not know on what day your Lord is coming. But know this, that if the master of the house had known in what part of the night the thief was coming, he would have stayed awake and would not have let his house be broken into. Therefore you also must be ready, for the Son of Man is coming at an hour you do not expect (Matthew 24:42-44 *ESV*)

Half-way down one side of the house stood out a projection like a very low shed; it was, as [Father Brown] afterwards discovered, a large dustbin. Round the corner of this came a figure, at first a mere shadow in the haze, apparently bending and peering about. Then, coming nearer, it solidified into a figure that was, indeed, rather unusually solid. Major Putnam was a bald-headed, bull-necked man, short and very broad, with one of those rather apoplectic faces that are produced by a prolonged attempt to combine the oriental climate with the occidental luxuries. But the face was a good-humoured one, and even now, though evidently puzzled and inquisitive, wore a kind of innocent grin. He had a large palm-leaf hat on the back of his head (suggesting a halo that was by no means appropriate to the face), but otherwise he was clad only in a very vivid suit of striped scarlet and yellow pyjamas; which, though glowing enough to behold, must have been, on a fresh morning, pretty chilly to wear. He had evidently come out of his house in a hurry, and the priest was not surprised when he called out without further ceremony: 'Did you hear that noise?'

'Yes,' answered Father Brown; 'I thought I had better look in, just in case anything was the matter.'

The Major looked at him rather queerly with his good-humoured gooseberry eyes. 'What do you think the noise was?' he asked.

'It sounded like a gun or something,' replied the other, with some hesitation; 'but it seemed to have a singular sort of echo.'*

STRIPED PYJAMAS OR not, Lord Jesus, keep me ready for your arrival. Help me to expect the unexpected!

* *The Salad of Colonel Cray.*

13 MAY

See to it that no one takes you captive through hollow and deceptive philosophy, which depends on human tradition and the elemental spiritual forces of this world rather than on Christ (Colossians 2:8 *NIV*)

The colossal American daily called the *Western Sun* . . . was full of the most solemn matters treated in the most farcical way. William James [*] figured there as well as 'Weary Willie,' and pragmatists alternated with pugilists in the long procession of its portraits.

Thus, when a very unobtrusive Oxford man named John Boulnois wrote in a very unreadable review called the *Natural Philosophy Quarterly* a series of articles on alleged weak points in Darwinian evolution, it fluttered no corner of the English papers; though Boulnois's theory (which was that of a comparatively stationary universe visited occasionally by convulsions of change) had some rather faddy fashionableness at Oxford, and got so far as to be named 'Catastrophism.' But many American papers seized on the challenge and the *Sun* threw the shadow of Mr Boulnois quite gigantically across its pages. By the paradox already noted, articles of valuable intelligence and enthusiasm were presented with headlines apparently written by an illiterate maniac; headlines such as 'Darwin Chews Dirt; Critic Boulnois says He Jumps the Shocks' – or 'Keep Catastrophic, says Thinker Boulnois.' And Mr Calhoun Kidd [emissary in England] of the *Western Sun*, was bidden to take his butterfly tie and lugubrious visage down to the little house outside Oxford where Thinker Boulnois lived in happy ignorance of such a title.[†]

THEORIES AND PHILOSOPHIES come and go, Lord. Some are fads, and some are facts. I don't pretend to understand everything that comes my way, Lord, in terms of theology and philosophy, so I ask you to guide me in ways of truth. Keep my mind hungry, but guard it too, I ask.

* American philosopher, historian and psychologist.

† *The Strange Crime of John Boulnois.*

14 MAY

My tongue is like the pen of a ready scribe (Psalm 45:1 *ESV*)

The fated philosopher had consented, in a somewhat dazed manner, to receive the interviewer, and had named the hour of nine that evening. The last of a summer sunset clung about Cumnor and the low wooded hills; the romantic Yankee was both doubtful of his road and inquisitive about his surroundings; and seeing the door of a genuine feudal old-country inn, The Champion Arms, standing open, he went in to make some inquiries.

In the bar parlour he rang the bell, and had to wait some little time for a reply to it. The only other person was a lean man with close red hair and loose, horsey-looking clothes, who was drinking very bad whisky, but smoking a very good cigar. The whisky, of course, was the choice brand of The Champion Arms; the cigar he had probably brought with him from London. Nothing could more different than his cynical *négligé* * from the dapper dryness of the young American; but something in his pencil and open notebook, and perhaps in the expression of his alert blue eye, caused Kidd to guess, correctly, that he was a brother journalist.†

JOURNALISTS, REPORTERS AND correspondents carry special responsibilities, Lord; to convey reports and stories to thousands – if not millions – of readers and/or listeners. In a world that can easily be dominated by newspaper reports and broadcasts shared over the airwaves, I pray that truth would prevail and that sensationalism would diminish. On a personal note, grant me wisdom to distinguish which is which and to be selective in my reading, listening and viewing.

* Old meaning: Informal attire.

† *The Strange Crime of John Boulnois.*

15 MAY

When I was a child, I talked like a child, I thought like a child, I reasoned like a child (1 Corinthians 13:11 *NIV*)

Despite his prosaic appearance and generally practical walk of life, Father Brown was not without a certain streak of romance in his composition, though he generally kept his day-dreams to himself, as many children do. . .

He took a childish pleasure, as a younger brother might, in the formidable sword-stick which Flambeau always flung as he walked, and which now stood upright beside his tall mug of Münich. Nay, in his sleepy irresponsibility, he even found himself eyeing the knobbed and clumsy head of his own shabby umbrella, with some faint memories of the ogre's club in a coloured toy-book. But he never composed anything in the form of fiction.*

WHAT A TRULY wonderful gift, Heavenly Father, is the gift of imagination! It is one of the treasures of childhood. Thank you for inventing something so delightful. Bless those children known to me personally today, Lord. Touch their childhood days in all kinds of lovely ways as I name them before you now.

* *The Fairy Tale of Father Brown.*

16 MAY

One day Elisha went to Shunem. And a well-to-do woman was there, who urged him to stay for a meal. So whenever he came by, he stopped there to eat. She said to her husband, 'I know that this man who often comes our way is a holy man of God' (2 Kings 4:8, 9 *NIV*)

'They tell me that not long ago [Heinrich] could still be seen about the neighbourhood occasionally, a man in a black cloak, nearly blind, with very wild, white hair, but a face of astonishing softness.'

'I know,' said Father Brown. 'I saw him once.'

[Flambeau] looked at him in some surprise.*

TODAY'S CHALLENGE IN personal holiness!

* *The Fairy Tale of Father Brown.*

17 MAY

The wicked flee when no one pursues (Proverbs 28:1 *ESV*)

'You must understand that towards the end of his life [Prince Otto] began to have those tricks of the nerves not uncommon with tyrants. He multiplied the ordinary daily and nightly guard round his castle till there seemed to be more sentry-boxes than houses in the town, and doubtful characters were shot without mercy. He lived almost entirely in a little room that was in the very centre of the enormous labyrinth of all the other rooms, and even in this he erected another sort of central cabin or cupboard, lined with steel, like a safe or a battleship. Some say that under the floor of this again was a secret hole in the earth, no more than large enough to hold him, so that, in his anxiety to avoid the grave, he was willing to go into a place pretty much like it. But he went further yet. The populace had been supposed to be disarmed ever since the suppression of the revolt, but Otto now insisted, as governments very seldom insist, on an absolute and literal disarmament. It was carried out, with extraordinary thoroughness and severity, by very well-organised officials over a small and familiar area, and, so far as human strength and science can be absolutely certain of anything, Prince Otto was absolutely certain that nobody could introduce so much as a toy pistol into [the city and state of] Heiligwaldstein.'*

HEAVENLY FATHER, MY thoughts and prayers turn towards those of your people who are living under the shadow of paranoid and tyrannical despots, whose fear and insecurity leads them to lock people up, oppress them and even execute them. Grant your Suffering Church daily enabling grace, I pray, that a witness might somehow continue. Bless those who persecute, and bless too those who are persecuted.

* *The Fairy Tale of Father Brown.*

18 MAY

No weapon formed against you shall prosper, And every tongue which rises against you in judgment You shall condemn. This is the heritage of the servants of the Lord, And their righteousness is from Me,' Says the LORD (Isaiah 54:17 *NKJV*)

'Human science can never be quite certain of things like that,' said Father Brown . . . 'if only because of the difficulty about definition and connotation. What is a weapon? People have been murdered with the mildest domestic comforts; certainly with tea-kettles, probably with tea-cosies. On the other hand, if you showed an Ancient Briton a revolver, I doubt if he would know it was a weapon – until it was fired into him, of course.'*

PATENTLY NOT, LORD, an assurance that individual Christians are immune from the perils and tragedies of warfare – history clearly tells us otherwise – but a promise for your Church, your corporate body. Thank you for such inspiring confidence, Heavenly Father, that victory – ultimate victory – belongs to you and, therefore, us. We might lose battles along the way, but we believe the war is won! Hallelujah!

* *The Fairy Tale of Father Brown.*

19 MAY

The people that do know their God shall be strong, and do exploits (Daniel 11:32 *KJV*)

There was a brief period during which Father Brown enjoyed, or rather did not enjoy, something like fame. He was nine days' wonder in the newspapers; he was even a common topic of controversy in the weekly reviews; his exploits were narrated eagerly and inaccurately in any number of clubs and drawing-rooms, especially in America. Incongruous and indeed incredible as it may seem to anyone who knew him, his adventures as a detective were even made the subject of short stories appearing in a magazine.

Strangely enough, this wandering limelight struck him in the most obscure, or at least the most remote, of his many places of residence. He had been sent out to officiate, as something between a missionary and a parish priest, in one of those sections of the northern coast of South America, where strips of country still cling insecurely to European powers, under the gigantic shadow of President Monroe. The population was . . . Spanish-American, and largely Spanish-American-Indian, but there was a considerable and increasing infiltration of Americans of the northern sort – Englishmen, Germans and the rest. And the trouble seems to have begun when one of these visitors, very recently landed and very much annoyed at having lost one of his bags, approached the first building of which he came in sight – which happened to be the mission-house and chapel attached to it.*

TO BE HONEST, Lord, it's hard to imagine any spiritual exploits of mine making the headlines. By your grace, I try to serve you to the best of my ability, but I seek no special reputation or credit. However, if you wish to use me in some way that might possibly be regarded as exploits, then please do; not so that stories might be written about me, but simply so that I may demonstrate your strength at work.

* *The Resurrection of Father Brown.*

20 MAY

The cloths of service, to do service in the holy place, the holy garments for Aaron the priest, and the garments of his sons, to minister in the priest's office (Exodus 35:19 *KJV*)

Standing out there in the strong sunshine, a spick-and-span figure in his Panama hat, his grip-sack held in a steely grip [the visitor to the mission-house] began to shout at the people in the shadow. He began to explain to them very loudly why they were lazy and filthy, and bestially ignorant and lower than the beasts that perish, in case this problem should previously have exercised their minds. In his opinion it was the deleterious influence of priests that had made them so miserably poor and so hopelessly oppressed that they were able to sit in the shade and smoke and do nothing. 'And a mighty soft crowd you must be at that,' he said, 'to be bullied by these stuck-up josses because they walk about in their mitres and their tiaras and their gold copes and other glad rags, looking down on everybody else like dirt – being bamboozled by crowns and canopies and sacred umbrellas like a kid at a pantomime; just because a pompous old High Priest of Mumbo-Jumbo looks as if he was lord of the earth. What about you? What do you look like, you poor simps? I tell you, that's why you're way-back in barbarism and can't read or write and – '

At this the High Priest of Mumbo-Jumbo came in an undignified hurry out of the door of the mission-house, not looking very like a lord of the earth, but rather like a bundle of black second-hand clothes buttoned round a short bolster in the semblance of a guy. He was not wearing his tiara, supposing him to possess one, but a shabby broad hat not very dissimilar from those of the Spanish Indians, and it was thrust to the back of his head with a gesture of botheration.

He seemed just about to speak to the motionless natives when he caught sight of the stranger and said quickly: 'Oh, can I be of any assistance? Would you like to come inside?'*

* *The Resurrection of Father Brown.*

WHAT AN INTERESTING perception some people have of priests and ministers – and Christians in general! Misconceptions abound and stereotypes often prevail. There's not a lot that can be done about that, I suppose, except for me to pray that genuine, authentic spirituality might shine through, as sunshine burning mist in order to show everything in its proper light. Shine, Jesus, shine!

21 MAY

In a wealthy home some utensils are made of gold and silver, and some are made of wood and clay. The expensive utensils are used for special occasions (2 Timothy 2:20 *NLT*)

Three murdered millionaires, which some may regard as an *embarrass de richesse* ... had all fallen victims to some vendetta or curse attaching to the possession of a relic of great value both intrinsically and historically: a sort of chalice inlaid with precious stones and commonly called the Coptic Cup.

Its origin was obscure, but its use was conjectured to be religious; and some attributed the fate that followed its possessors to the fanaticism of some Oriental Christian horrified at its passing through such materialistic hands.*

HEAVENLY FATHER, WHETHER or not such relics are of sacred worth is probably a matter of personal opinion; some people regard them with great awe, while to others they are of lesser religious significance. Please help me, not only to respect different points of view, but also, to reserve a special place in my heart for reverence, whatever that means to me personally. Furthermore, open my eyes so that I may spot the sacred in the everyday, especially as I live in a materialistic world, for doing so will enrich my life considerably.

* *The Arrow of Heaven.*

22 MAY

Jesus said to them, 'A prophet is not without honour except in his own town, among his relatives and in his own home' (Mark 6:4 *NIV*)

When Father Brown first stepped off an Atlantic liner on to American soil, he discovered as many another Englishman has done, that he was a much more important person than he had ever supposed.

His short figure, his short-sighted and undistinguished countenance, his rather rusty-black clerical clothes, could pass through any crowd in his own country without being noticed as anything unusual, except perhaps unusually significant. But America has a genius for the encouragement of fame; and his appearance in one or two curious criminal problems, together with his long association with Flambeau, the ex-criminal and detective, had consolidated a reputation in America out of what was little more than a rumour in England. His round face was blank with surprise when he found himself up on the quay by a group of journalists, as by a gang of brigands, who asked him questions about all the subjects on which he was least likely to regard himself as an authority, such as the details of female dress and the criminal statistics of the country that he had only that moment clapped his eyes upon.*

WHAT A STRANGE (and quite sad) thought, Lord Jesus – that you came to us as Almighty God made flesh, yet were largely ignored, and treated without prophetic honour. Thank you for such humility, that you were prepared to undergo such indignity, all for the sake of reaching the lost. A gracious God indeed.

* *The Arrow of Heaven.*

23 MAY

A son honours his father, and a servant his master. Then if I am a father, where is My honour? And if I am a master, where is My respect?' says the Lord of hosts to you (Malachi 1:6 *NIV*)

The deputation of distinguished geologists and mineralogists from Paris and Berlin were there in the most magnificent and appropriate dress, for there are no men who like wearing their decorations so much as the men of science – as anybody knows who has ever been to a soirée of the Royal Society. It was a brilliant gathering.*

LORD JESUS, YOU were never invited to soirées or anything of the kind. You weren't regarded as an honoured invitee at formal dinners and the like, whose presence was eagerly sought. Those who were proud of their decorations and honours didn't care to be seen with you. Yet, the irony is, you single-handedly outshine them all! Yet, there could be no more important or prestigious guest at any function! Forgive us, Lord, if ever we lose sight of your royal status. May you always be more than welcome in our homes, our hearts, and our hallowed places.

* *The Fairy Tale of Father Brown.*

24 MAY

And He said to them, 'Come aside by yourselves to a deserted place and rest a while.' For there were many coming and going, and they did not even have time to eat (Mark 6:31 *NKJV*)

The little pink clouds, that looked rather like sweet-stuff, had floated up to crown the turrets of the gilt gingerbread castle, and the pink baby fingers of the budding trees seemed spreading and stretching to reach them; the blue sky began to take a bright violet of evening, when Father Brown suddenly spoke again:

'It was on a dismal night, with rain still dropping from the trees and dew already clustering, that Prince Otto of Grossenmark stepped hurriedly out of a side door of the castle and walked swiftly into the wood. One of the innumerable sentries saluted him, but he did not notice it. He had no wish to be specially noted himself. He was glad when the great trees, grey and already greasy with rain, swallowed him up like a swamp. He had deliberately chosen the least frequented side of his palace, but even that was more frequented than he liked. But there was no particular chance of officious or diplomatic pursuit, for his exit had been a sudden impulse. All the full-dressed diplomatists he left behind were unimportant. He had realised suddenly that he could do without them.'*

TEACH ME, MY Heavenly Father, to spend much time in secret with Jesus. Teach me the worth and benefit of spiritual solitude. Teach me too, just how much those times mean to you, and how they thrill your heart; time in sweet communion spent.

* *The Fairy Tale of Father Brown.*

25 MAY

Call to me and I will answer you, and will tell you great and hidden things that you have not known (Jeremiah 33:3 *ESV*)

Mr Paul Snaith came inside; and it was the beginning of a considerable increase of that journalist's information on many things. Presumably his journalistic instinct was stronger than his prejudices, as, indeed, it often is in clever journalists; and he asked a good many questions, the answers to which interested and surprised him. He discovered that the Indians could read and write, for the simple reason that the priest had taught them, but that they did not read or write any more than they could help, from a natural preference for more direct communications. He learned that these strange people, who sat about in heaps, could work quite hard on their own patches of land; especially those of them who were more than half Spanish; and he learned with still more astonishment that they all had patches of land that were really their own. That much was part of a stubborn tradition that seemed quite native to natives.*

I thank you, Heavenly Father, for your grace in allowing me to ask as many questions as I like in pursuit of a greater knowledge of your being and your love. You handle my ignorance with patience, and you answer my queries with generous wisdom and authority. Thank you for being an approachable God; not remote, not distant, not afar, but willing to help.

* *The Resurrection of Father Brown.*

26 MAY

Enter not into the fields of the fatherless (Proverbs 23:10 *KJV*)

The priest had . . . taken perhaps what was his first and last part in politics, if it was only local politics. There had recently swept through that region one of those fevers of atheist and almost anarchist Radicalism which break out periodically in countries of the Latin culture, generally beginning in a secret society and generally ending in a civil war and in very little else. The local leader of the iconoclastic party was a certain Alvarez, a rather picturesque adventurer of Portugese nationality . . . the head of any number of lodges and temples of initiation of the sort that in such places clothe even atheism with something mystical.

The leader on the more conservative side was a much more commonplace person, a very wealthy man named Mendoza, the owner of many factories and quite respectable, but not very exciting. It was the general opinion that the cause of law and order would have been entirely lost if it had not adopted a more popular policy of its own, in the form of securing land for the peasants; and the movement had mainly originated from the little mission-station of Father Brown.*

O LORD! HOW very complicated and controversial it can sometimes become, when the Church at large becomes intertwined with politics. Having said that, so much of theology is, essentially, political! Issues of wealth and poverty, for example, or the fair distribution of land; Christian ethics often demand social action and intervention. My prayers today, therefore, are with Christians whose vocation leads them to speak truth to power. Bless and guide their holy influence, I pray.

* *The Resurrection of Father Brown.*

27 MAY

They came to Philip, who was from Bethsaida in Galilee, with a request. 'Sir,' they said, 'we would like to see Jesus' (John 12:21 *NIV*)

Perhaps it was the contrast with the black embattled solidarity of this group that made more vivid another figure that stood apart from it, equally black against the burning white daylight of that brilliant place and season, but entirely solitary; a tall, yellow-faced man in great goggles, who arrested him with a gesture when the journalists had finished and said: 'Excuse me, but maybe you are looking for Captain Wain.'

Some apology may be made for Father Brown; for he himself would have been sincerely apologetic. It must be remembered that he had never seen that sort of tortoise-shell spectacles before; for the fashion at this time had not spread to England. His first sensation was that of gazing at some goggling sea-monster with a faint suggestion of a diver's helmet. Otherwise this man was exquisitely dressed; and to Brown, in his innocence, the spectacles seemed the queerest disfigurement for a dandy. It was as if a dandy had adorned himself with a wooden leg as an extra touch of elegance.*

MY PRAYERS TODAY, Lord Jesus, are for those who are looking for you – seekers after truth, so to speak. I pray for them at whatever part of their search they may be; close to finding you, or just embarking on their pursuit. Bless their seeking. I include within my prayer those who are exploring different avenues of spirituality, even if they aren't specifically investigating the Christian faith. Lead them, Heavenly Father, lead them.

* *The Arrow of Heaven.*

28 MAY

For God is not *the* author of confusion (1 Corinthians 14:33 *NKJV*)

'I beg your pardon,' [Father Brown] said doubtfully, 'are you Captain Wain? Do you – do you know him?'

'Well, I'm pretty confident I'm not Captain Wain,' said the man in goggles, with a face of wood. 'I was pretty clear about that when I saw him waiting for you over there in the car. But the other question's a bit more problematical. I reckon I know Wain and his uncle, and old man Merton, too. I know old man Merton, but old man Merton don't know me. And he thinks he has the advantage, and I think I have the advantage. See?'

Father Brown did not quite see. He blinked at the glittering landscape and the pinnacles of the city, and then at the man in goggles.*

O LORD! HOW often life is confusing; as though it were one gigantic riddle. I bring to you all my perplexities; the things I cannot understand, my unanswered questions. I lay them at your feet in the hope that you will exchange confusion for comprehension. Draw close to those who are confused today, Lord; those for whom life and faith just don't seem to make sense at present. Ease their concerns.

* *The Arrow of Heaven.*

29 MAY

If you had really known me, you would know who my Father is (John 14:7 *NLT*)

'My chief danger is in my brother's high-and-dry notions, *noblesse oblige* and all that. Well, my name is Christabel Carstairs; and my father was that Colonel Carstairs you've probably heard of, who made the famous Carstairs Collection of Roman coins. I could never describe my father to you; the nearest I can say is that he was very like a Roman coin himself. He was as handsome and as genuine and as valuable and as metallic and as out-of-date. He was prouder of his Collection than of his coat-of-arms – nobody could say more than that. His extraordinary character came out in his will. He had two sons and one daughter. He quarrelled with one son, my brother Giles, and sent him to Australia on a small allowance. He then made a will leaving the Carstairs Collection, actually with a yet smaller allowance, to my brother Arthur. He meant it as a reward, as the highest honour he could offer, in acknowledgment of Arthur's loyalty and rectitude and the distinctions he had already gained in mathematics and economics at Cambridge. He left me practically all his pretty large fortune; and I am sure he meant it in contempt.'*

THANK YOU, LORD Jesus, that because you came to us as man, we can know the Father. In your life of love, we see a God of compassion and mercy. In your example (the exact representation of the Father's being), we see faithfulness, grace and holiness. We need not guess; you have shown us God.

* *The Head of Caesar.*

30 MAY

Have mercy on those who doubt (Jude 22 *ESV*)

The girl sprang to her feet and stood quite quietly, but with clenched hands, like one about to stride away; then her hands loosened slowly, and she sat down again.

'You are more of a mystery than all the others,' she said desperately; 'but I feel there might be a heart in your mystery.'

'What we all dread most,' said the priest in a low voice, 'is a maze with *no* centre. That is why atheism is only a nightmare.'*

WHAT DAILY GRACE you demonstrate, Lord, towards those who scorn you and doubt or deny your existence. You simply keep on loving! What daily grace you demonstrate, Lord, to all of us. Lord of our doubts and fears, we look to you for mercy. In what are our un-centred lives, trying to figure out the mysteries of life and eternity, each of us stands in need. Hear our prayers.

* *The Head of Caesar.*

31 MAY

And lead us not into temptation (Matthew 6:13 *NIV*)

'You see,' said Father Brown, blinking modestly, 'I'm not sure that the Armstrong cheerfulness is so very cheerful – for other people. You say that nobody could kill such a happy old man, but I'm not sure; ne nos inducas in tentationem. * If ever I murdered somebody,' he added quite simply, 'I dare say it might be an Optimist.'

'Why?' cried Merton amused. 'Do you think people dislike cheerfulness?'

'People like frequent laughter,' answered Father Brown, 'but I don't think they like a permanent smile. Cheerfulness without humour is a very trying thing.'†

AN AMUSING LITTLE excerpt, Lord, but it does go to show how surprisingly easy it might be to fall into sin, even a sin such as murder. All it takes is for the context and the provocation to be in place, and anything might happen, however unlikely that might seem in the normal run of things; a deadly flash of temper, for example. That being the case, I pray Matthew 6:13 for myself today, and for those who are sorely tempted. Deliver us from such evils.

* From Latin to English: 'And please do not lead us into temptation'.

† *The Three Tools of Death.*

1 JUNE

Stop being angry! Turn from your rage!
Do not lose your temper – it only leads to harm (Psalm 37:8 *NLT*)

'Be careful what you say,' said Royce gruffly, 'you'll frighten Miss Armstrong.'

'I hope so,' said the man with the clear voice.

As the woman winced and everyone else wondered, he went on:

'I am somewhat used to Miss Armstrong's tremors. I have seen her trembling off and on for years. And some said she was shaking with cold and some she was shaking with fear, but I know she was shaking with hate and wicked anger.'*

EASIER SAID THAN done at times, Lord! However, if this is the advice of the psalmist, then I want to try to follow it, with your help. At the moment of my weakness, help me not to be like Miss Armstrong. Grant me that enabling grace, especially when my patience has worn thin and tempers are frayed.

* *The Three Tools of Death.*

2 JUNE

Harden not your heart (Psalm 95:8 *KJV*)

Pauline Stacey . . . was actually the heiress of a crest and half a county, as well as great wealth; she had been brought up in castles and gardens, before a frigid fierceness (peculiar to the modern woman) had driven her to what she considered a harsher and a higher existence.

She had not, indeed, surrendered her money; in that there would have been a romantic or monkish abandon quite alien to her masterful utilitarianism. She held her wealth, she would say, for use upon practical social objects. Part of it she had put into her business, the nucleus of a model typewriting emporium; part of it was distributed in various leagues and causes for the advancement of such work among women.

How far Joan, her sister and partner, shared this slightly prosaic idealism no one could be very sure. But she followed her leader with a dog-like affection which was somehow more attractive, with its touch of tragedy, than the hard, high spirits of the elder. For Pauline Stacey had nothing to say to tragedy; she was understood to deny its existence.*

HOW HORRIBLY SAD and poignant, Lord, that anyone should feel the need to deny the existence of tragedy, as though life should always be un-tragic and entirely positive, which it certainly isn't. Rain falls into each and every life, and as human beings we are all the better, and kinder, for acknowledging the very real part that tragic events have to play in our formation as feeling, empathetic, sensitive individuals. Anything else is pretence. Lord, preserve us from hardness of heart, for that has nothing to do with Christ, whose heart was broken.

* *The Eye of Apollo.*

3 JUNE

We set our hearts at rest in his presence (1 John 3:19 *NIV*)

[Pauline Stacey] certainly had a temper, of a snappy, practical sort; the gestures of her thin, elegant hands were abrupt or even destructive.

Once Flambeau entered her office on some typewriting business, and found she had just flung a pair of spectacles belonging to her sister into the middle of the floor and stamped on them. She was already in the rapids of an ethical tirade about the 'sickly medical notions' and the morbid admission of weakness implied in such an apparatus. She dared her sister to bring such artificial, unhealthy rubbish into the place again. She asked if she was expected to wear wooden legs or false hair or glass eyes; and as she spoke her eyes sparkled . . .

Flambeau, quite bewildered with this fanaticism, could not refrain from asking Miss Pauline (with direct French logic) why a pair of spectacles was a more morbid sign of weakness than a lift, and why, if science might help us in the one effort, it might not help us in the other.

'That is so different,' said Pauline Stacey, loftily. 'Batteries and motors and all those things are marks of the force of man – yes, Mr Flambeau, and the force of woman, too! We shall take our turn at these great engines that devour distance and defy time. That is high and splendid – that is really science. But these nasty props and plasters the doctors sell – why, they are just badges of poltroonery. Doctors stick on legs and arms as if we were born cripples and sick slaves. But I was free-born, Mr Flambeau! People only think they need these things because they have been trained in fear instead of being trained in power and courage, just as the silly nurses tell children not to stare at the sun, and so they can't do it without blinking. But why among the stars should there be one star I may not see? The sun is not my master, and I will open my eyes and stare at him whenever I choose.'

'Your eyes,' said Flambeau, with a foreign bow, 'will dazzle the sun.' He took pleasure in complimenting this strange stiff beauty, partly because it threw her a little off her balance.*

* *The Eye of Apollo.*

O LORD! TODAY I pray for the uptight and overwrought. Mellow and soften their general approach to life, Lord, before something goes horribly wrong. A rope that is permanently too taut, Heavenly Father, is a rope that will more than likely snap at some point, and I wouldn't wish that analogy to apply to anyone I know and love. Impart your gifts of rest and relaxation.

4 JUNE

Thou hidest thy face, they are troubled:
thou takest away their breath, they die (Psalm 104:29 *KJV*)

[Pauline Stacey's] rigid rapidity and cold impatience had amused Flambeau very much on the first occasion of his entering the flats.

He had lingered outside the lift in the entrance hall waiting for the lift-boy, who generally conducts strangers to the various floors. But this bright-eyed falcon of a girl had openly refused to endure such official delay. She said sharply that she knew all about the lift, and was not dependent on boys – or men either.

Though her flat was only three floors above, she managed in the few seconds of ascent to give Flambeau a great many of her fundamental views in an off-hand manner; they were to the general effect that she was a modern working woman and loved modern working machinery. Her bright black eyes blazed with abstract anger against those who rebuke mechanic science and ask for the return of romance.

Everyone, she said, ought to be able to manage machines, just as she could manage the lift. She seemed almost to resent the fact of Flambeau opening the lift-door for her; and that gentleman went up to his own apartments smiling with somewhat mingled feelings at the memory of such spit-fire self-dependence.*

INDEPENDENCE IS ONE thing, Lord, and in many ways is to be admired; better independent, I suppose, than always expecting others to do everything for you. Having said that, we make a terrible decision if we ever once think we can live – or even do so much as breathe – without your help. Help us to find that happy balance, I pray, of working as though everything depended on us, but praying (and secretly realising) that everything, actually, depends on you.

* *The Eye of Apollo.*

5 JUNE

God saw everything that he had made, and behold, it was very good (Genesis 1:31 *ESV*)

[Flambeau and Father Brown] pushed slowly up the brightening river; the glowing violet of the sky and the pale gold of the moon grew fainter and fainter, and faded into that vast colourless cosmos that precedes the colours of the dawn. When the first faint stripes of red and gold and grey split the horizon from end to end they were broken by the black bulk of a town or village which sat on the river just ahead of them. It was already an easy twilight, in which all things were visible, when they came under the hanging roofs and bridges of this riverside hamlet.

The houses, with their long, low, stooping roofs, seemed to come down to drink at the river, like huge grey and red cattle. The broadening and whitening dawn had already turned to working daylight before they saw any living creature on the wharves and bridges of that silent town . . .

The boat took many such grassy corners and followed many such reedy and silent reaches of river; but before the search had become monotonous they had swung round a specially sharp angle and come into the silence of a sort of pool or lake, the sight of which instinctively arrested them. For in the middle of this wider piece of water, fringed on every side with rushes, lay a long, low islet, along which ran a long, low house or bungalow built of bamboo or some kind of tough tropic cane. The upstanding rods of bamboo which made the walls were pale yellow, the sloping rods that made the roof were of darker red or brown, otherwise the long house was a thing of repetition and monotony. The early morning breeze rustled the reeds round the island and sang in the strange ribbed house as in a giant pan-pipe.*

* *The Sins of Prince Saradine.*

CREATOR GOD, FORBID that this day should pass without me noticing at least one example of your creative handiwork and genius. There are, after all, quite a few to choose from! Forbid that this day should pass without me pausing to thank you for something that catches my eye, or my ear. Help me to worship by noticing.

6 JUNE

Offer hospitality to one another without grumbling (1 Peter 4:9 *NIV*)

The house stood with its back, as it were, to the river and the only landing-stage; the main entrance was on the other side, and looked down the long island garden. The visitors approached it, therefore, by a small path running round nearly three sides of the house, close under the low eaves.

Through three different windows on three different sides they looked in on the same long, well-lit room, panelled in light wood, with a large number of looking-glasses, and laid out as for an elegant lunch. The front door, when they came round to it at last, was flanked by two turquoise-blue flower pots. It was opened by a butler of the drearier type – long, lean, grey and listless – who murmured that Prince Saradine was away from home at present, but was expected hourly; the house being kept ready for him and his guests.

The exhibition of the card with the scrawl of green ink awoke a flicker of life in the parchment face of the depressed retainer, and it was with a certain shaky courtesy that he suggested that the strangers should remain. 'His Highness may be here any minute,' he said, 'and would be distressed to have just missed any gentleman he had invited. We have orders always to keep a little cold lunch for him and his friends, and I am sure he would wish it to be offered.'

Moved with curiosity to this minor adventure, Flambeau assented gracefully, and followed the old man, who ushered him ceremoniously into the long, lightly panelled room.*

HOW VERY WELCOME a cold lunch would be to a hungry caller! You would know all about the importance of hospitality, Lord Jesus, given the culture in which you were raised. Maybe offering a plate of food to unexpected guests (strangers) was second nature to your parents. May that be the case in my life too; a heart whose impulse is to share, and a home where all are welcomed and fed ... even when there's not a great deal in the cupboards or the fridge.

* *The Sins of Prince Saradine.*

7 JUNE

There was a famine in the land, and Abram went down to Egypt to live there for a while because the famine was severe. As he was about to enter Egypt, he said to his wife Sarai, 'I know what a beautiful woman you are. When the Egyptians see you, they will say, 'This is his wife.' Then they will kill me but will let you live. Say you are my sister, so that I will be treated well for your sake and my life will be spared because of you' (Genesis 12:10-13 *NIV*)

As [Flambeau and Father Brown] paused on the door-step, before taking a turn in the garden, the front garden gate was thrown open with violence, and a young man with a billycock hat on the back of his head tumbled up the steps in his eagerness. He was a dissipated-looking youth with a gorgeous red necktie all awry, as if he had slept in it, and he kept fidgeting and lashing about with one of those little jointed canes. 'I say,' he said breathlessly, 'I want to see old Quinton. I must see him. Has he gone?' 'Mr Quinton is in, I believe,' said Father Brown, cleaning his pipe, 'but I do not know if you can see him. The doctor is with him at present.'

The young man, who seemed not to be perfectly sober, stumbled into the hall; and at the same moment the doctor came out of Quinton's study, shutting the door and beginning to put on his gloves. 'See Mr Quinton?' said the doctor coolly. 'No, I'm afraid you can't. In fact, you mustn't on any account. Nobody must see him; I've just given him his sleeping draught.' 'No, but look here, old chap,' said the youth in the red tie, trying affectionately to capture the doctor by the lapels of his coat. 'Look here. I'm simply sewn up, I tell you. I – ' 'It's no good, Mr Atkinson,' said the doctor, forcing him to fall back; 'when you can alter the effects of a drug I'll alter my decision,' and, settling on his hat, he stepped out into the sunlight with the other two. He was a bull-necked, good-tempered little man with a small moustache, inexpressibly ordinary, yet giving an impression of capacity.

The young man in the billycock, who did not seem to be gifted with any tact in dealing with people beyond the general idea of clutching hold of their coats, stood outside the door, as dazed as if he had been thrown out bodily, and silently watched the other three walk away together through the garden.

'That was a sound, spanking lie I told just now,' remarked the medical man, laughing. 'In point of fact, poor Quinton doesn't have his sleeping draught for nearly half an hour. But I'm not going to have him bothered with that little beast, who only wants to borrow money that he wouldn't pay back if he could. He's a dirty little scamp, though he is Mrs Quinton's brother, and she's as fine a woman as ever walked.'*

A VERY TRICKY theological and moral point, this one, Lord – telling a blatant lie on account of a reasonable and worthwhile motive; in this case, protecting someone from an unwelcome drunken intruder who might even have posed a threat. Is kindness more important than truth? Help me with this, please, Lord.

* *The Wrong Shape.*

8 JUNE

The one who is in you is greater than the one who is in the world (1 John 4:4 *NIV*)

'In that case, Dr Harris,' said Flambeau, 'we might as well walk round at the back by the end of the conservatory. There's no entrance to it that way, but it's worth seeing, even from the outside.' 'Yes, and I might get a squint at my patient,' laughed the doctor, 'for he prefers to lie on an ottoman right at the end of the conservatory amid all those blood-red poinsettias; it would give me the creeps. But what are you doing?'

Father Brown had stopped for a moment, and picked up out of the long grass, where it had almost been wholly hidden, a queer, crooked Oriental knife, inlaid exquisitely in coloured stones and metals. 'What is this?' asked Father Brown, regarding it with some disfavour. 'Oh, Quinton's, I suppose,' said Dr Harris carelessly; 'he has all sorts of Chinese knickknacks about the place' . . .

'It's very beautiful,' said the priest in a low, dreaming voice; 'the colours are very beautiful. But it's the wrong shape.' 'What for?' asked Flambeau, staring.

'For anything. It's the wrong shape in the abstract. Don't you ever feel that about Eastern art? The colours are intoxicatingly lovely; but the shapes are mean and bad – deliberately mean and bad. I have seen wicked things in a Turkey carpet.' 'Mon Dieu!' cried Flambeau, laughing. 'They are letters and symbols in a language I don't know; but I know they stand for evil words,' went on the priest, his voice growing lower and lower. 'The lines go wrong on purpose – like serpents doubling to escape.'

'What the devil are you talking about?' said the doctor with a loud laugh.

Flambeau spoke quietly to him in answer. 'The Father sometimes gets this mystic's cloud on him,' he said; 'but I give you fair warning that I have never known him to have it except when there was some evil quite near.' 'Oh, rats!' said the scientist.*

* *The Wrong Shape.*

THE EVER-CROUCHING presence of evil, Almighty God – a very real and present entity. Wisdom instructs me never to underestimate Satan's power; to acknowledge it for what it is, but, simultaneously, to remember that you are a mighty God and that I live within the shadow of your protection. Those are the terms of conflict. Jesus is Lord!

9 JUNE

They will do no wrong; they will tell no lies. A deceitful tongue will not be found in their mouths (Zephaniah 3:13 *NIV*)

'Suppose a person in a position of trust,' went on the priest, 'began to give the enemy information because it was false information. Suppose he even thought he was saving his country by misleading the foreigner. Suppose this brought him into spy circles, and little loans were made to him, and little ties tied on to him. Suppose he kept up his contradictory position in a confused way by never telling the foreign spies the truth, but letting it more and more be guessed. The better part of him (what was left of it) would still say: `I have not helped the enemy; I said it was the left drawer.' The meaner part of him would already be saying: `But they may have the sense to see that means the right.' I think it is psychologically possible – in an enlightened age, you know.'*

O LORD! THIS is certainly not for me to judge; I simply pray today for anyone who is, for one reason or another, caught up in a web of lies and deceptions. I pray for anyone who is trapped and having to cover their tracks by telling one lie after another; at home, in a relationship, at work, or maybe in the political sphere – possibly even in a military setting. Whatever the context, I pray that you would lead them to freedom, however seriously ensnared they might be. Have mercy and untie the knots.

* *The Duel of Dr Hirsch.*

10 JUNE

Why should you die before your time? (Ecclesiastes 7:17 *ESV*)

The Duke looked at the priest. 'Dubosc's escape is more elaborate than we thought,' he said; 'but I suppose he is escaping from France.'

'He is escaping from everywhere,' answered Father Brown.

Valognes's eyes brightened, but his voice sank. 'Do you mean suicide?' he asked.

'You will not find his body,' replied the other.*

LORD OF LIFE and Lord of death, you are a God of enormous and untold compassion. You have walked this way, in Christ, and you know full well how the human journey goes; the plains and the mountainsides. I ask you to draw especially close to anyone who is contemplating suicide today. Prompt someone to visit them. I pray for those for whom it has all become too much. God of our desperation, meet with them.

* *The Duel of Dr Hirsch.*

11 JUNE

People will come from all over the world – from east and west, north and south – to take their places in the Kingdom of God (Luke 13:29 *NLT*)

Behind the lectern, and looking across the valley, stood a very old man in a black robe that fell as straight as the cliffs around him, but whose white hair and weak voice seemed alike to waver in the wind. He was evidently reading some daily lesson as part of his religious exercises. 'They trust in their horses...'

'Sir,' said the Prince of Heiligwaldenstein, with quite unusual courtesy, 'I should like only one word with you.'

'. . . and in their chariots,' went on the old man weakly, 'but we will trust in the name of the Lord of Hosts. . . '

His last words were inaudible, but he closed the book reverently and, being nearly blind, made a groping movement and gripped the reading-stand. Instantly his two servants slipped out of the low-browed cavern and supported him. They wore dull-black gowns like his own, but they had not the frosty silver on the hair, nor the frost-bitten refinement of the features. They were peasants, Croat or Magyar, with broad, blunt visages and blinking eyes.*

LORD OF THE Church, this word-picture leads me to think of my brothers and sisters who belong to the Orthodox tradition, and whose expression of faith and belief is ancient and distinct. As they serve you in their way, Lord Jesus, I ask your rich blessing upon them. May their witness, within their culture, bear much fruit for the Kingdom. Bless those in black robes who revere your word!

* *The Fairy Tale of Father Brown.*

12 JUNE

Yea, though I walk through the valley of the shadow of death, I will fear no evil: for thou art with me; thy rod and thy staff they comfort me (Psalm 23:4 *KJV*)

Turning the corner by the open lodge-gates, [Calhoun Kidd] set off, stumping up the long avenue of black pine-woods that pointed in abrupt perspective towards the inner gardens of Pendragon Park. The trees were as black and orderly as plumes upon a hearse; there were still a few stars.

He was a man with more literary than direct natural associations; the word 'Ravenswood' came into his head repeatedly. It was partly the raven colour of the pine-woods; but partly also an indescribable atmosphere almost described in Scott's great tragedy; the smell of something that died in the eighteenth century; the smell of dank gardens and broken urns, of wrongs that will never now be righted; of something that is none the less incurably sad because it is strangely unreal.

More than once, as he went up that strange, black road of tragic artifice, he stopped, startled, thinking he heard steps in front of him. He could see nothing in front but the twin sombre walls of pine and the wedge of starlit sky above them. At first he thought he must have fancied it or been mocked by a mere echo of his own tramp. But as he went on he was more and more inclined to conclude, with the remains of his reason, that there really were other feet upon the road.

He thought hazily of ghosts; and was surprised how swiftly he could see the image of an appropriate and local ghost, one with a face as white as Pierrot's, but patched with black. The apex of the triangle of dark-blue sky was growing brighter and bluer, but he did not realize as yet that this was because he was coming nearer to the lights of the great house and garden. He only felt that the atmosphere was growing more intense, there was in the sadness more violence and secrecy.*

* *The Strange Crime of John Bulnois.*

WHAT MARVELLOUS, WONDERFUL comfort this is, Lord, that even though I will be dead and therefore utterly powerless to change my circumstances, I need fear no evil, for you will be with me. As you have walked alongside me in this life, so you will accompany me in the next, to see me safely through death's travail. God of eternity, I worship you and I place my entire trust in you for that final journey. All will be well.

13 JUNE

Let us consider how we may spur one another on toward love and good deeds, not giving up meeting together, as some are in the habit of doing, but encouraging one another – and all the more as you see the Day approaching (Hebrews 10:24, 25 *NIV*)

'I don't believe you men can manage alone.'

'Oh yes, we can, my dear,' said the Major, looking at her very amiably. 'Marco has all the sauces, and we've often done ourselves well in very rough places, as you might know by now. And it's time you had a treat, Audrey; you mustn't be a housekeeper every hour of the day; and I know you want to hear the music.'

'I want to go to church,' she said, with rather severe eyes.*

FATHER GOD, THE COVID-19 pandemic has hit your Church hard, with many people reviewing their regular attendance and/or membership. For some, faith has deepened. For others, it has faltered. Some have resolved to build things up, while others have discovered a spiritual life that no longer includes physically attending a place of worship. Maybe this is a time for reflective review, Lord? How is your Spirit leading us? Keep us well within your will, I pray, for the days we cannot see.

* *The Salad of Colonel Cray.*

14 JUNE

I have become all things to all people so that by all possible means I might save some (1 Corinthians 9:22 *NIV*)

Putnam . . . not to be done out of a final feast with an old crony, had arranged for a special dejeuner to be set out and consumed in the course of the morning, while Audrey and other graver persons were at morning service.

She was going there under the escort of a relative and old friend of hers, Dr Oliver Oman, who, though a scientific man of a somewhat bitter type, was enthusiastic for music, and would go even to church to get it.*

GOD OF LOVE, I don't suppose it matters too much how people come to church in the first place, as much as the fact they do. What does it matter if a person first crosses the threshold of a church building because they are primarily attracted by the music, even if there is no initial faith interest? Surely it is well within the wit and wisdom of your grace and influence to take it from there and woo that person for Christ? I pray, therefore, that our churches will be attractive places, full of good 'entrance points' whereby people might come to know us, and then, subsequently, you. Fill our hearts with ideas and our buildings with converts.

* *The Salad of Colonel Cray.*

15 JUNE

Be sober, be vigilant; because your adversary the devil, as a roaring lion, walketh about, seeking whom he may devour (1 Peter 5:8 *KJV*)

The heady tempest without drove a dreadful wrack of clouds across Glengyle and threw the long room into darkness as Father Brown picked up the little illuminated pages to examine them. He spoke before the drift of darkness had passed; but it was the voice of an utterly new man.

'Mr Craven,' said he, talking like a man ten years younger, 'you have got a legal warrant, haven't you, to go up and examine that grave? The sooner we do it the better, and get to the bottom of this horrible affair. If I were you I should start now.'

'Now,' repeated the astonished detective, 'and why now?'

'Because this is serious,' answered Brown; 'this is not spilt snuff or loose pebbles, that might be there for a hundred reasons. There is only one reason I know of for this being done; and the reason goes down to the roots of the world. These religious pictures are not just dirtied or torn or scrawled over, which might be done in idleness or bigotry, by children or by Protestants. These have been treated very carefully – and very queerly. In every place where the great ornamented name of God comes in the old illuminations it has been elaborately taken out. The only other thing that has been removed is the halo round the head of the Child Jesus. Therefore, I say, let us get our warrant and our spade and our hatchet, and go up and break open that coffin.'

'What do you mean?' demanded the London officer.

'I mean,' answered the little priest, and his voice seemed to rise slightly in the roar of the gale. 'I mean that the great devil of the universe may be sitting on the top tower of this castle at this moment, as big as a hundred elephants, and roaring like the Apocalypse. There is black magic somewhere at the bottom of this.'*

* *The Honour of Israel Gow.*

LORD, GIVE ME Father Brown's sensitivity to such matters, I pray, that I might correctly discern the presence of evil. I don't want to be seeing demons around every corner, but neither do I want to be complacent. As there is no discharge in this warfare, help me to remain alert.

16 JUNE

I lay down and slept; I woke again, for the LORD sustained me (Psalm 3:5 *ESV*)

'Father,' said Flambeau in that infantile and heavy voice he used very seldom, 'what are we to do?'

His friend's reply came with the pent promptitude of a gun going off.

'Sleep!' cried Father Brown. 'Sleep. We have come to the end of the ways. Do you know what sleep is? Do you know that every man who sleeps believes in God? It is a sacrament; for it is an act of faith and it is a food. And we need a sacrament, if only a natural one.'*

LORD OF MY nights and days, I pray for: Those who just can't get a good night's sleep, however hard they try and whatever they do. Help them. Those who have nowhere to sleep tonight; no bed or even a bedroom of their own. Help them. Those whose sleep is fractured because of nightmares and fears. Help them. I thank you so much, Heavenly Father, for my bed, for essential rest and sustenance. I thank you for the mercy of your vigilant protection, for watching over me while I am unconscious.

* *The Honour of Israel Gow.*

17 JUNE

When they came to the place called The Skull, there they crucified Him and the criminals, one on the right and the other on the left (Luke 23:33 *NASB*)

Despite his mystic praise of slumber, Father Brown was up earlier than anyone else except the silent gardener; and was found smoking a big pipe and watching that expert at his speechless labours in the kitchen garden.

Towards daybreak the rocking storm had ended in roaring rains, and the day came with a curious freshness. The gardener seemed even to have been conversing, but at sight of the detectives he planted his spade sullenly in a bed and, saying something about his breakfast, shifted along the lines of cabbages and shut himself in the kitchen.

'He's a valuable man, that,' said Father Brown. 'He does the potatoes amazingly. Still,' he added, with a dispassionate charity, 'he has his faults; which of us hasn't? He doesn't dig this bank quite regularly. There, for instance,' and he stamped suddenly on one spot. 'I'm really very doubtful about that potato.'

'And why?' asked Craven, amused with the little man's hobby.

'I'm doubtful about it,' said the other, 'because old Gow was doubtful about it himself. He put his spade in methodically in every place but just this. There must be a mighty fine potato just here.'

Flambeau pulled up the spade and impetuously drove it into the place. He turned up, under a load of soil, something that did not look like a potato, but rather like a monstrous, over-domed mushroom. But it struck the spade with a cold click; it rolled over like a ball, and grinned up at them.

'The Earl of Glengyle,' said Brown sadly, and looked down heavily at the skull.*

LORD JESUS, YOU went to the place of The Skull for me. For me! You went to the rubbish tip, to the garbage heap, there to be crucified and heaped with the trash; there to die the death of common criminals. God on the cross – for me.

* *The Honour of Israel Gow.*

18 JUNE

One day is with the Lord as a thousand years, and a thousand years as one day (2 Peter 3:8 *KJV*)

The man's motor was small and swift like himself . . . The sense of something tiny and flying was accentuated as they swept up long white curves of road in the dead but open daylight of evening.

Soon the white curves came sharper and dizzier; they were upon ascending spirals, as they say in the modern religions. For, indeed, they were cresting a corner of London which is almost as precipitous as Edinburgh, if not quite so picturesque.

Terrace rose above terrace, and the special tower of flats they sought, rose above them all to almost Egyptian height, gilt by the level sunset. The change, as they turned the corner and entered the crescent known as Himalaya Mansions, was as abrupt as the opening of a window; for they found that pile of flats sitting above London as above a green sea of slate.

Opposite to the mansions, on the other side of the gravel crescent, was a bushy enclosure more like a steep hedge or dyke than a garden, and some way below that ran a strip of artificial water, a sort of canal, like the moat of that embowered fortress.

As the car swept round the crescent it passed, at one corner, the stray stall of a man selling chestnuts; and right away at the other end of the curve, Angus could see a dim blue policeman walking slowly. These were the only human shapes in that high suburban solitude; but he had an irrational sense that they expressed the speechless poetry of London. He felt as if they were figures in a story.*

HOW SWIFTLY LIFE itself moves along, Lord. The years pass, almost in the blink of an eye, so it seems, and the 'dream' of our human existence is over. We feel as though we are, somehow, figures in a story not of our own making; created to live this life to

* *The Invisible Man.*

the best of our ability, yet aware of the fact that the larger narrative belongs entirely to you. Hold my hand, I pray, as I straddle the mystery of this little time here on earth followed by eternity in your presence. What a remarkable continuum!

19 JUNE

Suddenly the fingers of a human hand appeared and wrote on the plaster of the wall, near the lampstand in the royal palace. The king watched the hand as it wrote. His face turned pale and he was so frightened that his legs became weak and his knees were knocking (Daniel 5:5, 6 *NIV*)

[Mr Smythe] pointed his polished walking-stick at the window . . . and [Mr Angus] was astonished to see along the front of the glass a long strip of paper pasted, which had certainly not been on the window when he looked through it some time before.

Following the energetic Smythe outside into the street, he found that some yard and a half of stamp paper had been carefully gummed along the glass outside, and on this was written in straggly characters, 'If you marry Smythe, he will die' . . .

'It's the writing of that fellow Welkin,' said Smythe gruffly. 'I haven't seen him for years, but he's always bothering me. Five times in the last fortnight he's had threatening letters left at my flat, and I can't even find out who leaves them, let alone if it is Welkin himself. The porter of the flats swears that no suspicious characters have been seen, and here he has pasted up a sort of dado on a public shop window, while the people in the shop –'

'Quite so,' said Angus modestly, 'while the people in the shop were having tea. Well, sir, I can assure you I appreciate your common sense in dealing so directly with the matter. We can talk about other things afterwards. The fellow cannot be very far off yet, for I swear there was no paper there when I went last to the window, ten or fifteen minutes ago. On the other hand, he's too far off to be chased, as we don't even know the direction. If you'll take my advice, Mr Smythe, you'll put this at once in the hands of some energetic inquiry man, private rather than public. I know an extremely clever fellow, who has set up in business five minutes from here in your car. His name's Flambeau, and though his youth was a bit stormy, he's a strictly honest man now, and his brains are worth money. He lives in Lucknow Mansions, Hampstead.'*

* *The Invisible Man.*

MANY ARE THE things I cannot understand! Mystery is all around me! That being so, I pray also to be surrounded by the contentment that comes from knowing I am upheld by your gracious omnipotence every single day. In other words, I need not fear that which I cannot comprehend, for I am embraced in love, and that will suffice, and does suffice. I need not know everything in order to know that.

20 JUNE

When Jesus came down from the mountainside, large crowds followed him. A man with leprosy came and knelt before him and said, 'Lord, if you are willing, you can make me clean.' Jesus reached out his hand and touched the man. 'I am willing,' he said. 'Be clean!' Immediately he was cleansed of his leprosy (Matthew 8:1-4 *NIV*)

'I won't have you talking like that,' cried the girl, who was in a curious glow. 'You've only talked like that since you became a horrid what's-his-name. You know what I mean. What do you call a man who wants to embrace the chimney-sweep?'

'A saint,' said Father Brown.

'I think,' said Sir Leopold, with a supercilious smile, 'that Ruby means a Socialist.'*

SAINT OR SOCIALIST? Open to debate! Saviour? That's not!

* *The Flying Stars.*

21 JUNE

When David realized that he had been recognized, he panicked, fearing the worst from Achish, king of Gath. So right there, while they were looking at him, he pretended to go crazy, pounding his head on the city gate and foaming at the mouth, spit dripping from his beard. Achish took one look at him and said to his servants, 'Can't you see he's crazy? Why did you let him in here? Don't you think I have enough crazy people to put up with as it is without adding another? Get him out of here!' (1 Samuel 21:12-15 *The Message*)

Father Brown, though he knew every detail done behind the scenes, and had even evoked applause by his transformation of a pillow into a pantomime baby, went round to the front and sat among the audience with all the solemn expectation of a child at his first matinee. The spectators were few, relations, one or two local friends, and the servants; Sir Leopold sat in the front seat, his full and still fur-collared figure largely obscuring the view of the little cleric behind him; but it has never been settled by artistic authorities whether the cleric lost much. The pantomime was utterly chaotic, yet not contemptible; there ran through it a rage of improvisation which came chiefly from Crook the clown.

Commonly he was a clever man, and he was inspired tonight with a wild omniscience, a folly wiser than the world, that which comes to a young man who has seen for an instant a particular expression on a particular face. He was supposed to be the clown, but he was really almost everything else, the author (so far as there was an author), the prompter, the scene-painter, the scene-shifter, and, above all, the orchestra. At abrupt intervals in the outrageous performance he would hurl himself in full costume at the piano and bang out some popular music equally absurd and appropriate.

The climax of this, as of all else, was the moment when the two front doors at the back of the scene flew open, showing the lovely moonlit garden, but showing more prominently the famous professional guest; the great Florian, dressed up as a policeman. The clown at the piano played the constabulary chorus in the *Pirates of Penzance*, but it was drowned in the deafening applause, for every gesture of the great comic actor was an admirable though restrained version of the carriage and manner of the police. The harlequin leapt upon him and hit him over the helmet; the pianist playing 'Where did you get that hat?' he faced about in admirably simulated astonishment, and then the leaping harlequin hit him again (the pianist suggesting a few bars of 'Then we had another one'). Then the harlequin rushed right into the arms of the policeman and fell on top of him, amid a roar of applause. Then it was that the strange actor gave that celebrated imitation of a dead man, of which the fame still lingers round Putney. It was almost impossible to believe that a living person could appear so limp.*

PLAY-ACTING, LORD! Pretending, mucking about! All a bit of a laugh, which is fair enough, and good fun in its own way, but don't ever let your Church pretend, or play at mission. Keep us real, Lord. This old world needs an authentic witness.

* *The Flying Stars.*

22 JUNE

I pray that you may enjoy good health and that all may go well with you, even as your soul is getting along well (3 John 1:2 *NIV*)

Father Brown was in no mood for adventures. He had lately fallen ill with over-work, and when he began to recover, his friend Flambeau had taken him on a cruise in a small yacht with Sir Cecil Fanshaw, a young Cornish squire and an enthusiast for Cornish coast scenery.

But Brown was still rather weak; he was no very happy sailor; and though he was never of the sort that either grumbles or breaks down, his spirits did not rise above patience and civility.

When the other two men praised the ragged violet sunset or the ragged volcanic crags, he agreed with them. When Flambeau pointed out a rock shaped like a dragon, he looked at it and thought it very like a dragon. When Fanshaw more excitedly indicated a rock that was like Merlin, he looked at it, and signified assent. When Flambeau asked whether this rocky gate of the twisted river was not the gate of Fairyland, he said 'Yes.'*

O LORD! IT'S absolutely rotten, feeling sick and fed up when everyone else is enjoying themselves and just carrying on as normal. How dreadful to feel queasy and distinctly out-of-sorts, especially in company. How easily the stomach can affect the soul! I pray the prayer of 3 John 1:2 for anyone struggling with that predicament.

* *The Perishing of the Pendragons.*

23 JUNE

Will you not revive us again, that your people may rejoice in you? (Psalm 85:6 *NIV*)

After walking a mile or two farther, they found that the shore was beginning to be formally embanked, so as to form something like a parade; the ugly lamp-posts became less few and far between and more ornamental, though quite equally ugly.

Half a mile farther on Father Brown was puzzled first by little labyrinths of flowerless flower-pots, covered with the low, flat, quiet-coloured plants that look less like a garden than a tessellated pavement, between weak curly paths studded with seats with curly backs. He faintly sniffed the atmosphere of a certain sort of seaside town that he did not specially care about, and, looking ahead along the parade by the sea, he saw something that put the matter beyond a doubt. In the grey distance the big bandstand of a watering-place stood up like a giant mushroom with six legs.

'I suppose,' said Father Brown, turning up his coat-collar and drawing a woollen scarf rather closer round his neck, 'that we are approaching a pleasure resort.' 'I fear,' answered Flambeau, 'a pleasure resort to which few people just now have the pleasure of resorting. They try to revive these places in the winter, but it never succeeds except with Brighton and the old ones.'*

HOW WONDERFUL, LORD God, that revival appears to be breaking out in some parts of the world; people coming to faith, left, right and centre. Glory! I praise you for that, and I pray for revival to appear right where I live and move and have my being. I don't pretend to know how these things work in the spiritual realm, but I pray. Lord, in your mercy, come revive the old places.

* *The God of the Gongs.*

24 JUNE

Those who made melody, Heman, Asaph, and Ethan, were put in position, with brass instruments, sounding loudly (1 Chronicles 15:19 *BBE*)

They had come under the big bandstand, and the priest was looking up at it with a curiosity that had something rather odd about it, his head a little on one side, like a bird's. It was the conventional, rather tawdry kind of erection for its purpose: a flattened dome or canopy, gilt here and there, and lifted on six slender pillars of painted wood, the whole being raised about five feet above the parade on a round wooden platform like a drum. But there was something fantastic about the snow combined with something artificial about the gold that haunted Flambeau as well as his friend with some association he could not capture, but which he knew was at once artistic and alien.

'I've got it,' he said at last. 'It's Japanese. It's like those fanciful Japanese prints, where the snow on the mountain looks like sugar, and the gilt on the pagodas is like gilt on gingerbread. It looks just like a little pagan temple.'

'Yes,' said Father Brown. 'Let's have a look at the god.' And with an agility hardly to be expected of him, he hopped up on to the raised platform.*

LORD, IT IS hard not to read about bandstands without thinking of The Salvation Army! I envisage their brass bands marching to and fro, or playing in open-air meetings, encouraging people to listen to a gospel message. So, I pray for The Salvation Army today, and its worldwide mission. Use that movement to lead many to look at God.

* *The God of the Gongs.*

25 JUNE

Jesus took with him Peter, James and John the brother of James, and led them up a high mountain by themselves. There he was transfigured before them. His face shone like the sun, and his clothes became as white as the light. Just then there appeared before them Moses and Elijah, talking with Jesus. Peter said to Jesus, 'Lord, it is good for us to be here. If you wish, I will put up three shelters – one for you, one for Moses and one for Elijah.' While he was still speaking, a bright cloud covered them, and a voice from the cloud said, 'This is my Son, whom I love; with him I am well pleased. Listen to him!' When the disciples heard this, they fell facedown to the ground, terrified. But Jesus came and touched them. 'Get up,' he said. 'Don't be afraid.' When they looked up, they saw no one except Jesus (Matthew 17:1-8 *NIV*)

No one can calculate the turns of mood in convalescence: but Father Brown's depression must have had a great deal to do with his mere unfamiliarity with the sea. For as the river mouth narrowed like the neck of a bottle, and the water grew calmer and the air warmer and more earthly, he seemed to wake up and take notice like a baby.

They had reached that phase just after sunset when air and water both look bright, but earth and all its growing things look almost black by comparison. About this particular evening, however, there was something exceptional. It was one of those rare atmospheres in which a smoked-glass slide seems to have been slid away from between us and Nature; so that even dark colours on that day look more gorgeous than bright colours on cloudier days. The trampled earth of the river-banks and the peaty stain in the pools did not look drab but glowing umber, and the dark woods astir in the breeze did not look, as usual, dim blue with mere depth of distance, but more like wind-tumbled masses of some vivid violet blossom.

This magic clearness and intensity in the colours was further forced on Brown's slowly reviving senses by something romantic and even secret in the very form of the landscape.*

* *The Perishing of the Pendragons.*

HOW MARVELLOUS THOSE occasions are, Heavenly Father, when heaven seems so very close to earth that it could almost be touched. Those moments are rare, but all the more precious for being so. I thank you for 'thin places'; venues and locations (or experiences) that somehow lend themselves to spiritual sensitivity, and which are particularly conducive to blessing. I think of them now; cathedrals, for example, and sacred spaces and opportunities of various kinds, and as I think of them, I pray your deep anointing upon visitors and pilgrims. May they sense you present and see no one but Jesus.

26 JUNE

Deep calls to deep (Psalm 42:7 *NIV*)

At the extreme point nearest them stood up an odd-looking building, unlike anything they could remember or connect with any purpose. It was not specially high, but it was too high for its breadth to be called anything but a tower. Yet it appeared to be built entirely of wood, and that in a most unequal and eccentric way.

Some of the planks and beams were of good, seasoned oak; some of such wood cut raw and recent; some again of white pinewood, and a great deal more of the same sort of wood painted black with tar. These black beams were set crooked or crisscross at all kinds of angles, giving the whole a most patchy and puzzling appearance. There were one or two windows, which appeared to be coloured and leaded in an old-fashioned but more elaborate style.

The travellers looked at it with that paradoxical feeling we have when something reminds us of something, and yet we are certain it is something very different. Father Brown, even when he was mystified, was clever in analysing his own mystification. And he found himself reflecting that the oddity seemed to consist in a particular shape cut out in an incongruous material; as if one saw a top-hat made of tin, or a frock-coat cut out of tartan.*

HOW VERY FRUSTRATING and mystifying that can be, Lord – being somewhere that reminds one of somewhere else, or seeing something that brings to mind something else, without quite being able to put one's finger on any specific details! I wonder if that is something akin to the struggle of a soul or a spirit inhabiting a body, with all its finite limitations? A gentle collision, perhaps, from time to time, of that which is infinite and that which is bound by a physical context? As we manage that balance, help us to find you in both arenas.

* *The Perishing of the Pendragons.*

27 JUNE

He lifted me out of the slimy pit, out of the mud and mire; he set my feet on a rock and gave me a firm place to stand (Psalm 40:2 *NIV*)

Warren Wynd was a very little man with loose grey hair and a pointed beard, seemingly frail but fierily active. He had very wonderful eyes, brighter than stars and stronger than magnets, which nobody who had ever seen them could easily forget. And indeed in his work as a reformer and regulator of many good works he had shown at least that he had a pair of eyes in his head.

All sorts of stories and even legends were told of the miraculous rapidity with which he could form a sound judgement, especially of human character. It was said that he selected the wife who worked with him so long in so charitable a fashion, by picking her out of a whole regiment of women in uniform marching past at some official celebration, some said of the Girl Guides and some of the Women Police. Another story was told of how three tramps, indistinguishable from each other in their community of filth and rags, had presented themselves before him asking for charity. Without a moment's hesitation he had sent one of them to a particular hospital devoted to a certain nervous disorder, had recommended the second to an inebriates' home, and had engaged the third at a handsome salary as his own private servant, a position which he filled successfully for years afterwards.*

BLESS THOSE, LORD (charities, churches and individuals), who make it their business to do all they can to lift the less fortunate into situations whereby they can receive relief and support. In doing so, they – wittingly or unwittingly – represent you. Honour their goodwill and charity, I pray, and help those on the receiving end of their altruism. I pray especially today for any such groups or people known to me personally, and also for anyone I know who is in need of assistance.

* *The Miracle of Moon Crescent.*

28 JUNE

If we say we have fellowship with him while we walk in darkness, we lie and do not practice the truth. But if we walk in the light, as he is in the light, we have fellowship with one another, and the blood of Jesus his Son cleanses us from all sin (1 John 1:6, 7 *ESV*)

Silas T. Vandam, the millionaire and oil magnate, was a lean man with a long, yellow face and blue-black hair, colours which were the less conspicuous yet somehow the more sinister because his face and figure showed dark against the window and the white warehouse wall outside it; he was buttoned up tight in an elegant overcoat with strips of astrakhan.

The eager face and brilliant eyes of Wynd, on the other hand, were in the full light from the other window over-looking the little garden, for his chair and desk stood facing it; and though the face was preoccupied, it did not seem unduly preoccupied about the millionaire.

Wynd's valet or personal servant, a big, powerful man with flat fair hair, was standing behind his master's desk holding a sheaf of letters; and Wynd's private secretary, a neat, red-haired youth with a sharp face, had his hand already on the door handle, as if guessing some purpose or obeying some gesture of his employer. The room was not only neat, but austere to the point of emptiness; for Wynd, with characteristic thoroughness, had rented the whole floor above, and turned it into a loft or storeroom, where all his other papers and possessions were stacked in boxes and corded bales.*

AN INTERESTING (AND challenging) contrast here, Heavenly Father. Fiction, maybe, but food for thought, nonetheless: Vandam's face, which shows up dark and sinister, and Wynd's, which is shown in full light. Which is mine, Lord, in your sight, so to speak? Am I walking in the light today?

* *The Miracle of Moon Crescent.*

29 JUNE

Unless the Lord builds the house, those who build it labour in vain (Psalm 127:1 *ESV*)

'What on earth's this?' said Flambeau, who was still staring at the tower.

Fanshaw's eyes were shining, and he spoke triumphantly. 'Aha! you've not seen a place quite like this before, I fancy; that's why I've brought you here, my friend. Now you shall see whether I exaggerate about the mariners of Cornwall. This place belongs to Old Pendragon, whom we call the Admiral; though he retired before getting the rank.

The spirit of Raleigh and Hawkins is a memory with the Devon folk; it's a modern fact with the Pendragons. If Queen Elizabeth were to rise from the grave and come up this river in a gilded barge, she would be received by the Admiral in a house exactly such as she was accustomed to, in every corner and casement, in every panel on the wall or plate on the table. And she would find an English Captain still talking fiercely of fresh lands to be found in little ships, as much as if she had dined with Drake.'

'She'd find a rum sort of thing in the garden,' said Father Brown, 'which would not please her Renaissance eye. That Elizabethan domestic architecture is charming in its way; but it's against the very nature of it to break out into turrets.' 'And yet,' answered Fanshaw, 'that's the most romantic and Elizabethan part of the business. It was built by the Pendragons in the very days of the Spanish wars; and though it's needed patching and even rebuilding for another reason, it's always been rebuilt in the old way. The story goes that the lady of Sir Peter Pendragon built it in this place and to this height, because from the top you can just see the corner where vessels turn into the river mouth; and she wished to be the first to see her husband's ship, as he sailed home from the Spanish Main.'*

* *The Perishing of the Pendragons.*

LORD GOD, YOU really do own some marvellous properties! St Paul's Cathedral, St Peter's Basilica, the Gothic masterpiece that is Notre-Dame; all wonderfully beautiful places of worship that inspire a sense of awe and reverence. Help your people today to do all we can to 'build', in as many ways as we can, all that will speak of you; buildings, congregations, liturgies, services and, most of all, lives. With you as our guide and architect, we can hope to build well!

30 JUNE

Remember your leaders, who spoke the word of God to you. Consider the outcome of their way of life and imitate their faith (Hebrews 13:7 *NIV*)

While [Father Brown] was talking to the journalist, Mendoza, the Conservative leader, came in. He was a stout, dark man, with a bald head like a pear and a round body also like a pear; he was smoking a very fragrant cigar, but he threw it away, perhaps a little theatrically, when he came into the presence of the priest, as if he had been entering church; and bowed with a curve that in so corpulent a gentleman seemed quite improbable. He was always exceedingly serious in his social gestures, especially towards religious institutions. He was one of those laymen who are much more ecclesiastical than ecclesiastics. It embarrassed Father Brown a good deal, especially when carried thus into private life.*

RESPECT WHERE RESPECT is due, Lord, and of course a priest, as a spiritual leader, is entitled to my courtesy. Some of us belong to faith traditions in which is it commonplace to bow in the presence of ecclesiastical dignitaries, while others of us prefer a more relaxed and informal setting. Either way, Lord – with all shades of deference in-between – I once again have the honour of lifting clergy to you in prayer. I pray for those in my town; men and women of every denominational hue. I ask your blessing upon their Kingdom endeavours, and also upon them personally in their private lives.

* *The Resurrection of Father Brown.*

1 JULY

I delivered to you as of first importance what I also received: that Christ died for our sins in accordance with the Scriptures
(1 Corinthians 15:3 *ESV*)

It seemed as if this familiarity between Father Brown and a successful and even famous man of business completed the reconciliation between the priest and the practical Mr Snaith. He felt, it might be supposed, a new respectability clothe the station and the mission, and was ready to overlook such occasional reminders of the existence of religion as a chapel and a presbytery can seldom wholly avoid. He became quite enthusiastic about the priest's programme – at least on its secular and social side – and announced himself ready at any moment to act in the capacity of a live wire for its communication to the world at large. And it was at this point that Father Brown began to find the journalist rather more troublesome in his sympathy than in his hostility.

Mr Paul Snaith set out vigorously to feature Father Brown. He sent long and loud eulogies on him across the continent to his newspaper in the Middle West. He took snapshots of the unfortunate cleric in the most commonplace occupations, and exhibited them in gigantic photographs in the gigantic Sunday papers of the United States. He turned his sayings into slogans, and was continually presenting the world with 'A message' from the reverend gentleman in South America. Any stock less strong and strenuously receptive than the American race would have become very much bored with Father Brown. As it was, he received handsome and eager offers to go on a lecturing tour in the States; and when he declined, the terms were raised with expressions of respectful wonder. A series of stories about him, like the stories of Sherlock Holmes, were, by the instrumentality of Mr Snaith, planned out and put before the hero with requests for his assistance and encouragement. As the priest found they had started, he could offer no suggestion except that they should stop.*

* *The Resurrection of Father Brown.*

ANOTHER COMPLEXITY, LORD! Friendly goodwill towards the Church is one thing, but not quite so much if it favours secular and social work at the (inevitable) expense of any recognition of spiritual mission. Help us not to be seduced, I pray, by attention and interest that often flatters to deceive, and which is probably founded on ulterior motives. Remind us to keep the main thing the main thing; that is, the gospel, and to trust you for the rest; provision and publicity. The arms of flesh, however helpful to begin with, will almost certainly fail us. Grant us discernment.

2 JULY

When one says, 'I follow Paul,' and another, 'I follow Apollos,' are you not mere human beings? What, after all, is Apollos? And what is Paul? Only servants, through whom you came to believe – as the Lord has assigned to each his task. I planted the seed, Apollos watered it, but God has been making it grow. So neither the one who plants nor the one who waters is anything, but only God, who makes things grow. The one who plants and the one who waters have one purpose, and they will each be rewarded according to their own labour. For we are co-workers in God's service; you are God's field, God's building (1 Corinthians 3:4-9 *NIV*)

Needless to say, this strange boom in the North reacted on the little outpost in the South where he had expected to live in so lonely an exile. The considerable English and American population already on the spot began to be proud of possessing so widely advertised a person. American tourists, of the sort who land with a loud demand for Westminster Abbey, landed on that distant coast with a loud demand for Father Brown. They were within measurable distance of running excursion trains named after him, and bringing crowds to see him as if he were a public monument.

He was especially troubled by the active and ambitious new traders and shopkeepers of the place, who were perpetually pestering him to try their wares and to give them testimonials. Even if the testimonials were not forthcoming, they would prolong the correspondence for the purpose of collecting autographs. As he was a good-natured person they got a good deal of what they wanted out of him.*

GOD'S SERVICE, GOD'S field, God's building. It's all about you, God. That's all it ever was about, and that's all it will ever be about; you and you alone, world without end.

* *The Resurrection of Father Brown.*

3 JULY

The Spirit of the Sovereign Lord is on me, because the Lord has anointed me to proclaim good news to the poor. He has sent me to bind up the broken-hearted, to proclaim freedom for the captives and release from darkness for the prisoners, to proclaim the year of the Lord's favour and the day of vengeance of our God, to comfort all who mourn, and provide for those who grieve in Zion – to bestow on them a crown of beauty instead of ashes, the oil of joy instead of mourning, and a garment of praise instead of a spirit of despair (Isaiah 61:1-3 *NIV*)

While the Major strolled unobtrusively towards him, the priest took an equally indolent turn, which took him round the next corner of the house to within a yard or two of the projecting dustbin.

He stood regarding this dismal object for some minute and a half – then he stepped towards it, lifted the lid and put his head inside. Dust and other discolouring matter shook upwards as he did so; but Father Brown never observed his own appearance, whatever else he observed. He remained thus for a measurable period, as if engaged in some mysterious prayers. Then he came out again, with some ashes on his hair, and walked unconcernedly away.*

WHAT A LOVELY, gracious transaction you have organised, Heavenly Father; a crown of beauty in exchange for the ashes of my despair. This generous swap represents your love so beautifully. Help me simply and trustingly to accept what's on offer.

* *The Salad of Colonel Cray.*

4 JULY

A time to be silent (Ecclesiastes 3:7 *NIV*)

[Major Putnam] was talking to his cook – the swarthy son of Malta, whose lean, yellow and rather careworn face contrasted quaintly with his snow-white cap and costume. The cook might well be careworn, for cookery was the Major's hobby. He was one of those amateurs who always know more than the professional. The only other person he even admitted to be a judge of an omelette was his friend Cray.*

O LORD! IN your mercy, preserve us from amateur experts! Pew-critics, for example, who, quite remarkably, claim to know how to preach, despite never having done so; those who offer commentary on the multi-complexities of how a church should be led, even though they have never led so much as a parade, and so on! Experts and professionals are, of course, not immune from constructive criticism (and nor should they be), but for those of us who know very little about certain subjects, grant us the grace to keep our mouths shut and our opinions to ourselves, lest we inflict the burden of careworn-ness.

* *The Salad of Colonel Cray.*

5 JULY

There is now no condemnation for those who are in Christ Jesus, because through Christ Jesus the law of the Spirit who gives life has set you free from the law of sin and death (Romans 8:1, 2 *NIV*)

Being a hardened reporter, and it being apparently a public inn, I did not need to summon much of my impudence to sit down at the long table and order some cider. The big man in black seemed very learned, especially about local antiquities; the small man in black, though he talked much less, surprised me with a yet wider culture. So we got on very well together; but the third man, the old gentleman in the tight pantaloons, seemed rather distant and haughty, until I slid into the subject of the Duke of Exmoor and his ancestry.

I thought the subject seemed to embarrass the other two a little; but it broke the spell of the third man's silence most successfully. Speaking with restraint and with the accent of a highly educated gentleman, and puffing at intervals at his long churchwarden pipe, he proceeded to tell me some of the most horrible stories I have ever heard in my life: how one of the Eyres in the former ages had hanged his own father; and another had his wife scourged at the cart tail through the village; and another had set fire to a church full of children, and so on.

Some of the tales, indeed, are not fit for public print – such as the story of the Scarlet Nuns, the abominable story of the Spotted Dog, or the thing that was done in the quarry. And all this red roll of impieties came from his thin, genteel lips rather primly than otherwise, as he sat sipping the wine out of his tall, thin glass.

I could see that the big man opposite me was trying, if anything, to stop him; but he evidently held the old gentleman in considerable respect, and could not venture to do so at all abruptly. And the little priest at the other end of the table, though free from any such air of embarrassment, looked steadily at the table, and seemed to listen to the recital with great pain – as well as he might.*

* *The Purple Wig.*

O LORD! FAMILY secrets! Skeletons in the cupboard! How wonderful it is, therefore, that we can share our stories with you without fear of being rejected or cast adrift, however sordid or shameful the details. Remorse and penitence, of course; we must exercise those in contrition and repentance, but never (astonishingly) are we to dwell in the mire of condemnation. Such is grace; the vilest offenders are pardoned; set free to sin no more.

6 JULY

The Lord your God turned the curse into a blessing for you because the Lord your God loves you (Deuteronomy 23:5 *NASB*)

'You don't seem,' I said to the narrator, 'to be very fond of the Exmoor pedigree.'

He looked at me a moment, his lips still prim, but whitening and tightening; then he deliberately broke his long pipe and glass on the table and stood up, the very picture of a perfect gentleman with the framing temper of a fiend.

'These gentlemen,' he said, 'will tell you whether I have cause to like it. The curse of the Eyres of old has lain heavy on this country, and many have suffered from it. They know there are none who have suffered from it as I have.' And with that he crushed a piece of the fallen glass under his heel, and strode away among the green twilight of the twinkling apple-trees.

'That is an extraordinary old gentleman,' I said to the other two; 'do you happen to know what the Exmoor family has done to him? Who is he?' The big man in black was staring at me with the wild air of a baffled bull; he did not at first seem to take it in. Then he said at last, 'Don't you know who he is?'

I reaffirmed my ignorance, and there was another silence; then the little priest said, still looking at the table, 'That is the Duke of Exmoor.'

Then, before I could collect my scattered senses, he added equally quietly, but with an air of regularizing things: 'My friend here is Doctor Mull, the Duke's librarian. My name is Brown.' 'But,' I stammered, 'If that is the Duke, why does he damn all the old dukes like that?' 'He seems really to believe,' answered the priest called Brown, 'that they have left a curse on him.'*

* *The Purple Wig.*

CURSES NULLIFIED BY love; robbed of all their power by the intervention of a more-powerful God and Heavenly Father. Hear my prayers today, Lord, for all those who live in dread of a curse's influence. Be all that Deuteronomy 23:5 is, unto them, and in your mercy, turn fear into faith and cowering into confidence.

7 JULY

God blesses those who work for peace (Matthew 5:9 *NLT*)

'You are really in a land of strange stories [said the young squire to Father Brown]. King Arthur was here and Merlin and the fairies before him. The story goes that Sir Peter Pendragon, who (I fear) had some of the faults of the pirates as well as the virtues of the sailor, was bringing home three Spanish gentlemen in honourable captivity, intending to escort them to Elizabeth's court. But he was a man of flaming and tigerish temper, and coming to high words with one of them, he caught him by the throat and flung him by accident or design, into the sea. A second Spaniard, who was the brother of the first, instantly drew his sword and flew at Pendragon, and after a short but furious combat in which both got three wounds in as many minutes, Pendragon drove his blade through the other's body and the second Spaniard was accounted for. As it happened the ship had already turned into the river mouth and was close to comparatively shallow water. The third Spaniard sprang over the side of the ship, struck out for the shore, and was soon near enough to it to stand up to his waist in water. And turning again to face the ship, and holding up both arms to Heaven – like a prophet calling plagues upon a wicked city – he called out to Pendragon in a piercing and terrible voice, that he at least was yet living, that he would go on living, that he would live for ever; and that generation after generation the house of Pendragon should never see him or his, but should know by very certain signs that he and his vengeance were alive. With that he dived under the wave, and was either drowned or swam so long under water that no hair of his head was seen afterwards.'*

THE PERILS AND potential consequences of losing one's temper and flying off the handle, Lord – albeit an extreme scenario! It's difficult, Heavenly Father, to live peaceably all the time, especially when threats and dangers catch us unawares and hijack our

* *The Perishing of the Pendragons.*

insecurities. Help us, though, to aspire to peace, and to cultivate our tempers so that we are made into calm and reasonable people, even in moments of stress. Lord Jesus, you knew what it was to be held prisoner, and you knew what it was to be attacked, yet you never once lashed out. Help us (me), therefore, to strive after your example. Frankly, I can't do so unless you show me how.

8 JULY

In your hearts revere Christ as Lord. Always be prepared to give an answer to everyone who asks you to give the reason for the hope that you have. But do this with gentleness and respect (1 Peter 3:15 *NIV*)

'We are well acquainted,' went on the stranger firmly, 'with the alleged achievements of Dupin and others; and with those of Lecoq, Sherlock Holmes, Nicholas Carter, and other imaginative incarnations of the craft. But we observe there is in many ways, a marked difference between your own method of approach and that of these other thinkers, whether fictitious or actual. Some have spec'lated, sir, as to whether the difference of method may perhaps involve rather the absence of method.'

Father Brown was silent; then he started a little, almost as if he had been nodding over the stove, and said: 'I beg your pardon. Yes . . . Absence of method . . . Absence of mind, too, I'm afraid.'

'I should say of strictly tabulated scientific method,' went on the inquirer. 'Edgar Poe throws off several little essays in a conversational form, explaining Dupin's method, with its fine links of logic. Dr Watson had to listen to some pretty exact expositions of Holmes's method with its observation of material details. But nobody seems to have got on to any full account of your method, Father Brown, and I was informed you declined the offer to give a series of lectures in the States on the matter.'

'Yes,' said the priest, frowning at the stove; 'I declined.'

'Your refusal gave rise to a remarkable lot of interesting talk,' remarked Chace. 'I may say that some of our people are saying your science can't be expounded, because it's something more than just natural science. They say your secret's not to be divulged, as being occult in its character.'*

* *The Secret of Father Brown.*

SOMETIMES IT'S EASY, Lord, for those who wish to ridicule faith to deride it as something nonsensical, spooky and weird. That's a lazy go-to, but the suspicion often remains that people who talk to God and expect him to talk back to them are somehow unhinged or maybe even dabbling in the occult. Help me to know what to say, Lord, when any such accusations come my way. Help me to clarify matters for my inquirers, and to do so well.

9 JULY

I heard a loud voice in heaven, saying, 'Now the salvation and the power and the kingdom of our God and the authority of his Christ have come, for the accuser of our brothers has been thrown down, who accuses them day and night before our God' (Revelation 12:10 *ESV*)

'Being what?' asked Father Brown, rather sharply. 'Why, kind of esoteric,' replied the other. 'I can tell you, people got considerably worked up about Gallup's murder, and Stein's murder, and then old man Merton's murder, and now Judge Gwynne's murder, and a double murder by Dalmon, who was well known in the States. And there were you, on the spot every time, slap in the middle of it; telling everybody how it was done and never telling anybody how you knew. So some people got to think you knew without looking, so to speak. And Carlotta Brownson gave a lecture on Thought-Forms with illustrations from these cases of yours. The Second Sight Sisterhood of Indianapolis –'

Father Brown, was still staring at the stove; then he said quite loud yet as if hardly aware that anyone heard him: 'Oh, I say. This will never do.' 'I don't exactly know how it's to be helped,' said Mr Chace humorously. 'The Second Sight Sisterhood want a lot of holding down. The only way I can think of stopping it is for you to tell us the secret after all.' Father Brown groaned. He put his head on his hands and remained a moment, as if full of a silent convulsion of thought. Then he lifted his head and said in a dull voice: 'Very well. I must tell the secret.' His eyes rolled darkly over the whole darkling scene, from the red eyes of the little stove to the stark expanse of the ancient wall, over which were standing out, more and more brightly, the strong stars of the south. 'The secret is,' he said; and then stopped as if unable to go on. Then he began again and said: 'You see, it was I who killed all those people.' 'What?' repeated the other, in a small voice out of a vast silence. 'You see, I had murdered them all myself,' explained Father Brown patiently. 'So, of course, I knew how it was done.'

Grandison Chace had risen to his great height like a man lifted to the ceiling by a sort of slow explosion. Staring down at the other he repeated his incredulous question. 'I had planned out each of the crimes very carefully,' went on Father Brown, 'I had thought out exactly how a thing like that could be done, and in what style or state of mind a man could really do it. And when I was quite sure that I felt exactly like the murderer myself, of course I knew who he was.'

Chace gradually released a sort of broken sigh. 'You frightened me all right,' he said. 'For the minute I really did think you meant you were the murderer. Just for the minute I kind of saw it splashed over all the papers in the States: 'Saintly Sleuth Exposed as Killer: Hundred Crimes of Father Brown.' Why, of course, if it's just a figure of speech and means you tried to reconstruct the psychology –'*

A FALSE CONFESSION, Lord – of sorts! Not quite the sort of declaration of guilt that some are forced to make, but it leads me to pray for Christians who are pressurised to recant their faith; those of your people who are tortured and bullied into admitting to crimes they would never dream of committing. Once again, Lord, I pray: be with your Suffering Church.

* *The Secret of Father Brown.*

10 JULY

Jesus called them together and said, 'You know that the rulers of the Gentiles lord it over them, and their high officials exercise authority over them. Not so with you. Instead, whoever wants to become great among you must be your servant, and whoever wants to be first must be your slave – just as the Son of Man did not come to be served, but to serve, and to give his life as a ransom for many' (Matthew 20:24-28 *NIV*)

The big librarian had buried his big bald brow in his big red hands, like a man trying to think out his duty . . .

'Understand, I've no reason to defend him, or even keep faith with him. He has been a tyrant to me as to everybody else. Don't fancy because you see him sitting here that he isn't a great lord in the worst sense of the word. He would fetch a man a mile to ring a bell a yard off – if it would summon another man three miles to fetch a matchbox three yards off. He must have a footman to carry his walking-stick; a body servant to hold up his opera-glasses –'*

YOURS IS AN upside-down Kingdom, Lord! You are the Christ of counter-culture! Teach me these lessons of love.

* *The Purple Wig.*

11 JULY

The Almighty will not pervert justice (Job 43:2 *NASB*)

I opened my mouth to speak, but Mull went on in oblivion of me, speaking out of the cavern of his hands. 'I don't mind telling you, Father, because it's really more defending the poor Duke than giving him away. Didn't you ever hear of the time when he very nearly lost all the estates?'

The priest shook his head; and the librarian proceeded to tell the tale as he had heard it from his predecessor in the same post, who had been his patron and instructor, and whom he seemed to trust implicitly. Up to a certain point it was a common enough tale of the decline of a great family's fortunes – the tale of a family lawyer. His lawyer, however, had the sense to cheat honestly, if the expression explains itself. Instead of using funds he held in trust, he took advantage of the Duke's carelessness to put the family in a financial hole, in which it might be necessary for the Duke to let him hold them in reality.

The lawyer's name was Isaac Green, but the Duke always called him Elisha; presumably in reference to the fact that he was quite bald, though certainly not more than thirty. He had risen very rapidly, but from very dirty beginnings; being first a 'nark' or informer, and then a money-lender: but as solicitor to the Eyres he had the sense, as I say, to keep technically straight until he was ready to deal the final blow. The blow fell at dinner; and the old librarian said he should never forget the very look of the lampshades and the decanters, as the little lawyer, with a steady smile, proposed to the great landlord that they should halve the estates between them. The sequel certainly could not be overlooked; for the Duke, in dead silence, smashed a decanter on the man's bald head as suddenly as I had seen him smash the glass that day in the orchard. It left a red triangular scar on the scalp, and the lawyer's eyes altered, but not his smile.

He rose tottering to his feet, and struck back as such men do strike. 'I am glad of that,' he said, 'for now I can take the whole estate. The law will give it to me.'*

* *The Purple Wig.*

SOMETIMES, LORD, IT seems as though the system of criminal justice is tilted, unfairly, in favour of those who have wronged, rather than those who have been wronged. News reports quite often carry stories of what appear to be miscarriages of justice, when the law is made to look stupid. I'm not suggesting it's right to go about smashing decanters on people's heads, but in situations where there has been a serious degree of provocation, surely that must count for something, legally? Given all that, I thank you that we can take comfort in the knowledge that your judgments are scrupulous, accurate and sound. You are a just God who takes everything into consideration, fairly and squarely.

12 JULY

The heartfelt counsel of a friend is as sweet as perfume and incense (Proverbs 27: *NLT*)

'Flambeau,' said Father Brown, 'there is a long seat there under the veranda, where we can smoke out of the rain. You are my only friend in the world, and I want to talk to you. Or, perhaps, be silent with you.'

They established themselves comfortably in the veranda seat; Father Brown, against his common habit, accepted a good cigar and smoked it steadily in silence, while the rain shrieked and rattled on the roof of the veranda.*

A VERY SIMPLE prayer today, Heavenly Father: a prayer of grateful thanks for friends, for confidants, and for those who accompany me on my way. Thank you.

* *The Wrong Shape.*

13 JULY

God did extraordinary miracles through Paul, so that even handkerchiefs and aprons that had touched him were taken to the sick, and their illnesses were cured and the evil spirits left them (Acts 19:11, 12 *NIV*)

'The modern mind always mixes up two different ideas [said Father Brown]: mystery in the sense of what is marvellous, and mystery in the sense of what is complicated. That is half its difficulty about miracles. A miracle is startling; but it is simple. It is simple because it is a miracle. It is power coming directly from God (or the devil) instead of indirectly through nature or human wills.'*

WONDER-WORKING GOD, to be honest, I regard my salvation as a miracle, never mind anything else, but I pray today for those standing in need of miraculous action of another kind; for healing, maybe, when all else has failed, or for your provision in a moment of dire need, or for a breakthrough in a particular situation, when all seems lost. God of miracles, show us your power afresh.

* *The Wrong Shape.*

14 JULY

The prudent hold their tongues (Proverbs 10:19 *NIV*)

Father Brown, though commonly a silent, was an oddly sympathetic little man, and . . . had that knack of friendly silence which is so essential to gossip; and saying scarcely a word, he probably obtained from his new acquaintances all that in any case they would have told.

The butler indeed was naturally uncommunicative. He betrayed a sullen and almost animal affection for his master; who, he said, had been very badly treated. The chief offender seemed to be his highness's brother, whose name alone would lengthen the old man's lantern jaws and pucker his parrot nose into a sneer. Captain Stephen was a ne'er-do-weel, apparently, and had drained his benevolent brother of hundreds and thousands; forced him to fly from fashionable life and live quietly in this retreat.

That was all Paul, the butler, would say, and Paul was obviously a partisan.*

THE CHALLENGE IS, I suppose, Lord, to speak of others behind their back as I would do to their face. Obviously, there are those times when confidentiality is called for, but in the normal run of things, let openness and honesty be my norm, I pray.

* *The Sins of Prince Saradine.*

15 JULY

Be kindly affectioned one to another with brotherly love (Romans 12:10 *KJV*)

The Italian housekeeper was somewhat more communicative, being, as Brown fancied, somewhat less content. Her tone about her master was faintly acid; though not without a certain awe. Flambeau and his friend were standing in the room of the looking-glasses examining the red sketch of the two boys, when the housekeeper swept in swiftly on some domestic errand. It was a peculiarity of this glittering, glass-panelled place that anyone entering was reflected in four or five mirrors at once; and Father Brown, without turning round, stopped in the middle of a sentence of family criticism. But Flambeau, who had his face close up to the picture, was already saying in a loud voice, 'The brothers Saradine, I suppose. They both look innocent enough. It would be hard to say which is the good brother and which the bad.' Then, realising the lady's presence, he turned the conversation with some triviality, and strolled out into the garden. But Father Brown still gazed steadily at the red crayon sketch; and Mrs Anthony still gazed steadily at Father Brown.

She had large and tragic brown eyes, and her olive face glowed darkly with a curious and painful wonder – as of one doubtful of a stranger's identity or purpose. Whether the little priest's coat and creed touched some southern memories of confession, or whether she fancied he knew more than he did, she said to him in a low voice as to a fellow plotter, 'He is right enough in one way, your friend. He says it would be hard to pick out the good and bad brothers. Oh, it would be hard, it would be mighty hard, to pick out the good one.'*

SIBLING RIVALRIES, LORD! Differences between siblings; characteristics, traits and personalities. Those born of the same womb, Lord, need not necessarily be anything like each other. Today I pray for brothers and sisters; those whose branches

* *The Sins of Prince Saradine.*

might well stretch out in different directions but whose root is their common ground. I pray for harmony amongst them, even if they don't always see eye-to-eye and even if they live miles apart. I pray that brotherly and sisterly love might prevail. Strengthen such bonds, for they are uniquely special.

16 JULY

If we are faithless, he remains faithful, for he cannot disown himself (2 Timothy 3:13 *NIV*)

Father Brown had been thus rapidly summoned at the request of Patrick Royce, the big ex-Bohemian secretary. Royce was an Irishman by birth; and that casual kind of Catholic that never remembers his religion until he is really in a hole.*

O LORD! NEVER mind Patrick Royce – this rings a bell with me too, if I'm telling the truth! How often do I turn to you in an emergency, having perhaps neglected my prayer-life for a day or two, or even a little while! Pardon me those moments, I pray, when maybe I move, say, from Sunday to Sunday without making time for you in my week, only to find I need you for something urgent. Forgive me.

* *The Three Tools of Death.*

17 JULY

Whatever house you enter, first say, 'Peace be to this house!'
(Luke 10:5 *ESV*)

[Armstrong's] was in itself a depressing house. The rooms were very high and very cold; the decoration mean and provincial; the draughty corridors were lit by electricity that was bleaker than moonlight. And though the old man's scarlet face and silver beard had blazed like a bonfire in each room or passage in turn, it did not leave any warmth behind it. Doubtless this spectral discomfort in the place was partly due to the very vitality and exuberance of its owner; he needed no stoves or lamps, he would say, but carried his own warmth with him. But when [the young detective] Merton recalled the other inmates, he was compelled to confess that they also were as shadows of their lord.

The moody man-servant, with his monstrous black gloves, was almost a nightmare; Royce, the secretary, was solid enough, a big bull of a man, in tweeds, with a short beard; but the straw-coloured beard was startlingly salted with grey like the tweeds, and the broad forehead was barred with premature wrinkles. He was good-natured enough also, but it was a sad sort of good-nature, almost a heart-broken sort – he had the general air of being some sort of failure in life. As for Armstrong's daughter, it was almost incredible that she was his daughter; she was so pallid in colour and sensitive in outline. She was graceful, but there was a quiver in the very shape of her that was like the lines of an aspen. Merton had sometimes wondered if she had learnt to quail [*] at the crash of the passing trains.[†]

HOUSES AND HOMES, Lord; some as warm and welcoming as can be, others cold and cheerless. I pray for those like Armstrong's daughter, whose home life sounds pretty bleak; children, for example, who are raised without much love, or whose parents prefer them to live somewhere else. I pray too for those whose

* Old meaning: 'to cower'.
† *The Three Tools of Death.*

homes are lonely places in which they rattle around for long hours on end. Lord, you know all that takes place behind closed doors; joy and laughter as well as tears and misery. Bless our houses and homes, whether they be palaces or cottages.

18 JULY

Jesus said: 'A man was going down from Jerusalem to Jericho, when he was attacked by robbers. They stripped him of his clothes, beat him and went away, leaving him half dead. A priest happened to be going down the same road, and when he saw the man, he passed by on the other side. So too, a Levite, when he came to the place and saw him, passed by on the other side. But a Samaritan, as he travelled, came where the man was; and when he saw him, he took pity on him. He went to him and bandaged his wounds, pouring on oil and wine. Then he put the man on his own donkey, brought him to an inn and took care of him. The next day he took out two denarii and gave them to the innkeeper. 'Look after him,' he said, 'and when I return, I will reimburse you for any extra expense you may have.' 'Which of these three do you think was a neighbour to the man who fell into the hands of robbers?' The expert in the law replied, 'The one who had mercy on him.' Jesus told him, 'Go and do likewise' (Luke 10:30-37 *NIV*)

'They say,' she cried, with the awful relish of a schoolgirl, 'that all that country isn't ruled by the King of Italy, but by the King of Thieves. Who is the King of Thieves?'

'A great man,' replied Muscari, 'worthy to rank with your own Robin Hood, Signorina. Montano, the King of Thieves, was first heard of in the mountains some ten years ago, when people said brigands were extinct. But his wild authority spread with the swiftness of a silent revolution. Men found his fierce proclamations nailed in every mountain village; his sentinels, gun in hand, in every mountain ravine. Six times the Italian Government tried to dislodge him, and was defeated in six pitched battles as if by Napoleon.'*

* *The Paradise of Thieves.*

LORD OF THE years, given that nothing much has changed over the course of human history, and that banditry, thuggery and theft are just as common nowadays as they were in Bible times, and as there is not much, realistically-speaking, that I can do about that, let it be the case that I live a life of mercy. If, of course, I can help in some way, then I am at your disposal.

19 JULY

The desert and the parched land will be glad; the wilderness will rejoice and blossom. Like the crocus, it will burst into bloom; it will rejoice greatly and shout for joy. The glory of Lebanon will be given to it, the splendour of Carmel and Sharon; they will see the glory of the Lord, the splendour of our God (Isaiah 35:1, 2 *NIV*)

The white road climbed like a white cat; it spanned sunless chasms like a tight-rope; it was flung round far-off headlands like a lasso.

And yet, however high they went, the desert still blossomed like the rose. The fields were burnished in sun and wind with the colour of kingfisher and parrot and humming-bird, the hues of a hundred flowering flowers.

There are no lovelier meadows and woodlands than the English, no nobler crests or chasms than those of Snowdon and Glencoe. But Ethel Harrogate had never before seen the southern parks tilted on the splintered northern peaks; the gorge of Glencoe laden with the fruits of Kent. There was nothing here of that chill and desolation that in Britain one associates with high and wild scenery. It was rather like a mosaic palace, rent with earthquakes; or like a Dutch tulip garden blown to the stars with dynamite.*

LORD, IF GARDENS and parks can provoke such word-pictures, how much more the joy of the redeemed! The prospect of Paradise! Let that be our thrill!

* *The Paradise of Thieves.*

20 JULY

Do not store up for yourselves treasures on earth, where moths and vermin destroy, and where thieves break in and steal. But store up for yourselves treasures in heaven, where moths and vermin do not destroy, and where thieves do not break in and steal. For where your treasure is, there your heart will be also (Matthew 6:19-21 *NIV*)

Father Brown was dragged in a somewhat dazed condition towards a car at some little distance, in which a young man with tufts of untidy yellow hair and a rather harassed and haggard expression, hailed him from afar, and presented himself as Peter Wain. Before he knew where he was he was stowed in the car and travelling with considerable speed through and beyond the city. He was unused to the impetuous practicality of such American action, and felt about as bewildered as if a chariot drawn by dragons had carried him away into fairyland. It was under these disconcerting conditions that he heard for the first time, in long monologues from Wain, and short sentences from Drage, the story of the Coptic Cup and the two crimes already connected with it.

It seemed that Wain had an uncle named Crake who had a partner named Merton, who was number three in the series of rich business men to whom the cup had belonged. The first of them, Titus P. Trant, the Copper King, had received threatening letters from somebody signing himself Daniel Doom. The name was presumably a pseudonym, but it had come to stand for a very public if not a very popular character; for somebody as well known as Robin Hood and Jack the Ripper combined. For it soon became clear that the writer of the threatening letter did not confine himself to threatening. Anyhow, the upshot was that old Trant was found one morning with his head in his own lily-pond, and there was not the shadow of a clue. The cup was, fortunately, safe in the bank; and it passed with the rest of Trant's property to his cousin, Brian Horder, who was also a man of great wealth and who was also threatened by the nameless enemy. Brian Horder was picked up dead at the foot of a cliff outside his seaside residence, at which there was a burglary, this time on a large scale. For though the cup apparently again escaped, enough bonds and securities were stolen to leave Horder's financial affairs in confusion.*

WHAT CURIOUS CREATURES we really are, Lord! How highly we prize things like jewels and gold and silver cups! They are lovely, of course, and all to be admired, but today's Bible verses are all about priorities. As I pray, Heavenly Father, guide me by your gracious Spirit and allow me to assess the pecking order, so to speak, of matters within my heart.

* *The Arrow of Heaven.*

21 JULY

The LORD gives wisdom; from his mouth come knowledge and understanding (Proverbs 2:6 *NIV*)

'Brian Horder's widow,' explained Wain, 'had to sell most of his valuables, I believe, and Brander Merton must have purchased the cup at that time, for he had it when I first knew him. But you can guess for yourself that it's not a very comfortable thing to have.'

'Has Mr Merton ever had any of the threatening letters?' asked Father Brown, after a pause.

'I imagine he has,' said Mr Drage; and something in his voice made the priest look at him curiously, until he realized that the man in goggles was laughing silently, in a fashion that gave the newcomer something of a chill.

'I'm pretty sure he has,' said Peter Wain, frowning. 'I've not seen the letters, only his secretary sees any of his letters, for he is pretty reticent about business matters, as big business men have to be. But I've seen him real upset and annoyed with letters; and letters that he tore up, too, before even his secretary saw them. The secretary himself is getting nervous and says he is sure somebody is laying for the old man; and the long and the short of it is, that we'd be very grateful for a little advice in the matter. Everybody knows your great reputation, Father Brown, and the secretary asked me to see if you'd mind coming straight out to the Merton house at once.'

'Oh, I see,' said Father Brown, on whom the meaning of this apparent kidnapping began to dawn at last.*

ONLY FICTION, LORD, but perhaps today's story provides some kind of insight into the real and complex issues that church ministers often face; not only theological or spiritual matters, but pastoral concerns brought to their attention by anxious parishioners, for example. I pray, therefore, for my own church leaders as they grapple with sensitive affairs that require confidentiality and tact. Lord, grant them knowledge and understanding.

* *The Arrow of Heaven.*

22 JULY

There is neither Jew nor Gentile, neither slave nor free, nor is there male and female, for you are all one in Christ Jesus (Galatians 3:28 *NIV*)

Six people sat around a small table, seeming almost as incongruous and accidental as if they had been shipwrecked separately on the same small desert island. At least the sea surrounded them; for in one sense their island was enclosed in another island, a large and flying island like Laputa. For the little table was one of many little tables dotted about in the dining saloon of that monstrous ship the Moravia, speeding through the night and the everlasting emptiness of the Atlantic. The little company had nothing in common except that all were travelling from America to England. Two of them at least might be called celebrities; others might be called obscure, and in one or two cases even dubious. The first was the famous Professor Smaill, an authority on certain archaeological studies touching the later Byzantine Empire. His lectures, delivered in an American University, were accepted as of the first authority even in the most authoritative seats of learning in Europe. His literary works were so steeped in a mellow and imaginative sympathy with the European past, that it often gave strangers a start to hear him speak with an American accent. Yet he was, in his way, very American; he had long fair hair brushed back from a big square forehead, long straight features and a curious mixture of preoccupation with a poise of potential swiftness, like a lion pondering absent-mindedly on his next leap.

There was only one lady in the group; and she was (as the journalists often said of her) a host in herself; being quite prepared to play hostess, not to say empress, at that or any other table. She was Lady Diana Wales, the celebrated lady traveller in tropical and other countries; but there was nothing rugged or masculine about her appearance at dinner. She was herself handsome in an almost tropical fashion, with a mass of hot and heavy red hair; she was dressed in what the journalists call a daring fashion, but her face was intelligent and her eyes had that bright and rather prominent appearance which belongs to the eyes of ladies who ask questions at political meetings.*

* *The Curse of the Golden Cross.*

'THERE WAS ONLY one lady in the group': Thank you, Lord, for the leaps and bounds that have been made in terms of female emancipation around the world, in terms of social and political progress. Thank you too, for the significant strides that have been taken within the Church, in terms of female leadership. There is, though, quite some way to go on both fronts! Grant, therefore, wisdom, grace and courage to all who discuss and negotiate what can be a thorny topic. May courtesy, dignity and respect be the prevailing hallmarks of continued dialogue around this issue.

23 JULY

I am sending you out like sheep among wolves. Therefore be as shrewd as snakes and as innocent as doves (Matthew 10:16 *NIV*)

The Professor lingered and the little priest was the last to leave the table, carefully folding up his napkin. And as they were thus left alone together the Professor said suddenly to his companion: 'What would you say was the point of that little talk?'

'Well,' said Father Brown, smiling, 'since you ask me, there was something that amused me a little. I may be wrong; but it seemed to me that the company made three attempts to get you to talk about an embalmed body said to be found in Sussex. And you, on your side, very courteously offered to talk – first about algebra, and then about the Fascisti, * and then about the landscape of the Downs.'

'In short,' replied the Professor, 'you thought I was ready to talk about any subject but that one. You were quite right.'

The Professor was silent for a little time, looking down at the tablecloth; then he looked up and spoke with that swift impulsiveness that suggested the lion's leap.

'See here. Father Brown,' he said, 'I consider you about the wisest and whitest † man I ever met.'‡

WHAT A LOVELY compliment, Lord. May that be said and thought of me too.

* The National Fascisti (NF), renamed British National Fascists (BNF) in 1926, were a splinter group from the British Fascisti formed in 1924.

† *Used here to mean transparent, innocent, and guileless. Nothing to do with skin colour.*

‡ *The Curse of the Golden Cross.*

24 JULY

Righteousness exalts a nation (Proverbs 14:34 *ESV*)

Father Brown was very English. He had all the normal national helplessness about what to do with a serious and sincere compliment suddenly handed to him to his face in the American manner. His reply was a meaningless murmur.*

NATIONAL CHARACTERISTICS, LORD! I pray for my homeland today.

* *The Curse of the Golden Cross.*

25 JULY

Love does no wrong to a neighbour (Romans 13:10 *ESV*)

'The Great Scandal began thus. In the house called The Grange, situated at the extreme end of The Grove, there lives a lady. A lonely lady. She calls herself Mrs Maltravers (that is how we put it); but she only came a year or two ago and nobody knows anything about her. 'I can't think why she wants to live here,' said Miss Carstairs-Carew; 'we do not visit her'.'

''Perhaps that's why she wants to live there,' said Father Brown.

'Well, her seclusion is considered suspicious. She annoys them by being good-looking and even what is called good style. And all the young men are warned against her as a vamp.'

'People who lose all their charity generally lose all their logic,' remarked Father Brown. 'It's rather ridiculous to complain that she keeps to herself; and then accuse her of vamping the whole male population.'*

UNKINDNESS IS NOT often logical, Lord, yet that flaw is conveniently overlooked whenever unkindness is the order of the day! Is there anyone new to my neighbourhood, Lord? Someone who is settling in but not finding it all that easy, having relocated, perhaps? A family whose children are anxious at the prospect of starting at a new school? What can I do to make them welcome?

* *The Vampire of the Village.*

26 JULY

Love . . . rejoices with the truth (1 Corinthians 13:6 *NIV*)

'She is really rather a puzzling person [said the Doctor]. I saw her and found her intriguing; one of those brown women, long and elegant and beautifully ugly, if you know what I mean. She is rather witty, and though young enough certainly gives me an impression of what they call – well, experience. What the old ladies call a Past.'

'All the old ladies having been born this very minute,' observed Father Brown. 'I think I can assume she is supposed to have vamped the parson's son.'

'Yes, and it seems to be a very awful problem to the poor old parson. She is supposed to be a widow.'

Father Brown's face had a flash and spasm of his rare irritation. 'She is supposed to be a widow, as the parson's son is supposed to be the parson's son, and the solicitor is supposed to be a solicitor and you are supposed to be a doctor. Why in thunder shouldn't she be a widow? Have they one speck of prima facie evidence for doubting that she is what she says she is?'*

A TENDENCY TO mistrust (or misconstrue) what people tell me. Is that something I might need to check? I don't want to be naïve, and there is no virtue in gullibility, but by the same token, I am not entitled to cast doubt upon what might very well be the good word of others. Equally, they are entitled to my trust and courtesy. Please help me on this one, I pray. Preserve my heart from cynicism.

* *The Vampire of the Village.*

27 JULY

Let your conversation be always full of grace, seasoned with salt (Colossians 4:6 *NIV*)

Rock also gazed round the room and could see no sign of life less vegetable than the orange trees, except what looked like a large black mushroom, which he recognized as the hat of some native priest or other, stolidly smoking a black local cigar, and otherwise as stagnant as any vegetable. He looked for a moment at the heavy, expressionless features, noting the rudeness of that peasant type from which priests so often come, in Latin and especially Latin-American countries; and lowered his voice a little as he laughed.

'I don't imagine that Mexican padre knows our language,' he said. 'Catch those lumps of laziness learning any language but their own. Oh, I can't swear he's a Mexican; he might be anything . . . I suppose. But I'll answer for it he's not an American. Our ministries don't produce that debased type.'

'As a matter of fact,' said the debased type, removing his black cigar, 'I'm English and my name is Brown. But pray let me leave you if you wish to be private.'*

OOPS! LET ME stock up on salt, please, Lord.

* *The Scandal of Father Brown.*

28 JULY

Jesus answered, 'I am the way and the truth and the life. No one comes to the Father except through me' (John 14:6 *NIV*)

'I tell you any scheme that leaves out the new Great Spirit movement in Texas and Oklahoma, is leaving out the religion of the future.'

'Oh; I've sized up those religions of the future,' said the millionaire, contemptuously. 'I've been through them with a tooth-comb and they're as mangy as yellow dogs. There was that woman called herself Sophia: ought to have called herself Sapphira, I reckon. Just a plum fraud. Strings tied to all the tables and tambourines. Then there were the Invisible Life bunch; said they could vanish when they liked, and they did vanish, too, and a hundred thousand of my dollars vanished with them. I knew Jupiter Jesus out in Denver; saw him for weeks on end; and he was just a common crook. So was the Patagonian Prophet; you bet he's made a bolt for Patagonia. No, I'm through with all that; from now on I only believe what I see. I believe they call it being an atheist.'

'I guess you got me wrong,' said the man from Oklahoma, almost eagerly. 'I guess I'm as much of an atheist as you are. No supernatural or superstitious stuff in our movement; just plain science. The only real right science is just health, and the only real right health is just breathing. Fill your lungs with the wide air of the prairie and you could blow all your old eastern cities into the sea. You could just puff away their biggest men like thistledown. That's what we do in the new movement out home: we breathe. We don't pray; we breathe.'*

FRAUDSTERS AND CHARLATANS, Lord – there are plenty of those out there! Money-grabbers and con artists – quite a few of those too! Having said that, not every representation of superstition and spirituality is founded upon out-and-out deception; quite a bit of it is sincere, albeit some way from truth. As I try to live for you, Lord Jesus, in what appears to be a culture of 'pick and mix' spiritual belief, grant me wisdom and discernment and help me to be a good witness.

* *The Miracle of Moon Crescent.*

29 JULY

'If their purpose or activity is of human origin, it will fail. But if it is from God, you will not be able to stop these men; you will only find yourselves fighting against God' (Acts 4:38, 39 *NIV*)

The keen face of the secretary, rather pale against his red hair, showed a flicker of some odd feeling suggestive of a secret bitterness.

'I'm not glad,' he said, 'I'm just sure. You seem to like being atheists; so you may be just believing what you like to believe. But. I wish to God there were a God; and there ain't. It's just my luck.'*

A RELUCTANT ATHEIST, Lord! My prayers today reach out to atheists (and agnostics) who may be doubting their stance. Draw close to them by your Holy Spirit, I pray, and gently nudge their thoughts towards faith and belief. Have mercy.

* *The Miracle of Moon Crescent.*

30 JULY

David triumphed over the Philistine with a sling and a stone; without a sword in his hand he struck down the Philistine and killed him. David ran and stood over him. He took hold of the Philistine's sword and drew it from the sheath. After he killed him, he cut off his head with the sword (1 Samuel 17:50, 51 *NIV*)

'Otto, Prince of Heiligwaldenstein and Grossenmark [said Flambeau], was lying in the dews of the darkening twilight in the woods beyond the castle, with his arms flung out and his face flung up to the moon. The blood still pulsed from his shattered temple and jaw, but it was the only part of him that moved like a living thing. He was clad in his full white and yellow uniform, as to receive his guests within, except that the sash or scarf had been unbound and lay rather crumpled by his side. Before he could be lifted he was dead. But, dead or alive, he was a riddle – he who had always hidden in the inmost chamber out there in the wet woods, unarmed and alone.'

'Who found his body?' asked Father Brown. 'Some girl attached to the Court named Hedwig von something or other,' replied his friend, 'who had been out in the wood picking wild flowers.'

'Had she picked any?' asked the priest, staring rather vacantly at the veil of the branches above him.*

NOT A PLEASANT subject by any means, Heavenly Father – the discovery of a corpse. Nevertheless, a reminder today, in the larger narrative of David and Goliath, of the truth that in your name, we can, if needs by, slay giants; not necessarily literally, as in this story, but metaphorically – fear, for example, or any number of things that would seek to knock us off track. May we who are attached to the Courts of Heaven, as it were, learn to live in that knowledge.

* *The Fairy Tale of Father Brown.*

31 JULY

Continue to remember those in prison as if you were together with them in prison (Hebrews 13:3 *NIV*)

'Yes,' replied Flambeau. 'I particularly remember that the Chamberlain, or old Grimm or somebody, said how horrible it was, when they came up at her call, to see a girl holding spring flowers' . . .

'Had the flowers got long stalks?' asked Father Brown.

Flambeau stared at him. 'What an odd person you are!' he said. 'That's exactly what old Grimm said. He said the ugliest part of it, he thought – uglier than the blood and bullet – was that the flowers were quite short, plucked close under the head.'

'Of course,' said the priest, 'when a grown up girl is really picking flowers, she picks them with plenty of stalk. If she just pulled their heads off, as a child does, it looks as if –' And he hesitated.

'Well?' inquired the other.

'Well, it looks rather as if she had snatched them nervously, to make an excuse for being there after – well, after she was there.'*

UNDER SUSPICION! AN unusual prayer today, Heavenly Father, but one which I sense is close to your heart; suspects awaiting trial, those on remand, whose fate is still to be decided by judge or jury. Have great mercy, Lord. I know justice must prevail, and rightly so, but I believe you to be a God of compassion. Look upon those who are under arrest, those in holding cells, and those in the dock. Guilty or not, may they all somehow sense your love.

* *The Fairy Tale of Father Brown.*

1 AUGUST

On Herod's birthday the daughter of Herodias danced for the guests and pleased Herod so much that he promised with an oath to give her whatever she asked. Prompted by her mother, she said, 'Give me here on a platter the head of John the Baptist.' The king was distressed, but because of his oaths and his dinner guests, he ordered that her request be granted and had John beheaded in the prison. His head was brought in on a platter and given to the girl, who carried it to her mother (Matthew 14:6-10 *NIV*)

Flambeau turned abruptly at an exclamation behind him. It seemed to come from lower down than might have been expected, and to be addressed to his heels rather than his head. He instantly held out his hand, but he could hardly help laughing at what he saw. For some reason or other the platform had given way under Father Brown, and the unfortunate little man had dropped through to the level of the parade. He was just tall enough, or short enough, for his head alone to stick out of the hole in the broken wood, looking like St John the Baptist's head on a charger. The face wore a disconcerted expression, as did, perhaps, that of St John the Baptist.*

A LIGHT-HEARTED STORY of Father Brown today, Lord Jesus, but it turns my thoughts to those who are martyred for the sake of righteousness, John the Baptist being a prime example. I think of Christians in countries where their steadfast witness might well result in beheading. Lord, grant them a special place in the life to come. What heroes and heroines of the faith they are! I am humbled before them.

* *The God of the Gongs.*

2 AUGUST

She brought forth her firstborn son, and wrapped him in swaddling clothes, and laid him in a manger; because there was no room for them in the inn (Luke 2:7 *KJV*)

[Father Brown] was staring, with a knot in his forehead, at the landscape; and he suddenly pointed at it. 'What's that house over there?' he asked. Following his finger, Flambeau saw for the first time the corners of a building nearer than the farmhouse, but screened for the most part with a fringe of trees. It was not a large building, and stood well back from the shore . . .

Almost the whole frontage was of gilt plaster and figured glass, and between that grey seascape and the grey, witch-like trees, its gimcrack quality had something spectral in its melancholy. They both felt vaguely that if any food or drink were offered at such a hostelry, it would be the paste-board ham and empty mug of the pantomime. In this, however, they were not altogether confirmed. As they drew nearer and nearer to the place they saw in front of the buffet, which was apparently closed, one of the iron garden-seats with curly backs that had adorned the gardens, but much longer, running almost the whole length of the frontage. Presumably, it was placed so that visitors might sit there and look at the sea, but one hardly expected to find anyone doing it in such weather. Nevertheless, just in front of the extreme end of the iron seat stood a small round restaurant table, and on this stood a small bottle of Chablis and a plate of almonds and raisins. Behind the table and on the seat sat a dark-haired young man, bareheaded, and gazing at the sea in a state of almost astonishing immobility. But though he might have been a waxwork when they were within four yards of him, he jumped up like a jack-in-the-box when they came within three, and said in a deferential, though not undignified, manner: 'Will you step inside, gentlemen? I have no staff at present, but I can get you anything simple myself.' 'Much obliged,' said Flambeau. 'So you are the proprietor?' 'Yes,' said the dark man, dropping back a little into his motionless manner.*

* *The God of the Gongs.*

ALMIGHTY GOD, YOU came to us in Bethlehem, yet there was no room for you at the inn. Come to my heart, Lord Jesus; there is room for you there. Will you step inside?

3 AUGUST

Let the word of Christ dwell in you richly in all wisdom; teaching and admonishing one another in psalms and hymns and spiritual songs, singing with grace in your hearts to the Lord (Colossians 3:16 *KJV*)

[Father Brown continued] 'Sir Arthur St Clare, as I have already said, was a man who read his Bible. That was what was the matter with him. When will people understand that it is useless for a man to read his Bible unless he also reads everybody else's Bible? A printer reads a Bible for misprints. A Mormon reads his Bible, and finds polygamy; a Christian Scientist reads his, and finds we have no arms and legs. St Clare was an old Anglo-Indian Protestant soldier. Now, just think what that might mean; and, for Heaven's sake, don't cant about it. It might mean a man physically formidable living under a tropic sun in an Oriental society, and soaking himself without sense or guidance in an Oriental Book. Of course, he read the Old Testament rather than the New. Of course, he found in the Old Testament anything that he wanted – lust, tyranny, treason. Oh, I dare say he was honest, as you call it. But what is the good of a man being honest in his worship of dishonesty? In each of the hot and secret countries to which the man went he kept a harem, he tortured witnesses, he amassed shameful gold; but certainly he would have said with steady eyes that he did it to the glory of the Lord.'*

ASSIST ME IN my Bible reading, Lord; to find you there. Holy Spirit, speak to me as I read and meditate. Protect me from misunderstanding and misinterpretation.

* *The Sign of the Broken Sword.*

4 AUGUST

Pilate took Jesus and flogged him. And the soldiers twisted together a crown of thorns and put it on his head and arrayed him in a purple robe. They came up to him, saying, 'Hail, King of the Jews!' and struck him with their hands. Pilate went out again and said to them, 'See, I am bringing him out to you that you may know that I find no guilt in him.' So Jesus came out, wearing the crown of thorns and the purple robe (John 19:1-5 *ESV*)

The attic, which was the secretary's private place (and rather a small cell for so large a hermit), had indeed all the vestiges of a violent drama. Near the centre of the floor lay a large revolver as if flung away; nearer to the left was rolled a whisky bottle, open but not quite empty. The cloth of the little table lay dragged and trampled, and a length of cord, like that found on the corpse, was cast wildly across the windowsill. Two vases were smashed on the mantelpiece and one on the carpet.*

WHAT BECAME OF your crown of thorns, Lord Jesus? And your purple robe? And the nails that were hammered into your hands? And your blood-stained cross, Lord? What became of all those vestiges of a violent drama? I may never know, but what I do know is that you endured unimaginable suffering for my sake, that I should be forgiven. Suffering God, I worship you.

* *The Three Tools of Death.*

5 AUGUST

Show perfect courtesy toward all people (Titus 3:2 *ESV*)

As he entered the church, hitherto always empty at that hour, a kneeling figure rose hastily to its feet and came towards the full daylight of the doorway. When the curate saw it he stood still with surprise. For the early worshipper was none other than the village idiot, a nephew of the blacksmith, one who neither would nor could care for the church or for anything else. He was always called 'Mad Joe,' and seemed to have no other name; he was a dark, strong, slouching lad, with a heavy white face, dark straight hair, and a mouth always open. As he passed the priest, his moon-calf countenance gave no hint of what he had been doing or thinking of. He had never been known to pray before. What sort of prayers was he saying now? Extraordinary prayers surely.*

GOD OF GRACE, political correctness is an imperfect science, and it is not without its flaws. However, I thank you for the way in which your Spirit has moved amongst us in modern times, to help us realise that phrases such as 'village idiot' and 'Mad Joe' are unacceptably rude and offensive. Help me, I pray, to be sensitive to your Spirit's leading in all such matters, and to be considerate in thought, word and deed.

* *The Hammer of God.*

6 AUGUST

Bear one another's burdens, and so fulfil the law of Christ (Galatians 6:2 *ESV*)

The cobbler was, as in many villages, an atheist, and his appearance in church was a shade more extraordinary than Mad Joe's. It was a morning of theological enigmas.

'What is it?' asked Wilfred Bohun rather stiffly, but putting out a trembling hand for his hat. The atheist spoke in a tone that, coming from him, was quite startlingly respectful, and even, as it were, huskily sympathetic. 'You must excuse me, sir,' he said in a hoarse whisper, 'but we didn't think it right not to let you know at once. I'm afraid a rather dreadful thing has happened, sir. I'm afraid your brother –' Wilfred clenched his frail hands. 'What devilry has he done now?' he cried in voluntary passion. 'Why, sir,' said the cobbler, coughing, 'I'm afraid he's done nothing, and won't do anything. I'm afraid he's done for. You had really better come down, sir.'

The curate followed the cobbler down a short winding stair which brought them out at an entrance rather higher than the street. Bohun saw the tragedy in one glance, flat underneath him like a plan. In the yard of the smithy were standing five or six men mostly in black, one in an inspector's uniform. They included the doctor, the Presbyterian minister, and the priest from the Roman Catholic chapel, to which the blacksmith's wife belonged. The latter was speaking to her, indeed, very rapidly, in an undertone, as she, a magnificent woman with red-gold hair, was sobbing blindly on a bench. Between these two groups, and just clear of the main heap of hammers, lay a man in evening dress, spread-eagled and flat on his face. From the height above Wilfred could have sworn to every item of his costume and appearance, down to the Bohun rings upon his fingers; but the skull was only a hideous splash, like a star of blackness and blood.*

* *The Hammer of God.*

AN HORRIFIC SCENARIO, Lord, yet the kind of scene that might, relatively often, greet, for example, police officers and/or members of the clergy, whose responsibility it sometimes is to be present at, say, a traffic accident or even the location of a murder or a sudden death. I pray for them as they process such tragedies, and especially as they care for shocked loved ones and relatives. Bless them as they not only cope with their own sense of shock, but need to be there for others too.

7 AUGUST

He is the image of the invisible God (Colossians 1:15 *NASB*)

They turned out into the street, the small priest trundling after them with the docility of a small dog. He merely said, in a cheerful way, like one making conversation, 'How quick the snow gets thick on the ground.' As they threaded the steep side streets already powdered with silver, Angus finished his story; and by the time they reached the crescent with the towering flats, he had leisure to turn his attention to the four sentinels. The chestnut seller, both before and after receiving a sovereign, swore stubbornly that he had watched the door and seen no visitor enter. The policeman was even more emphatic. He said he had had experience of crooks of all kinds, in top hats and in rags; he wasn't so green as to expect suspicious characters to look suspicious; he looked out for anybody, and, so help him, there had been nobody. And when all three men gathered round the gilded commissionaire, who still stood smiling astride of the porch, the verdict was more final still. 'I've got a right to ask any man, duke or dustman, what he wants in these flats,' said the genial and gold-laced giant, 'and I'll swear there's been nobody to ask since this gentleman went away.'

The unimportant Father Brown, who stood back, looking modestly at the pavement, here ventured to say meekly, 'Has nobody been up and down stairs, then, since the snow began to fall? It began while we were all round at Flambeau's.' 'Nobody's been in here, sir, you can take it from me,' said the official, with beaming authority.

'Then I wonder what that is?' said the priest, and stared at the ground blankly like a fish. The others all looked down also; and Flambeau used a fierce exclamation and a French gesture. For it was unquestionably true that down the middle of the entrance guarded by the man in gold lace, actually between the arrogant, stretched legs of that colossus, ran a stringy pattern of grey footprints stamped upon the white snow. 'The Invisible Man!' cried Angus involuntarily.*

* *The Invisible Man.*

TODAY'S BIBLE TEXT says it all, Lord Jesus, and I thank you for it. It tells us who you are, it reminds us of your greatness, and most of all it speaks of a wonderful love coming to us from heaven above. No longer invisible!

8 AUGUST

All you need to say is simply 'Yes' or 'No' anything beyond this comes from the evil one (Matthew 5:37 *NIV*)

'Have you ever noticed this – that people never answer what you say? They answer what you mean – or what they think you mean. Suppose one lady says to another in a country house, "Is anybody staying with you?" the lady doesn't answer "Yes; the butler, the three footmen, the parlourmaid, and so on," though the parlourmaid may be in the room, or the butler behind her chair. She says "There is nobody staying with us," meaning nobody of the sort you mean. But suppose a doctor inquiring into an epidemic asks, "Who is staying in the house?" then the lady will remember the butler, the parlourmaid, and the rest. All language is used like that; you never get a question answered literally, even when you get it answered truly.'*

AN INTERESTING OBSERVATION, Lord! Keep a guard on my speech today, so that I may speak and converse as you would have me do; nothing more, nothing less.

* *The Invisible Man.*

9 AUGUST

Jesus went with his disciples to a place called Gethsemane, and he said to them, 'Sit here while I go over there and pray.' He took Peter and the two sons of Zebedee along with him, and he began to be sorrowful and troubled. Then he said to them, 'My soul is overwhelmed with sorrow to the point of death. Stay here and keep watch with me.' Going a little farther, he fell with his face to the ground and prayed, 'My Father, if it is possible, may this cup be taken from me. Yet not as I will, but as you will' (Matthew 26:36-39 *NIV*)

Aristide Valentin, Chief of the Paris Police, was late for his dinner, and some of his guests began to arrive before him. These were, however, reassured by his confidential servant, Ivan, the old man with a scar, and a face almost as grey as his moustaches, who always sat at a table in the entrance hall – a hall hung with weapons.

Valentin's house was perhaps as peculiar and celebrated as its master. It was an old house, with high walls and tall poplars almost overhanging the Seine; but the oddity – and perhaps the police value – of its architecture was this: that there was no ultimate exit at all except through this front door, which was guarded by Ivan and the armoury. The garden was large and elaborate, and there were many exits from the house into the garden.

But there was no exit from the garden into the world outside; all round it ran a tall, smooth, unscalable wall with special spikes at the top; no bad garden, perhaps, for a man to reflect in whom some hundred criminals had sworn to kill.*

A GARDEN FROM which there was no exit, Lord Jesus. An inhabitant of that garden whom some had sworn to kill. How horribly reminiscent of Gethsemane. And yet, you could actually have left, but you didn't. There was an exit! You could have walked away, but you chose not to. Your anguish in the garden was all for me. My Saviour.

* *The Secret Garden.*

10 AUGUST

'Nazareth! Can anything good come from there?' Nathanael asked (John 1:46 *NIV*)

Valentin was an anti-clerical of some note. But O'Brien was an Irishman, with a kind of chastity even in his sins; and his gorge rose against that great brutality of the intellect which belongs only to France. He felt Paris as a whole, from the grotesques on the Gothic churches to the gross caricatures in the newspapers. He remembered the gigantic jests of the Revolution. He saw the whole city as one ugly energy.*

HOW CASUALLY, LORD, we (I) dip into stereotypes; to view, for example, an entire nation in stereotypical terms. Caricatures have their place, but not if they are used to distort truth and fact. Forgive me if I have dipped, unthinkingly, into lazy assumptions, using labels that are neither fair nor accurate.

* *The Secret Garden.*

11 AUGUST

How long wilt thou forget me, O Lord? for ever? how long wilt thou hide thy face from me? How long shall I take counsel in my soul, having sorrow in my heart daily? how long shall mine enemy be exalted over me? (Psalm 13:1, 2 *KJV*)

'Do you believe in doom?' asked the restless Prince Saradine suddenly.

'No,' answered his guest. 'I believe in Doomsday.'

The prince turned from the window and stared at him in a singular manner, his face in shadow against the sunset. 'What do you mean?' he asked.

'I mean that we here are on the wrong side of the tapestry,' answered Father Brown. 'The things that happen here do not seem to mean anything; they mean something somewhere else. Somewhere else retribution will come on the real offender. Here it often seems to fall on the wrong person.'*

IF I MAY BE perfectly honest, Lord, both the psalmist and Father Brown have a point. It does often seem as though righteousness and justice are slow in coming to pass. In world events, tyrants appear to run amok without hindrance or interruption. Bullies and crooks cause misery with seeming impunity. Help me not to lose heart, though, Lord. If nothing else, help me to remember Father Brown's perspective.

* *The Sins of Prince Saradine.*

12 AUGUST

He began again to teach by the sea side: and there was gathered unto him a great multitude, so that he entered into a ship, and sat in the sea; and the whole multitude was by the sea on the land (Mark 4:1 *KJV*)

He momentarily fulfilled all Fanshaw's fable of an old piratical Admiral; though the details seemed afterwards to decompose into accidents. For instance, he wore a broad-brimmed hat as protection against the sun; but the front flap of it was turned up straight to the sky, and the two corners pulled down lower than the ears, so that it stood across his forehead in a crescent like the old cocked hat worn by Nelson. He wore an ordinary dark-blue jacket, with nothing special about the buttons, but the combination of it with white linen trousers somehow had a sailorish look.

He was tall and loose, and walked with a sort of swagger, which was not a sailor's roll, and yet somehow suggested it; and he held in his hand a short sabre which was like a navy cutlass, but about twice as big. Under the bridge of the hat his eagle face looked eager, all the more because it was not only clean-shaven, but without eyebrows. It seemed almost as if all the hair had come off his face from his thrusting it through a throng of elements. His eyes were prominent and piercing. His colour was curiously attractive, while partly tropical; it reminded one vaguely of a blood-orange. That is, that while it was ruddy and sanguine, there was a yellow in it that was in no way sickly, but seemed rather to glow like gold apples of the Hesperides –Father Brown thought he had never seen a figure so expressive of all the romances about the countries of the Sun.*

LORD JESUS, YOU probably spent a fair amount of your time at sea, or at least on boats; sufficient to know the perils of the deep. First Sea Lord, I ask your blessing on those whose livelihood depends upon rivers and oceans. Theirs is often a thankless task,

* *The Perishing of the Pendragons.*

and is probably under-appreciated by those of us who remain on land. May they know your blessing. Be with their families too, if and when they are separated from their loved ones for weeks or months at a time.

13 AUGUST

As a face is reflected in water, so the heart reflects the real person (Proverbs 27:19 *NLT*)

'There's that girl in the canoe again,' said Flambeau irrelevantly, for good-looking young women would call him off any topic . . .

Indeed, the black-haired young lady was letting her canoe float slowly and silently past . . . with a strong glow of curiosity on her oval and olive face.*

LORD OF LOVE, bless relationships everywhere, I pray; those that are successful, as well as those that are struggling. I pray today for relationships known to me personally; family and friends, neighbours. Grant them your help and support according to their needs and the dynamics of their situation.

* *The Perishing of the Pendragons.*

14 AUGUST

Do not take revenge, my dear friends, but leave room for God's wrath, for it is written: 'It is mine to avenge; I will repay,' says the Lord (Romans 12:19 *NIV*)

'If you are Prince Saradine,' said the young man, 'I may tell you that my name is Antonelli.' 'Antonelli,' repeated the prince languidly. 'Somehow I remember the name.' 'Permit me to present myself,' said the young Italian. With his left hand he politely took off his old-fashioned top-hat; with his right he caught Prince Saradine so ringing a crack across the face that the white top hat rolled down the steps and one of the blue flower-pots rocked upon its pedestal. The prince, whatever he was, was evidently not a coward; he sprang at his enemy's throat and almost bore him backwards to the grass. But his enemy extricated himself with a singularly inappropriate air of hurried politeness. 'That is all right,' he said, panting and in halting English. 'I have insulted. I will give satisfaction. Marco, open the case.'

The man beside him with the earrings and the big black case proceeded to unlock it. He took out of it two long Italian rapiers, with splendid steel hilts and blades, which he planted point downwards in the lawn. The strange young man standing facing the entrance with his yellow and vindictive face, the two swords standing up in the turf like two crosses in a cemetery, and the line of the ranked towers behind, gave it all an odd appearance of being some barbaric court of justice. But everything else was unchanged, so sudden had been the interruption. The sunset gold still glowed on the lawn, and the bittern still boomed as announcing some small but dreadful destiny.

'Prince Saradine,' said the man called Antonelli, 'when I was an infant in the cradle you killed my father and stole my mother; my father was the more fortunate. You did not kill him fairly, as I am going to kill you. You and my wicked mother took him driving to a lonely pass in Sicily, flung him down a cliff, and went on your way. I could imitate you if I chose, but imitating you is too vile. I have followed you all over the world, and you have always fled from me. But this is the end of the world – and of you. I have you now, and I give you the chance you never gave my father. Choose one of those swords.'*

* *The Sins of Prince Saradine.*

GETTING MY OWN back, Lord! Revenge seems such a natural expression of justice; avenging a wrong that has been inflicted. Your word, though, says otherwise; to leave things to you. Help me with that, I pray, when it seems to go against the grain. Take from my heart any thoughts of tit-for-tat.

15 AUGUST

Speak out on behalf of the voiceless and for the rights of all who are vulnerable. Speak out in order to judge with righteousness and to defend the needy and the poor (Proverbs 31:8-10 *CEB*)

Men were already running from the street corners; there was a small but ever-clustering crowd. With the prompt French instinct for the politics of the street, the man with the black moustache had already run across to a corner of the cafe, sprung on one of the tables, and seizing a branch of chestnut to steady himself, shouted as Camille Desmoulins once shouted when he scattered the oak-leaves among the populace.

'Frenchmen!' he volleyed; 'I cannot speak! God help me, that is why I am speaking! The fellows in their filthy parliaments who learn to speak also learn to be silent – a silent as that spy cowering in the house opposite! Silent as he is when I beat on his bedroom door! Silent as he is now, though he hears my voice across this street and shakes where he sits! Oh, they can be silent eloquently – the politicians! But the time has come when we that cannot speak must speak.*

LORD JESUS, YOU were nothing if not a revolutionary, and on that basis I bring my prayers to you today, for those around the world who are engaged in the struggle for human rights, improved living conditions and basic justice. As they raise their voices on behalf of the oppressed and downtrodden, may they know your blessing and protection. Doubtless, they will attract the attention of powerful opponents and enemies as they seek to expose exploitation. Strengthen their cause.

* *The Duel of Dr Hirsch.*

16 AUGUST

Give us this day our daily bread (Matthew 6:11 *ESV*)

In the early evening a light dinner was spread at the back of the Cafe Charlemagne. Though unroofed by any glass or gilt plaster, the guests were nearly all under a delicate and irregular roof of leaves; for the ornamental trees stood so thick around and among the tables as to give something of the dimness and the dazzle of a small orchard. At one of the central tables a very stumpy little priest sat in complete solitude, and applied himself to a pile of whitebait with the gravest sort of enjoyment. His daily living being very plain, he had a peculiar taste for sudden and isolated luxuries; he was an abstemious epicure. He did not lift his eyes from his plate, round which red pepper, lemons, brown bread and butter, etc., were rigidly ranked, until a tall shadow fell across the table, and his friend Flambeau sat down opposite.*

JEHOVAH-JIREH: 'God my Provider'.

* *The Duel of Dr Hirsch.*

17 AUGUST

The secret things belong to the Lord our God (Deuteronomy 29:29 *ESV*)

The lane down which they followed him was one of those that seem to be at the back of things, and look like the wrong side of the stage scenery. A colourless, continuous wall ran down one flank of it, interrupted at intervals by dull-hued and dirt-stained doors, all shut fast and featureless save for the chalk scribbles of some passing gamin.*

The tops of trees, mostly rather depressing evergreens, showed at intervals over the top of the wall, and beyond them in the grey and purple gloaming could be seen the back of some long terrace of tall Parisian houses, really comparatively close, but somehow looking as inaccessible as a range of marble mountains. On the other side of the lane ran the high gilt railings of a gloomy park.

Flambeau was looking round him in rather a weird way. 'Do you know,' he said, 'there is something about this place that –'†

A FEELING, LORD, that something is not quite right; a sixth sense, as it were, or an instinct. Those times when it can be difficult to analyse a feeling of unease or even suspicion. Lord, as I travel down life's lanes and sometimes experience feelings like that, grant me your protection, if necessary, and the reassurance of your constant presence. There is more to this life than meets the eye, and some matters are beyond human comprehension, even though something tells us they are real. Calm any fears, and enable me, even at moments of mystery, to know that you are there.

* Street urchins.

† *The Duel of Dr Hirsch.*

18 AUGUST

Do not be deceived: God is not mocked, for whatever one sows, that will he also reap (Galatians 6:7 *ESV*)

'Our people aren't like the English [said Usher], who will forgive a man for being rich if he throws away money on hospitals or horses. Last-Trick Todd has made himself big by his own considerable abilities; and there's no doubt that many of those on whom he has shown his abilities would like to show theirs on him with a shotgun. Todd might easily get dropped by some man he'd never even heard of; some labourer he'd locked out, or some clerk in a business he'd busted. Last-Trick is a man of mental endowments and a high public character; but in this country the relations of employers and employed are considerably strained.'*

'LAST-TRICK TODD', Lord. It's almost as if con artists and criminals are regarded as comic-book heroes, in a way; 'Jack the Ripper', for example, or 'Scarface' Capone. Those nicknames seem to neutralise the crimes behind the legends, as though bandits, murderers and gangsters are fictional characters, somehow. Yet, the reality is something quite different altogether. Help me not to be seduced by that, Lord, and to regard sin as sin, first and foremost in my own life; not to make light of it in the light of your holiness.

* *The Mistake of the Machine.*

19 AUGUST

A woman who had been subject to bleeding for twelve years came up behind him and touched the edge of his cloak. She said to herself, 'If I only touch his cloak, I will be healed.' Jesus turned and saw her. 'Take heart, daughter,' he said, 'your faith has healed you.' And the woman was healed at that moment (Matthew 9:20-22 *NIV)*

'A door had opened in the dark bulk of the left wing [said Usher], and a figure appeared black against the illuminated interior – a muffled figure bending forward, evidently peering out into the night. It closed the door behind it, and I saw it was carrying a lantern, which threw a patch of imperfect light on the dress and figure of the wearer. It seemed to be the figure of a woman, wrapped up in a ragged cloak and evidently disguised to avoid notice; there was something very strange both about the rags and the furtiveness in a person coming out of those rooms lined with gold. She took cautiously the curved garden path which brought her within half a hundred yards of me – then she stood up for an instant on the terrace of turf that looks towards the slimy lake, and holding her flaming lantern above her head she deliberately swung it three times to and fro as for a signal. As she swung it the second time a flicker of its light fell for a moment on her own face, a face that I knew. She was unnaturally pale, and her head was bundled in her borrowed plebeian shawl; but I am certain it was Etta Todd, the millionaire's daughter.'*

PEERING OUT, HOPING not to be noticed, and moving furtively and cautiously: how graciously, Lord Jesus, you deal with those who tentatively approach you in such ways, anxious only to touch the hem of your garment and then disappear back into the shadows. You don't take offence, and neither do you seek to expose the anxious and shy. What grace this is, and how very reassuring.

* *The Mistake of the Machine.*

20 AUGUST

Remember the LORD your God, for it is he who gives you the ability to produce wealth (Deuteronomy 8:18 *NIV*)

'There is no reason why anybody in America should want to kill an English lord newly landed [said Usher], except for the one reason mentioned in the pink paper – that the lord is paying his attentions to the millionaire's daughter. Our crop-haired friend, despite his ill-fitting clothes, must be an aspiring lover. I know the notion will seem to you jarring and even comic; but that's because you are English. It sounds to you like saying the Archbishop of Canterbury's daughter will be married in St George's, Hanover Square, to a crossing-sweeper on ticket-of-leave. You don't do justice to the climbing and aspiring power of our more remarkable citizens. You see a good-looking grey-haired man in evening-dress with a sort of authority about him, you know he is a pillar of the State, and you fancy he had a father. You are in error. You do not realize that a comparatively few years ago he may have been in a tenement or (quite likely) in a jail. You don't allow for our national buoyancy and uplift. Many of our most influential citizens have not only risen recently, but risen comparatively late in life.*

PEOPLE OF INFLUENCE in society, Lord – movers and shakers, power brokers. We need them, if things are to get done and matters of business and commerce are to progress. Without such people, the economic life of nations risks becoming stagnant. So, I pray for them today; the rich, the powerful and influential, and I thank you for all that they do, without many of whom the world would, quite literally, be a poorer place. Help them to deal and negotiate in ways that are fair and just.

* *The Mistake of the Machine.*

21 AUGUST

Some of them also were appointed over the furniture and over all the utensils of the sanctuary (1 Chronicles 9:28 *NASB*)

He threw open the door of the flat and looked in. The first glimpse showed that Warren Wynd's chair was empty. The second glance showed that his room was empty also.

Fenner, electrified with energy in his turn, dashed past the other into the apartment.

'He's in his bedroom,' he said curtly, 'he must be.'

As he disappeared into the inner chamber the other men stood in the empty outer room staring about them. The severity and simplicity of its fittings, which had already been noted, returned on them with a rigid challenge. Certainly in this room there was no question of hiding a mouse, let alone a man. There were no curtains and, what is rare in American arrangements, no cupboards. Even the desk was no more than a plain table with a shallow drawer and a tilted lid. The chairs were hard and high-backed skeletons.*

HOW EASY IT is for me, Lord, to all-too-often overlook the ministry of those who prepare church furnishings week by week, whether they be sparse or ornate; those who arrange the chairs (and tidy them away again), those who clean and polish, those who make sure the heating is switched on, those who take care of the practical behind-the-scenes details that all help to enhance my worship experience. I would soon notice the difference, were they to quit or fail to do what they do so faithfully. Thank you for them, Heavenly Father. Bless them. And forgive me.

* *The Miracle of Moon Crescent.*

22 AUGUST

When Judas, who had betrayed him, saw that Jesus was condemned, he was seized with remorse and returned the thirty pieces of silver to the chief priests and the elders. 'I have sinned,' he said, 'for I have betrayed innocent blood.' 'What is that to us?' they replied. 'That's your responsibility.' So Judas threw the money into the temple and left. Then he went away and hanged himself (Matthew 27:3-5 *NIV*)

'It's partly all this moon and trees that get on one's nerves,' said Fenner obstinately. 'Trees always look queer by moonlight, with their branches crawling about. Look at that –'

'Yes,' said Father Brown, standing still and peering at the moon through a tangle of trees. 'That's a very queer branch up there.' When he spoke again he only said: 'I thought it was a broken branch.'

But this time there was a catch in his voice that unaccountably turned his hearers cold. Something that looked rather like a dead branch was certainly dependent in a limp fashion from the tree that showed dark against the moon; but it was not a dead branch.

When they came close to it to see what it was Fenner sprang away again with a ringing oath. Then he ran in again and loosened a rope from the neck of the dingy little body dangling with drooping plumes of grey hair. Somehow he knew that the body was a dead body before he managed to take it down from the tree. A very long coil of rope was wrapped round and round the branches, and a comparatively short length of it hung from the fork of the branch to the body. A long garden tub was rolled a yard or so from under the feet, like the stool kicked away from the feet of a suicide.*

* *The Miracle of Moon Crescent.*

WHAT A DESPERATELY sad end to a life, Lord. How tragic for the deceased, to have ended their days like this, and how unbearably awful for those left behind. My prayers today are for families, communities, churches and places of employment grieving the loss of someone who ended their own life; a loved one, a friend, a colleague. Have mercy, Lord, and draw alongside them as they attempt to make sense of such a tragedy.

23 AUGUST

Let us pursue what makes for peace and for mutual upbuilding (Romans 14:18 *ESV*)

'First of all,' said the doctor, 'they have made one discovery about Mrs Maltravers. She is an actress.'

'I fancied so,' said Father Brown. 'Never mind why. I had another fancy about her, that would seem even more irrelevant.'

'Well, at that instant it was scandal enough that she was an actress. The dear old clergyman of course is heartbroken, to think that his white hairs should be brought in sorrow to the grave by an actress and adventuress. The spinsters shriek in chorus. The Admiral admits he has sometimes been to a theatre in town; but objects to such things in what he calls 'our midst'. Well, of course I've no particular objections of that kind. This actress is certainly a lady, if a bit of a Dark Lady, in the manner of the Sonnets.'*

HOW TIMES HAVE changed, Lord! Nevertheless, how divisive such matters can (still) sometimes be! Should Christians be seen going to the theatre, or is that worldliness personified? Should Christians spend time watching television, or playing cards? Should we go shopping on Sundays, or is that unacceptable? For all that times have indeed changed (for better or for worse), opinions still vary and points of view can be markedly different. That being so, Heavenly Father, and even with differing denominational emphases, grant us your grace, that we may witness well, despite secondary points on which we disagree.

* *The Vampire of the Village.*

24 AUGUST

I have come that they may have life, and have it to the full (John 10:10 *NIV*)

'I suppose you've gone the dreary round,' began the doctor, 'and found it a very dull village.'

Father Brown's reply was sharp and almost shrill. 'Don't call your village dull. I assure you it's a very extraordinary village indeed.'*

THANK YOU, LORD Jesus, for the wonderful yet challenging promise of life in all its fullness – Life with a capital 'L'! Allow me to step into that extraordinary experience, I pray, on the basis that if you have promised it, then it must surely be available. I step forward to claim it. I bring you my lower-case 'l' and ask that I might exchange it for an upper-case one, please!

* *The Vampire of the Village.*

25 AUGUST

Who was your guide through that great and cruel waste, where there were poison-snakes and scorpions and a dry land without water; who made water come out of the hard rock for you? (Deuteronomy 8:15 *BBE*)

'I've been dealing with the only extraordinary thing that ever happened here, I should think,' observed Dr Mulborough. 'And even that happened to somebody from outside. I may tell you they managed the exhumation quietly last night; and I did the autopsy this morning. In plain words we've been digging up a corpse that's simply stuffed with poison.'*

THROUGH MANY DANGERS, Lord! I wonder just how many toils and snares your grace has brought me safely through without me even realising they were there in the first place. Thank you for doing so. As you were with your people in the wilderness all those years ago, so you are with your people today, great unchanging God. Thank you for all your unseen protection in life's treacherous landscape.

* *The Vampire of the Village.*

26 AUGUST

One generation shall commend your works to another (Psalm 145:4 *ESV*)

The lawyer was indeed . . . an archaic old bird, he seemed something more than a fossil. Perhaps it was the uniformity of the background; but the priest had again the curious feeling that he himself was transplanted back into the early nineteenth century, rather than that the solicitor had survived into the early twentieth. His collar and cravat contrived to look almost like a stock as he settled his long chin into them; but they were clean as well as clean-cut; and there was even something about him of a very dry old dandy. In short, he was what is called well preserved, even if partly by being petrified.*

THERE'S A LOT to be said for fine old tradition, and there is certainly a value in warmly acknowledging the virtues and victories of the past. We do indeed stand on the shoulders of giants, and that is not treated lightly. However, if we, your people, give the impression that we are living in a century that has long-since passed, while the rest of the world is busy navigating the present age, then something might need to be addressed. In that context, I pray for my own church today, and my leaders, seeking your guidance for all our tomorrows in mission and service.

* *The Vampire of the Village.*

27 AUGUST

Judgment without mercy will be shown to anyone who has not been merciful. Mercy triumphs over judgment (James 2:13 *NIV*)

'What I see is that these scoundrels are bringing Paganism to our country [said Agar Rock], and destroying all the Christianity there is. Also destroying all the common sense there is. All settled habits, all solid social order, all the way in which the farmers who were our fathers and grandfathers did manage to live in the world, melted into a hot mush by sensations and sensualities about film stars who divorced every month or so, and make every silly girl think that marriage is only a way of getting divorced.'

'You are quite right,' said Father Brown. 'Of course I quite agree with you there. But you must make some allowances. Perhaps these Southern people are a little prone to that sort of fault. You must remember that Northern people have other kinds of faults. Perhaps these surroundings do encourage people to give too rich an importance to mere romance.'

The whole integral indignation of Agar Rock's life rose up within him at the word.

'I hate Romance,' he said, hitting the little table before him. 'I've fought the papers I worked for for forty years about the infernal trash. Every blackguard bolting with a barmaid is called a romantic elopement or something.'*

HELP ME WITH this one, please, Lord. On the one hand, I cannot disagree with what is essentially righteous indignation and a concern for moral standards on the part of Agar Rock. On the other, I, like Father Brown, wish to be kind in making allowances. I don't want to be a Pharisee full of condemnation and harsh judgment, but neither do I want to be so lenient and easy-going that I fail to take a stand. I wait upon you in prayer. Show me a realistic middle ground.

* *The Scandal of Father Brown.*

28 AUGUST

A bribe is like a magic stone in the eyes of the one who gives it; wherever he turns he prospers (Proverbs 17:8 *ESV*)

'I heard him hollering at the management [said Agar Rock], telling them to keep that rascal out; and quite right too. The people here seem a sly and slinky lot; but I rather fancy he's put the fear of God into them already.'

'As a matter of fact,' said Father Brown, 'I rather agree with you about the manager and the men in this hotel . . . Also I fancy the gentleman you speak of has not only hollered, but handed round dollars enough to get the whole staff on his side. I saw them locking doors and whispering most excitedly. By the way, your plain straightforward friend seems to have a lot of money.'*

PROSPERITY AND INFLUENCE, Lord, but at what cost? A bribe here, a bung there, and lucrative short-term gains, no doubt, but at the expense of integrity and a clear conscience. Give me strength to resist such short cuts, I pray, and even to decline relative prosperity if needs be. Give me a contented heart, which will serve as my best defence in the hour of temptation. Guard me. Guide me.

* *The Scandal of Father Brown.*

29 AUGUST

Trust in the LORD with all your heart and lean not on your own understanding (Proverbs 3:5 *NIV*)

'Now you are romantic,' said Father Brown helpfully. 'For instance, you see somebody looking poetical, and you assume he is a poet. Do you know what the majority of poets look like? What a wild confusion was created by that coincidence of three good-looking aristocrats at the beginning of the nineteenth century: Byron and Goethe and Shelley! Believe me, in the common way, a man may write: "Beauty has laid her flaming lips on mine," or whatever that chap wrote, without being himself particularly beautiful. Besides, do you realize how old a man generally is by the time his fame has filled the world? Watts painted Swinburne with a halo of hair; but Swinburne was bald before most of his last American or Australian admirers had heard of his hyacinthine locks. So was D'Annunzio.'*

THAT'S AN INTERESTING point made by Father Brown, Lord – the power of hearsay and assumption; in other words, that which is assumed to be fact simply because the majority of people think it so, even though it might actually be some distance from the truth. I pray for your guidance in that sense, when I read my Bible. Remind me to check for what's there, as opposed to what I think I've heard might be there. Help me to confirm things for myself, as that will be quite a spiritual benefit. Fact-check my faith, Father!

* *The Scandal of Father Brown.*

30 AUGUST

May it never be that I would boast, except in the cross of our Lord Jesus Christ, through which the world has been crucified to me, and I to the world (Galatians 6:14 *NASB*)

'You see, up to a point it's all simple enough [said Professor Smaill]. A Christian tomb of the Dark Ages, apparently that of a bishop, has been found under a little church at Dulham on the Sussex coast. The Vicar happens to be a good bit of an archaeologist himself and has been able to find a good deal more than I know yet. There was a rumour of the corpse being embalmed in a way peculiar to Greeks and Egyptians but unknown in the West, especially at that date. So Mr Walters (that is the Vicar) naturally wonders about Byzantine influences. But he also mentions something else, that is of even more personal interest to me.'

His long grave face seemed to grow even longer and graver as he frowned down at the tablecloth. His long finger seemed to be tracing patterns on it like the plans of dead cities and their temples and tombs . . .

'It is also stated that in the coffin is a chain with a cross, common enough to look at, but with a certain secret symbol on the back found on only one other cross in the world. It is from the arcana of the very earliest Church, and is supposed to indicate St Peter setting up his See at Antioch before he came to Rome. Anyhow, I believe there is but one other like it, and it belongs to me. I hear there is some story about a curse on it; but I take no notice of that.'*

HOW BEAUTIFULLY AND how poignantly your cross is represented in churches all around the world, Lord Jesus; that rugged old instrument of execution transformed into gold and silver, and often bejewelled. As we survey that wondrous emblem of love, may we simultaneously view the cross of crimson that speaks of death and atonement, and the polished, shining artefact that tells us of resurrection and victory. And at we gaze, and as we ponder, may we also be led to worship.

* *The Curse of the Golden Cross.*

31 AUGUST

Your kingdom is an everlasting kingdom (Psalm 145:13 *NKJV*)

[Professor Smaill continued] . . .

'I found a maze of subterranean passages which led at last to a heap of rich refuse, broken ornaments and scattered gems which I took to be the ruins of some sunken altar, and in which I found the curious gold cross. I turned it over, and on the back of it I saw the Ichthus or fish, which was an early Christian symbol, but of a shape and pattern rather different from that commonly found; and, as it seemed to me, more realistic – more as if the archaic designer had meant it to be not merely a conventional enclosure or nimbus, but to look a little more like a real fish. It seemed to me that there was a flattening towards one end of it that was not like mere mathematical decoration, but rather like a sort of rude or even savage zoology . . .

I belong to the group which believed that these caverns had been used in the same way as the catacombs. That is, we believed that, during some of the persecutions which spread like a fire over the whole Empire, the Christians had concealed themselves in these ancient pagan labyrinths of stone. It was therefore with a thrill as sharp as a thunderclap that I found and picked up the fallen golden cross and saw the design upon it; and it was with still more of a shock of felicity that, on turning to make my way once more outwards and upwards into the light of day, I looked up at the walls of bare rock that extended endlessly along the low passages, and saw scratched in yet ruder outline, but if possible more unmistakable, the shape of the Fish.'*

AN ANCIENT AND very basic Christian symbol, Lord, that speaks of persecution and concealment, of fear and courage. A crude emblem, Lord, that echoes down the centuries with news of the downfall of an empire and the furtherance of your Kingdom. Empires come and empires go, Heavenly Father, yet your Kingdom stands for ever. Thank you for this reminder.

* *The Curse of the Golden Cross.*

1 SEPTEMBER

My dear brothers and sisters, take note of this: Everyone should be quick to listen (James 1:19 *NIV*)

'Father Brown,' said the secretary, who had recovered his quiet tone, 'you're very smart, but there's something more to you than smartness. Somehow you're the sort of man to whom one wants to tell the truth.'*

WHAT A LOVELY compliment for a priest to receive! It speaks of trustworthiness, wisdom and that great spiritual gift, unshockabiity! May I be found, by your grace, as one in whom others may easily confide; not fearing judgment or condemnation, but confidant of empathy, care and mercy. Lord, may Jesus be seen in me.

* *The Arrow of Heaven.*

2 SEPTEMBER

Hear me, my God, as I voice my complaint; protect my life from the threat of the enemy. Hide me from the conspiracy of the wicked, from the plots of evildoers. They sharpen their tongues like swords and aim cruel words like deadly arrows . . . But God will shoot them with his arrows; they will suddenly be struck down (Psalm 64:1-7 *NIV*)

Wilton rushed forward, and [he and Father Brown] plunged into the inner room together. It was a comparatively small room and simply though elegantly furnished. Opposite to them one wide window stood open, over-looking the garden and the wooded plain. Close up against the window stood a chair and a small table, as if the captive desired as much air and light as was allowed him during his brief luxury of loneliness.

On the little table under the window stood the Coptic Cup; its owner had evidently been looking at it in the best light. It was well worth looking at, for that white and brilliant daylight turned its precious stones to many-coloured flames so that it might have been a model of the Holy Grail.

It was well worth looking at; but Brander Merton was not looking at it. For his head had fallen back over his chair, his mane of white hair hanging towards the floor, and his spike of grizzled beard thrust up towards the ceiling, and out of his throat stood a long, brown painted arrow with red feathers at the other end.

'A silent shot,' said Father Brown, in a low voice; 'I was just wondering about those new inventions for silencing firearms. But this is a very old invention, and quite as silent.' Then, after a moment, he added: 'I'm afraid he is dead.'*

SOMEWHAT DRASTIC, LORD, and I can't honestly say I want you to strike anyone with an arrow on my behalf. What I do want (and need) is your fierce protection, and I call upon you to strike down those things that threaten to ambush my faith; doubt, fear, apathy, temptation, and so on: my daily enemies. Please, Lord, shoot them with your arrows.

* *The Arrow of Heaven.*

3 SEPTEMBER

He said to them, 'I saw Satan fall like lightning from heaven' (Luke 10:18 *NKJV*)

Father Brown went to the window by which the arrow had evidently entered and looked out. The garden, with its flat flower-beds, lay far below like a delicately coloured map of the world. The whole vista seemed so vast and empty, the tower seemed set so far up in the sky that as he stared out a strange phrase came back to his memory.

'A bolt from the blue,' he said.

'What was that somebody said about a bolt from the blue and death coming out of the sky? Look how far away everything looks; it seems extraordinary that an arrow could come so far, unless it were an arrow from heaven!'

Wilton had returned, but did not reply, and the priest went on as in soliloquy. 'One thinks of aviation. We must ask young Wain ... about aviation.'*

WHAT A SIGHT you must have witnessed, Lord Jesus! A bolt from the blue indeed! Tragic in one sense, in that Satan relinquished the life of an angel in the heavenly courts and became absolutely absorbed by evil and hatred, doomed to destruction. In another sense, though, a terrific victory, that stunning fall representing the power of God over the forces of darkness. What a clear and powerful message that would have sent reverberating all across the spiritual realms! Hallelujah! Our God reigns.

* *The Arrow of Heaven.*

4 SEPTEMBER

Two of them were going to a village called Emmaus, about seven miles from Jerusalem. They were talking with each other about everything that had happened. As they talked and discussed these things with each other, Jesus himself came up and walked along with them; but they were kept from recognizing him . . . As they approached the village to which they were going, Jesus continued on as if he were going farther. But they urged him strongly, 'Stay with us, for it is nearly evening; the day is almost over.' So he went in to stay with them. When he was at the table with them, he took bread, gave thanks, broke it and began to give it to them. Then their eyes were opened and they recognized him, and he disappeared from their sight. They asked each other, 'Were not our hearts burning within us while he talked with us on the road and opened the Scriptures to us?' (Luke 24:1-32 *NIV*)

Without a sound or stir they all became almost creepily conscious at this moment that the group, halted outside Wynd's door, had silently grown from three figures to four.

How long the fourth figure had stood there none of the earnest disputants could tell, but he had every appearance of waiting respectfully and even timidly for the opportunity to say something urgent. But to their nervous sensibility he seemed to have sprung up suddenly and silently like a mushroom. And indeed, he looked rather like a big, black mushroom, for he was quite short and his small, stumpy figure was eclipsed by his big, black clerical hat; the resemblance might have been more complete if mushrooms were in the habit of carrying umbrellas, even of a shabby and shapeless sort.

Fenner, the secretary, was conscious of a curious additional surprise at recognizing the figure of a priest.*

O LORD! WALKING along life's way, and not even realising you are there, right beside me, step-by-step, day-by-day. Forgive me, I pray, for not recognizing you and your presence perhaps as often as I should.

* *The Miracle of Moon Crescent.*

5 SEPTEMBER

Speak thou the things which become sound doctrine (Titus 2:1 *KJV*)

'Father Brown believes a good number of things, I take it,' said Vandam, whose temper was suffering from the past snub and the present bickering.

'Father Brown believes a hermit crossed a river on a crocodile conjured out of nowhere, and then he told the crocodile to die, and it sure did. Father Brown believes that some blessed saint or other died, and had his dead body turned into three dead bodies, to be served out to three parishes that were all intent on figuring as his home-town. Father Brown believes that a saint hung his cloak on a sunbeam, and another used his for a boat to cross the Atlantic. Father Brown believes the holy donkey had six legs and the house of Loretto flew through the air. He believes in hundreds of stone virgins winking and weeping all day long' . . .

'Well,' said the priest gravely, 'it is true enough that I believe in a good many things that you probably don't. But it would take a considerable time to explain all the things I believe in.'*

I THANK YOU today, Lord, for apologists and theologians who carefully defend Christian doctrine with robust intellectual commitment, even, sometimes, in the face of cheap ridicule and nonsensical accusations. I thank you for teachers and lecturers; those whom you have gifted with the ability to debate and discuss points of Christian teaching at an academic level. They are a gift to the Church, and I pray your blessing on them in their special and important ministry.

* *The Miracle of Moon Crescent.*

6 SEPTEMBER

They heard the sound of the LORD God walking in the garden in the cool of the day (Genesis 3:8 *ESV*)

'Father Brown's religion has always understood the psychology of atmospheres [said Professor Vair], and knows how to appeal to everything simultaneously; even, for instance, to the sense of smell. It understands those curious effects produced by music on animals and human beings . . .

He knows how to concentrate the essence of all these spiritual sounds and sights, and even smells, in a few restrained gestures; in an art or school of manners. He could contrive so to concentrate your minds on the supernatural by his mere presence, that natural things slipped off your minds to left and right unnoticed. Now you know,' he proceeded with a return to cheerful good sense, 'that the more we study it the more queer the whole question of human evidence becomes. There is not one man in twenty who really observes things at all. There is not one man in a hundred who observes them with real precision; certainly not one in a hundred who can first observe, then remember, and finally describe. Scientific experiments have been made again and again showing that men under strain have thought a door was shut when it was open, or open when it was shut. Men have differed about the number of doors or windows in a wall just in front of them. They have suffered optical illusions in broad daylight. They have done this even without the hypnotic effect of personality; but here we have a very powerful and persuasive personality bent upon fixing only one picture on your minds.'*

HOW WONDERFUL IT is, Heavenly Father, to be reminded that I can sense your perma-presence in so many ways, all for the want of a little effort and application. How graciously and how gently you fill the atmosphere, so that life is, if I let it be, full of God. Keep all my senses on daily alert, I pray, lest I inadvertently miss spiritual sounds, sights and impressions.

* *The Miracle of Moon Crescent.*

7 SEPTEMBER

I will go before thee, and make the crooked places straight: I will break in pieces the gates of brass, and cut in sunder the bars of iron: And I will give thee the treasures of darkness, and hidden riches of secret places, that thou mayest know that I, the Lord, which call thee by thy name, am the God of Israel (Isaiah 45:2, 3 *KJV*)

'But I thought you believed in miracles,' broke out the secretary.

'Yes,' answered Father Brown, 'I believe in miracles. I believe in man-eating tigers, but I don't see them running about everywhere. If I want any miracles, I know where to get them.'

'I can't understand your taking this line, Father Brown,' said Vandam, earnestly. 'It seems so narrow; and you don't look narrow to me, though you are a parson.'*

WHAT A REFRESHINGLY balanced approach to the miraculous, Lord! Not denying your wonder-working power, yet not looking for a miracle every five minutes. Show me that power at work when it suits you, Lord, as opposed to when it suits me and my curiosity. Let that be my submission and my satisfaction. Your will be done.

* *The Miracle of Moon Crescent.*

8 SEPTEMBER

Know well the condition of your flocks, and give attention to your herds (Proverbs 27:23 *ESV*)

'Yes,' said Father Brown, 'I always like a dog, so long as he isn't spelt backwards.'

Those who are quick in talking are not always quick in listening. Sometimes even their brilliancy produces a sort of stupidity. Father Brown's friend and companion was a young man with a stream of ideas and stories, an enthusiastic young man named Fiennes, with eager blue eyes and blond hair that seemed to be brushed back, not merely with a hair-brush but with the wind of the world as he rushed through it. But he stopped in the torrent of his talk in a momentary bewilderment before he saw the priest's very simple meaning.

'You mean that people make too much of them?' he said. 'Well, I don't know. They're marvellous creatures. Sometimes I think they know a lot more than we do.'

Father Brown said nothing, but continued to stroke the head of the big retriever in a half-abstracted but apparently soothing fashion.*

FATHER BROWN HAS a point, Lord, but today I want to pray about standards in animal welfare – dogs horribly mistreated and abused in puppy farms, for example, and livestock deprived of any semblance of a normal, happy life. We should hang our heads in shame, Heavenly Father, at so much routine mistreatment. Forgive our ways of cruelty and grant your blessing to those trying hard to change legislation.

* *The Oracle of the Dog.*

9 SEPTEMBER

The wind blows wherever it pleases. You hear its sound, but you cannot tell where it comes from or where it is going. So it is with everyone born of the Spirit (John 3:8 *NIV*)

As his guests, the biped and the quadruped, disappeared, Father Brown took up his pen and went back to his interrupted occupation of planning a course of lectures on the Encyclical Rerum Novarum.

The subject was a large one and he had to recast it more than once, so that he was somewhat similarly employed some two days later when the big black dog again came bounding into the room and sprawled all over him with enthusiasm and excitement. The master who followed the dog shared the excitement if not the enthusiasm. He had been excited in a less pleasant fashion, for his blue eyes seemed to start from his head and his eager face was even a little pale.*

INTERRUPTIONS, LORD! EVEN friendly ones like this can sometimes cut right across my best-laid plans for the day. They can be inconvenient, to be honest. Maybe, though, I need to revise my thinking and learn to go with the flow? What if, after all, those interruptions are from you? Another rhythm for my days, Lord?

* *The Oracle of the Dog.*

10 SEPTEMBER

I am reminded of your sincere faith, a faith that dwelt first in your grandmother Lois and your mother Eunice and now, I am sure, dwells in you as well (2 Timothy 1:5 *ESV*)

His name was John Adams Race, and he was an electrical engineer, employed by Mendoza to fit out the old town with all the new conveniences. He was a figure far less familiar in satire and international gossip than that of the American journalist. Yet, as a matter of fact, America contains a million men of the moral type of Race . . .

He was exceptional in being exceptionally good at his job, but in every other way he was very simple. He had begun life as a druggist's assistant in a Western village, and risen by sheer work and merit; but he still regarded his home town as the natural heart of the habitable world.

He had been taught a very Puritan, or purely Evangelical, sort of Christianity from the Family Bible at his mother's knee; and in so far as he had time to have any religion, that was still his religion. Amid all the dazzling lights of the latest and even wildest discoveries, when he was at the very edge and extreme of experiment, working miracles of light and sound like a god creating new stars and solar systems, he never for a moment doubted that the things 'back home' were the best things in the world; his mother and the Family Bible and the quiet and quaint morality of his village. He had as serious and noble a sense of the sacredness of his mother as if he had been a frivolous Frenchman. He was quite sure the Bible religion was really the right thing.*

A SOLID FOUNDATION, an upbringing in the faith. Those things, Lord, have an inestimable and eternal value. Hear my prayers today for Christian mothers (parents) everywhere, who are doing their best to instil spiritual values that will last.

* *The Resurrection of Father Brown.*

11 SEPTEMBER

I have given them the glory that you gave me, that they may be one as we are one (John 17:22 *NIV*)

[Race] could hardly be expected to sympathize with the religious externals of Catholic countries; and in a dislike of mitres and croziers he sympathized with Mr Snaith . . .

Anyhow, when he said there was nothing to touch his home town, he was not boasting. He really meant that there was somewhere something plain and unpretentious and touching, which he really respected more than anything else in the world. Such being the mental attitude of John Adams Race in a South American station, there had been growing on him for some time a curious feeling, which contradicted all his prejudices and for which he could not account. For the truth was this: that the only thing he had ever met in his travels that in the least reminded him of the old wood-pile and the provincial proprieties and the Bible on his mother's knee was (for some inscrutable reason) the round face and black clumsy umbrella of Father Brown.

He found himself insensibly watching that commonplace and even comic black figure as it went bustling about; watching it with an almost morbid fascination, as if it were a walking riddle or contradiction. He had found something he could not help liking in the heart of everything he hated; it was as if he had been horribly tormented by lesser demons and then found that the Devil was quite an ordinary person.*

A LOVELY HINT of ecumenical warmth and goodwill in this story. More of the same, please, Lord.

* *The Resurrection of Father Brown.*

12 SEPTEMBER

I am the LORD, and there is none else, there is no God beside me (Isaiah 45:5 *KJV*)

'The Pyramids are mighty material, and they hold down the dead kings all right,' grinned the man in the goggles. 'I think there's a lot to be said for these old material religions. There's old carvings that have lasted for thousands of years, showing their gods and emperors with bended bows; with hands that look as if they could really bend bows of stone. Material, perhaps – but what materials! Don't you sometimes stand staring at those old Eastern patterns and things, till you have a hunch that old Lord God is still driving like a dark Apollo, and shooting black rays of death?'

'If he is,' replied Father Brown, 'I might call him by another name.'*

ONE GOD. MANY imposters, but one God, now and for ever. Amen.

* *The Arrow of Heaven.*

13 SEPTEMBER

Beware of false prophets, who come to you in sheep's clothing but inwardly are ravenous wolves (Matthew 7:15 *ESV*)

'Who in the world is Norman Drage?' asked his uncle. 'That's what I want to know,' replied the young man. 'I practically asked him, but he has got a wonderful trick of twisting every straight question crooked; it's like lunging at a fencer. He hooked on to me with hints about the flying-ship of the future; but I never trusted him much.' 'But what sort of a man is he?' asked Crake. 'He's a mystagogue,'* said Father Brown, with innocent promptitude. 'There are quite a lot of them about; the sort of men about town who hint to you in Paris cafes and cabarets that they've lifted the veil of Isis or know the secret of Stonehenge. In a case like this they're sure to have some sort of mystical explanations.'

The smooth, dark head of Mr Barnard Blake, the lawyer, was inclined politely towards the speaker, but his smile was faintly hostile. 'I should hardly have thought, sir,' he said, 'that you had any quarrel with mystical explanations.'

'On the contrary,' replied Father Brown, blinking amiably at him. 'That's just why I can quarrel with 'em. Any sham lawyer could bamboozle me, but he couldn't bamboozle you; because you're a lawyer yourself . . .

A swindler could pretend to me that he knew all about aeroplanes, but not to Captain Wain. And it's just the same with the other, don't you see? It's just because I have picked up a little about mystics that I have no use for mystagogues. Real mystics don't hide mysteries, they reveal them. They set a thing up in broad daylight, and when you've seen it it's still a mystery. But the mystagogues hide a thing in darkness and secrecy, and when you find it, it's a platitude.'†

SOPHISTICATED, LORD, AND most likely eloquent and clever. Still, though, false. I thank you, Lord Jesus, for your utter trustworthiness. You have no intention of tricking anyone. You are truth embodied, and I need look to no one else.

* A proponent of mystical doctrines.

† *The Arrow of Heaven.*

14 SEPTEMBER

Simon Peter, who had a sword, drew it and struck the high priest's servant, cutting off his right ear. (The servant's name was Malchus.) Jesus commanded Peter, 'Put your sword away!' (John 18:10, 11 *NIV*)

'Oh, I've no patience with all this sentimental whitewashing of worthless, murderous blackguards,' cried Wain, heatedly. 'If Wilton croaked the criminal he did a jolly good day's work, and there's an end of it.'

'Quite so, quite so,' said his uncle, nodding vigorously.

Father Brown's face had a yet heavier gravity as he looked slowly round the semicircle of faces.

'Is that really what you all think?' he asked.

Even as he did so he realized that he was an Englishman and an exile. He realized that he was among foreigners, even if he was among friends. Around that ring of foreigners ran a restless fire that was not native to his own breed; the fiercer spirit of the western nation that can rebel and lynch, and above all, combine. He knew that they had already combined.*

VIGILANTE LAW AND jurisdiction, Lord – mob rule. It's a dangerous thing, with edicts being imposed by people without credible authority or accountability. Street gangs, Lord, with their own private codes of ethics, and crime bosses who operate according to their home-made rules. Protection rackets. Heavenly Father, God of justice, these are powder keg, incendiary options, and I pray, therefore, for towns and cities – county lines – where police forces are ignored or usurped, and where violence can erupt without warning. We need you there, Lord. Bless those who seek to negotiate between rival factions. Help them, I pray.

* *The Arrow of Heaven.*

15 SEPTEMBER

Jael, Heber's wife, picked up a tent peg and a hammer and went quietly to him while he lay fast asleep, exhausted. She drove the peg through his temple into the ground, and he died (Judges 4:21 *NIV*)

'The disappearance of the dagger,' said Father Brown, nodding. He seemed to have become suddenly attentive.

'Well,' continued Fiennes, 'I told you that man Traill had a trick of fidgeting with his tie and tie-pin – especially his tie-pin. His pin, like himself, was at once showy and old-fashioned. It had one of those stones with concentric coloured rings that look like an eye; and his own concentration on it got on my nerves, as if he had been a Cyclops with one eye in the middle of his body. But the pin was not only large but long; and it occurred to me that his anxiety about its adjustment was because it was even longer than it looked; as long as a stiletto in fact.'

Father Brown nodded thoughtfully. 'Was any other instrument ever suggested?' he asked.*

A TIE-PIN USED as a dagger? A tent peg used as a murder weapon? Extreme examples, Lord, but nevertheless examples of perfectly innocent items misused, with tragic consequences; a tie-pin meant only to adorn a tie, and a tent peg meant only to secure a tent. How awful and how perverted the ordinary can become when used for the wrong purposes; a pen that can be deployed to write notes of friendship and encouragement (or sermons!) can also be used to sign a Declaration of War. Books that can be published to educate and edify can sit alongside books that spread hatred and evil. That which I have at my disposal today, Lord – my time, my possessions, my words –; help me to deploy wisely and kindly.

* *The Oracle of the Dog.*

16 SEPTEMBER

A hot-tempered person stirs up conflict, but the one who is patient calms a quarrel (Proverbs 15:18 *NIV*)

'I'm bound to say that the secretary is something of a busybody. He's one of those hot and headlong people whose warmth of temperament has unfortunately turned mostly to pugnacity and bristling suspicion; to distrusting people instead of to trusting them. That sort of red-haired red-hot fellow is always either universally credulous or universally incredulous; and sometimes both. He was not only a Jack-of-all-trades, but he knew better than all tradesmen. He not only knew everything, but he warned everybody against everybody.'*

O LORD! THE pros and cons of a hot-headed temperament – certainly not confined to red-haired individuals! Walk with me this day, I pray, and be the guardian of my reactions; if someone cuts ahead of me in the car park, so be it. If a shop assistant makes a mess of my perfectly straightforward order, so be it. If an uninvited caller on the telephone interrupts my work with some kind of scam, so be it. Keep me cool.

* *The Oracle of the Dog.*

17 SEPTEMBER

Pray for those who spitefully use you and persecute you (Matthew 5:44 NKJV)

'He was a . . . bloody assassin, no doubt,' said Fenner quietly. 'I'm not defending him; but I suppose it's Father Brown's business to pray for all men, even for a man like – '

'Yes,' assented Father Brown, 'it's my business to pray for all men, even for a man like Warren Wynd.'*

TODAY'S CHALLENGE IN devotional living, Lord! Grant me the grace of heart and mind to pray for all (not only those I like); people who have upset me or hurt me, people whose lifestyle irritates me, political leaders whose decisions and policies make me angry. There's the rub: to pray for them. Even them.

* *The Miracle of Moon Crescent.*

18 SEPTEMBER

Fear not, for I am with you; Be not dismayed, for I am your God. I will strengthen you, Yes, I will help you, I will uphold you with My righteous right hand (Isaiah 41:10 *NKJV*)

'Everyone walking along stone passages knows what it is to be followed by phantom feet [said Professor Smaill]. The echo follows flapping or clapping behind or in front, so that it is almost impossible for the man who is really lonely to believe in his loneliness. I had got used to the effects of this echo and had not noticed it much for some time past, when I caught sight of the symbolical shape scrawled on the wall of rock. I stopped, and at the same instant it seemed as if my heart stopped, too; for my own feet had halted, but the echo went marching on. I ran forward, and it seemed as if the ghostly footsteps ran also, but not with that exact imitation which marks the material reverberation of a sound. I stopped again, and the steps stopped also; but I could have sworn they stopped an instant too late; I called out a question; and my cry was answered; but the voice was not my own. It came round the corner of a rock just in front of me; and throughout that uncanny chase I noticed that it was always at some such angle of the crooked path that it paused and spoke. The little space in front of me that could be illuminated by my small electric torch was always as empty as an empty room. Under these conditions I had a conversation with I know not whom, which lasted all the way to the first white gleam of daylight, and even there I could not see in what fashion he vanished into the light of day. But the mouth of the labyrinth was full of many openings and cracks and chasms, and it would not have been difficult for him to have somehow darted back and disappeared again into the underworld of the caves. I only know that I came out on the lonely steps of a great mountain like a marble terrace, varied only with a green vegetation that seemed somehow more tropical than the purity of the rock, like the Oriental invasion that has spread sporadically over the fall of classic Hellas. I looked out on a sea of stainless blue, and the sun shone steadily on utter loneliness and silence; and there was not a blade of grass stirred with a whisper of flight nor the shadow of a shadow of man.'*

* *The Curse of the Golden Cross.*

DIVINE COMPANION, 'FEARING not' is sometimes easier said, than done! Especially, to be honest, when the uncertainties and vagaries of life are a little bit frightening, or when we cannot see our way very clearly, or when we are haunted by fears. Nevertheless, despite all that, I want to take you at your word today. Honour that, Lord, please. Answer that cry, I pray, on behalf of any who are frightened of today.

19 SEPTEMBER

Do not be afraid of those who kill the body but cannot kill the soul. Rather, be afraid of the One who can destroy both soul and body in hell (Matthew 10:28 *NIV*)

'It had been a terrible conversation; so intimate and so individual and in a sense so casual. This being, bodiless, faceless, nameless and yet calling me by my name, had talked to me in those crypts and cracks where we were buried alive with no more passion or melodrama than if we had been sitting in two armchairs at a club. But he had told me also that he would unquestionably kill me or any other man who came into the possession of the cross with the mark of the fish. He told me frankly he was not fool enough to attack me there in the labyrinth, knowing I had a loaded revolver, and that he ran as much risk as I. But he told me, equally calmly, that he would plan my murder with the certainty of success, with every detail developed and every danger warded off, with the sort of artistic perfection that a Chinese craftsman or an Indian embroiderer gives to the artistic work of a life-time. Yet he was no Oriental; I am certain he was a white man. I suspect that he was a countryman of my own.'*

UNDOUBTEDLY, LORD, THERE is a rightful place for fear in my psyche; it is a useful part of my make-up if it leads me to suddenly jump out of the way of a speeding vehicle, for example. Nevertheless, misplaced fear is a distortion of that positive element, so I pray for any realignment that might be necessary within my thinking. As I ponder today's Bible text, work with me, I pray, to realign. Teach me awe of you, and in doing so, impart confidence and courage regarding that which should not be feared.

* *The Curse of the Golden Cross.*

20 SEPTEMBER

I saw the souls of those who had been beheaded for the testimony of Jesus and for the word of God (Revelation 20:4 *ESV*)

'Why should I worry because one madman among a million of sane men, leagued in a great society against him, chooses to brag of persecuting me or pursuing me to death? The man who drew in the dark catacomb the secret symbol of Christ was persecuted in a very different fashion. He was the solitary madman; the whole sane society was leagued together not to save but to slay him.'*

AN ECHO OF Roman persecution, Lord, when the ground was saturated in the blood of your martyrs. An echo, Lord Jesus, of the time in human history that cost you your life. And yet, nothing has died: your Church has outlasted the Roman Empire by some considerable distance, and you yourself are alive and reigning in Glory. This is all a salutary lesson in faith and perspective, and I thank you for it. The voice of the martyrs calls to me today, and is as inspiring as ever.

* *The Curse of the Golden Cross.*

21 SEPTEMBER

I have other sheep that are not of this sheep pen. I must bring them also. They too will listen to my voice (John 10:16 *NIV*)

Dr Boyne was a big dark Irishman, one of those rather baffling Irishmen to be found all over the world, who will talk scientific scepticism, materialism, and cynicism at length and at large, but who never dream of referring anything touching the ritual of religion to anything except the traditional religion of their native land. It would be hard to say whether their creed is a very superficial varnish or a very fundamental substratum; but most probably it is both, with a mass of materialism in between.*

THE TRADITIONAL RELIGION of one's native land. That's an important and significant matter, Lord, for it represents so much that is precious; culture and upbringing, friends and family. I pray for grace and tact in my witnessing for Jesus, so that if and when I happen to be in dialogue with someone whose faith is not the same as mine, I will witness with attentive charm, respect and courtesy. Help me to be a learner, as well as an imparter.

* *The Dagger with Wings.*

22 SEPTEMBER

Rejoice greatly, Daughter Zion! Shout, Daughter Jerusalem! See, your king comes to you, righteous and victorious, lowly and riding on a donkey, on a colt, the foal of a donkey (Zechariah 9:9 *NIV*)

Father Brown buttoned up his commonplace overcoat to the neck, for the night was stormy, and took his commonplace umbrella from the stand . . .

And saying 'Good evening,' he pushed open the heavy doors of that palace of pleasures. The golden gates closed behind him, and he went at a brisk walk through the damp, dark streets in search of a penny omnibus.*

THIS IS QUITE a lovely little picture, Lord – a priest, a man of God, a person closely in touch with spiritual matters and familiar with the sacred, walking in search of a bus! It's a fascinating juxtaposition of the divine and the commonplace. What a poignant reminder, Lord Jesus, of the fact that you came to us as God Almighty, yet lowly and riding on a donkey. That indeed is the grand juxtaposition of divine love and humility, and it causes me to rejoice greatly.

* *The Queer Feet.*

23 SEPTEMBER

Early on the first day of the week, while it was still dark, Mary Magdalene went to the tomb and saw that the stone had been removed from the entrance. So she came running to Simon Peter and the other disciple, the one Jesus loved, and said, 'They have taken the Lord out of the tomb, and we don't know where they have put him!' (John 20:1, 2 *NIV*)

The hall had grown darker, though it was still struck here and there with the last crimson shafts of sunset, and one or two of the headless machines had been moved from their places for this or that purpose, and stood here and there about the twilit place. The green and red of their coats were all darkened in the dusk; and their likeness to human shapes slightly increased by their very shapelessness. But in the middle of them all . . . there lay something that looked like red ink spilt out of its bottle. But it was not red ink.

With a French combination of reason and violence Flambeau simply said 'Murder!' and, plunging into the flat, had explored, every corner and cupboard of it in five minutes. But if he expected to find a corpse he found none . . .

'My friend,' said Flambeau, talking French in his excitement, 'not only is your murderer invisible, but he makes invisible also the murdered man.'*

UP FROM THE grave you arose! The murdered Lamb is not there! Death unable to hold its prey! All glory to you, Risen Christ, for this, the ultimate victory. Life and love have triumphed! Death has lost its sting!

* *The Invisible Man.*

24 SEPTEMBER

We do not want you to be unaware, brethren, of our affliction which came to us in Asia, that we were burdened excessively, beyond our strength, so that we despaired even of life (2 Corinthians 1:8 *NASB*)

'An invisible man?' inquired Angus, raising his red eyebrows.

'A mentally invisible man,' said Father Brown.

A minute or two after he resumed in the same unassuming voice, like a man thinking his way. 'Of course you can't think of such a man, until you do think of him.'*

LORD, THIS MAKES me think of those people I have accidentally and inadvertently treated as though they were invisible – perhaps because, subconsciously, I have made them mentally invisible. The beggar in the shop doorway when I need to be about my business, for example. Forgive me. The colleague whose concerns and troubles I have (deliberately?) ignored, lest I become embroiled. And situations too; wars in lands far from my own, injustices I have failed to notice. Forgive me. May I never again regard anyone as invisible.

* *The Invisible Man.*

25 SEPTEMBER

Unobserved, they perish forever (Job 4:20 *NASB*)

'Reverend sir,' cried Angus, standing still, 'are you raving mad, or am I?'

'You are not mad,' said Brown, 'only a little unobservant. You have not noticed such a man as this, for example.'

He took three quick strides forward, and put his hand on the shoulder of an ordinary passing postman who had bustled by them unnoticed under the shade of the trees.

'Nobody ever notices postmen somehow,' he said thoughtfully; 'yet they have passions like other men, and even carry large bags where a small corpse can be stowed quite easily.'

The postman, instead of turning naturally, had ducked and tumbled against the garden fence.*

GRANT ME AN observant heart, Lord Jesus. I don't necessarily want people to duck and tumble in my presence, but I pray, nevertheless, for a sensitivity that causes me to notice the unnoticed as they travel life's way beside me.

* *The Invisible Man.*

26 SEPTEMBER

Stay always within the boundaries where God's love can reach and bless you (Jude 21 *LB*)

Flambeau went back to his sabres, purple rugs and Persian cat, having many things to attend to.

John Turnbull Angus went back to the lady at the shop, with whom that imprudent young man contrives to be extremely comfortable.

But Father Brown walked those snow-covered hills under the stars for many hours.*

EACH TO THEIR own, Lord; pastimes, preferences, people. May those I love and care for find great satisfaction in all they do today. I will go my way, I will do my thing, and they will go theirs, and do theirs. Keep us all, Lord, within the boundaries of your love, however we are spending these hours, and with whomever, satisfied and content within the ordinary pleasures of the day, relaxed within your goodwill.

* *The Invisible Man.*

27 SEPTEMBER

The LORD is my shepherd, I lack nothing (Psalm 23:1 *NIV*)

'[The mad lord] swore he was Diogenes, that had long sought an honest man, and at last had found one. He made a new will, which I have seen. He took the literal youth into his huge, neglected house, and trained him up as his solitary servant and – after an odd manner – his heir. And whatever that queer creature understands, he understood absolutely . . . that he himself was to have the gold of Glengyle. So far, that is all; and that is simple. He has stripped the house of gold, and taken not a grain that was not gold; not so much as a grain of snuff. He lifted the gold leaf off an old illumination, fully satisfied that he left the rest unspoilt. All that I understood; but I could not understand this skull business. I was really uneasy about that human head buried among the potatoes. It distressed me – till Flambeau said the word.'

'It will be all right. He will put the skull back in the grave, when he has taken the gold out of the tooth.' And, indeed, when Flambeau crossed the hill that morning, he saw that strange being, the just miser, digging at the desecrated grave, the plaid round his throat thrashing out in the mountain wind; the sober top hat on his head.*

O LORD! A crazed, frenzied pursuit of gold! Release my heart and mind from any such madness, I pray. Grant me a contentment in life that will prevent me from ever scratching around in the dirt for grains of gold, so to speak. Some people's ambition might well be gold. That's their business, and I commend them to you. Make my ambition, though, not gold, but souls, which are of far greater worth.

* *The Honour of Israel Gow.*

28 SEPTEMBER

Peter was kept in prison, but the church was earnestly praying to God for him. The night before Herod was to bring him to trial, Peter was sleeping between two soldiers, bound with two chains, and sentries stood guard at the entrance. Suddenly an angel of the Lord appeared and a light shone in the cell. He struck Peter on the side and woke him up. 'Quick, get up!' he said, and the chains fell off Peter's wrists. Then the angel said to him, 'Put on your clothes and sandals.' And Peter did so. 'Wrap your cloak around you and follow me,' the angel told him. Peter followed him out of the prison, but he had no idea that what the angel was doing was really happening; he thought he was seeing a vision. They passed the first and second guards and came to the iron gate leading to the city. It opened for them by itself, and they went through it. When they had walked the length of one street, suddenly the angel left him (Acts 12:5-10 *NIV*)

They had turned the corner of the front facade, and were approaching the front doorway. As they turned into it they saw the man in the white robe for the third time. He came so straight towards the front door that it seemed quite incredible that he had not just come out of the study opposite to it. Yet they knew that the study door was locked.

Father Brown and Flambeau, however, kept this weird contradiction to themselves, and Dr Harris was not a man to waste his thoughts on the impossible.*

IT SEEMS AS though locked doors and iron gates are as nothing to you, Almighty God! Graciously hear my prayers today, then, for those who are locked in, in one way or another. Not necessarily physically or literally, but spiritually, emotionally, mentally, and seemingly unable to escape the prisons of their

* *The Wrong Shape.*

minds and, therefore, their behaviours. Even if, like Dr Harris in the story, they do not contemplate the (apparently) impossible, have mercy and lead them to freedom, just as you led Peter when all seemed lost.

29 SEPTEMBER

Ahasuerus . . . reigned from India to Ethiopia over 127 provinces (Esther 1:1 *NASB*)

'My father,' said Flambeau in French, 'what is the matter with you?'

Father Brown was silent and motionless for half a minute, then he said: 'Superstition is irreligious, but there is something in the air of this place. I think it's that Indian – at least, partly.' He sank into silence, and watched the distant outline of the Indian, who still sat rigid as if in prayer.

At first sight he seemed motionless, but as Father Brown watched him he saw that the man swayed ever so slightly with a rhythmic movement, just as the dark tree-tops swayed ever so slightly in the wind that was creeping up the dim garden paths and shuffling the fallen leaves a little.*

LORD CHRIST, QUITE a bit of Indian superstition and religion is incompatible with Christianity. Hindus and Sikhs, for example, would present different ideas about your Being than a Christian traditionally would. An Indian mystic guru might contend that you, Jesus, are but one of many deities. Clearly, there is a gulf in terms of belief, but there need be no gulf at all in terms of friendship and common goodwill. Furthermore, Christians have much to learn from those whose beliefs are steeped in, for example, meditation and solitude. To that end, I pray for your people engaged in outreach in lands such as India, where their faith is very much in the minority. Season their witness, I pray, that it may reap a harvest. May many Indians come to call you their Father.

* *The Wrong Shape.*

30 SEPTEMBER

In the beginning God created the heaven and the earth. And the earth was without form, and void; and darkness was upon the face of the deep. And the Spirit of God moved upon the face of the waters (Genesis 1:1, 2 *KJV*)

'When that Indian spoke to us,' went on Brown in a conversational undertone, 'I had a sort of vision, a vision of him and all his universe. Yet he only said the same thing three times. When first he said "I want nothing," it meant only that he was impenetrable, that Asia does not give itself away. Then he said again, "I want nothing," and I knew that he meant that he was sufficient to himself, like a cosmos, that he needed no God, neither admitted any sins. And when he said the third time, "I want nothing," he said it with blazing eyes. And I knew that he meant literally what he said; that nothing was his desire and his home; that he was weary for nothing as for wine; that annihilation, the mere destruction of everything or anything – '*

THAT SEEMS TO be a strange kind of ambition, Lord, the destruction of everything and a literal nothing. It's a puzzling hope on the part of the Indian, but it does at least lead me to consider the stunning fact that you, Almighty God, created entire universes out of precisely that – nothing at all. Uncreated and unaided, you set to work on an extraordinary miracle; bring into existence that which had never existed. I cannot hope to comprehend even a fraction of what you did there, but I can at least praise you and worship you, in awe, Creator God.

* *The Wrong Shape.*

1 OCTOBER

He who repeats a matter separates close friends (Proverbs 17:9 *ESV*)

'Will you do me a favour?' said the priest quietly. 'The truth is, I make a collection of these curious stories, which often contain . . . elements which can hardly be put into a police report. Now, I want you to write out a report of this case for my private use. Yours is a clever trade,' he said, looking the doctor gravely and steadily in the face.

'I sometimes think that you know some details of this matter which you have not thought fit to mention. Mine is a confidential trade like yours, and I will treat anything you write for me in strict confidence. But write the whole.'

The doctor, who had been listening thoughtfully with his head a little on one side, looked the priest in the face for an instant, and said: 'All right,' and went into the study, closing the door behind him.*

I PRAY FOR those, such as doctors and priests, who are expected to keep confidences. This must take quite a toll on them at times, given some of the matters they discuss, so I pray that you will help to keep their minds clear (unpolluted, even) and their hearts light, even though they handle heavy issues. Theirs is quite a responsibility.

* *The Wrong Shape.*

2 OCTOBER

As long as it is day, we must do the works of him who sent me. Night is coming, when no one can work (John 9:4 *NIV*)

'Father,' said Flambeau suddenly, 'do you think it was all a dream?'

The priest shook his head, whether in dissent or agnosticism, but remained mute.

A smell of hawthorn and of orchards came to them through the darkness, telling them that a wind was awake; the next moment it swayed their little boat and swelled their sail, and carried them onward down the winding river to happier places and the homes of harmless men.*

RELATIVELY SPEAKING, ETERNAL Father, life – human existence, even the sum total of it – is like a dream, in terms of eternity. Our little day is soon gone. It isn't, of course, a dream in a literal sense, but in terms of brevity, it has that feeling about it; one life that will soon be past. Given that perspective, help me to live out this day – this miniscule but important twenty-four hours – in eternity's light. The day you have given will soon be over, and then we shall go Home.

* *The Sins of Prince Saradine.*

3 OCTOBER

Some faced jeers and flogging, and even chains and imprisonment. They were put to death by stoning; they were sawed in two; they were killed by the sword. They went about in sheepskins and goatskins, destitute, persecuted and mistreated – the world was not worthy of them. They wandered in deserts and mountains, living in caves and in holes in the ground (Hebrews 11:36-38 *NIV*)

The little priest was not an interesting man to look at, having stubbly brown hair and a round and stolid face.*

HOW UNNOTICED, AND how unmentioned, Lord, are your saints of old; largely anonymous in a culture that favours celebrity or material gain as hallmarks of recognition. Your world-changers aren't famous. Their names barely merit a mention in the pages of human history. Yet, gloriously, despite that earthly, worldly anonymity, they are remembered in the annals of heaven, where vastly different criteria apply. Here, they are unheard of. There, they shine. What a perspective for me to bear in mind as I go about my own life and times.

* *The Hammer of God.*

4 OCTOBER

They will suffer the punishment of eternal destruction, away from the presence of the Lord and from the glory of his might (2 Thessalonians 1:9 *ESV*)

'I won't ask you, Mr Barnes,' he said, 'whether you know anything about what has happened here. You are not bound to say. I hope you don't know, and that you will be able to prove it. But I must go through the form of arresting you in the King's name for the murder of Colonel Norman Bohun.'

'You are not bound to say anything,' said the cobbler in officious excitement. They've got to prove everything. They haven't proved yet that it is Colonel Bohun, with the head all smashed up like that.'

'That won't wash,' said the doctor aside to the priest. 'That's out of the detective stories. I was the colonel's medical man, and I knew his body better than he did. He had very fine hands, but quite peculiar ones. The second and third fingers were the same length. Oh, that's the colonel right enough.'

As he glanced at the brained corpse upon the ground the iron eyes of the motionless blacksmith followed them and rested there also.

'Is Colonel Bohun dead?' said the smith quite calmly. 'Then he's damned.'*

IT SOMETIMES APPEARS, Lord, as though any mention of the damned is regarded as politically incorrect and unacceptable, within church life at large. So too, any mention of hell and damnation. Nevertheless, lest they fall from the Christian agenda altogether one day, let me (at least privately) contemplate the reality of such matters. They might not be palatable, but they are there, in the Bible, Lord, and it therefore behoves me to ponder them. Dreadful, awful concepts they may be, but they are, for all that, part and parcel of my belief system as a follower of Christ. Be with me as I think and pray.

* *The Hammer of God.*

5 OCTOBER

The Lord added to their number daily those who were being saved (Acts 2:47 *NIV*)

'Don't say anything! Oh, don't say anything,' cried the atheist cobbler, dancing about in an ecstasy of admiration of the English legal system. For no man is such a legalist as the good Secularist.

The blacksmith turned on him over his shoulder the august face of a fanatic. 'It's well for you infidels to dodge like foxes because the world's law favours you,' he said; 'but God guards His own in His pocket, as you shall see this day.' Then he pointed to the colonel and said: 'When did this dog die in his sins?' 'Moderate your language,' said the doctor. 'Moderate the Bible's language, and I'll moderate mine. When did he die?' 'I saw him alive at six o'clock this morning,' stammered Wilfred Bohun.

'God is good,' said the smith. 'Mr Inspector, I have not the slightest objection to being arrested. It is you who may object to arresting me. I don't mind leaving the court without a stain on my character. You do mind perhaps leaving the court with a bad set-back in your career.' The solid inspector for the first time looked at the blacksmith with a lively eye; as did everybody else, except the short, strange priest, who was still looking down at the little hammer that had dealt the dreadful blow.

'There are two men standing outside this shop,' went on the blacksmith with ponderous lucidity, 'good tradesmen in Greenford whom you all know, who will swear that they saw me from before midnight till daybreak and long after in the committee room of our Revival Mission, which sits all night, we save souls so fast. In Greenford itself twenty people could swear to me for all that time. If I were a heathen, Mr Inspector, I would let you walk on to your downfall. But as a Christian man I feel bound to give you your chance, and ask you whether you will hear my alibi now or in court.'

The inspector seemed for the first time disturbed, and said, 'Of course I should be glad to clear you altogether now.' The smith walked out of his yard with the same long and easy stride, and returned to his two friends from Greenford, who were indeed friends of nearly everyone present. Each of them said a few words which no one ever thought of disbelieving.*

SOULS BEING SAVED so fast that midnight sittings are called for. Yes please, Lord.

* *The Hammer of God.*

6 OCTOBER

Mary treasured up all these things and pondered them in her heart (Luke 2:19 *NIV*)

One of those silences struck the group which are more strange and insufferable than any speech. Madly, in order to make conversation, the curate said to the Catholic priest:

'You seem very much interested in that hammer, Father Brown.'

'Yes, I am,' said Father Brown; 'why is it such a small hammer?'

The doctor swung round on him. 'By George, that's true,' he cried; 'who would use a little hammer with ten larger hammers lying about?'

Then he lowered his voice in the curate's ear and said:

'Only the kind of person that can't lift a large hammer. It is not a question of force or courage between the sexes. It's a question of lifting power in the shoulders. A bold woman could commit ten murders with a light hammer and never turn a hair. She could not kill a beetle with a heavy one.'*

JUMPING TO CONCLUSIONS, Lord – and in doing so, missing the important obvious. Preserve me from being a jumper to conclusions, I pray. Rather, let me ponder things slowly and carefully, lest I miss a detail or overlook a relevant point. I pray this especially in regard to my devotional life. Help me to take my time over the pages of Holy Scripture, that I may carefully excavate and in doing so, discover buried treasure that I might otherwise not have noticed.

* *The Hammer of God.*

7 OCTOBER

My beloved, flee from idolatry (1 Corinthians 10:14 *ESV*)

Flambeau had seen quite enough of these daily salutations of Phoebus, and plunged into the porch of the tall building without even looking for his clerical friend to follow.

But Father Brown, whether from a professional interest in ritual or a strong individual interest in tomfoolery, stopped and stared up at the balcony of the sun-worshipper, just as he might have stopped and stared up at a Punch and Judy. Kalon the Prophet was already erect, with argent garments and uplifted hands, and the sound of his strangely penetrating voice could be heard all the way down the busy street uttering his solar litany.

He was already in the middle of it; his eyes were fixed upon the flaming disc. It is doubtful if he saw anything or anyone on this earth; it is substantially certain that he did not see a stunted, round-faced priest who, in the crowd below, looked up at him with blinking eyes. That was perhaps the most startling difference between even these two far divided men. Father Brown could not look at anything without blinking; but the priest of Apollo could look on the blaze at noon without a quiver of the eyelid.

'O sun,' cried the prophet, 'O star that art too great to be allowed among the stars! O fountain that flowest quietly in that secret spot that is called space. White Father of all white unwearied things, white flames and white flowers and white peaks. Father, who art more innocent than all thy most innocent and quiet children; primal purity, into the peace of which –'*

ALMIGHTY GOD, PURIFY my heart from idolatry of any kind. Grant that my focus in liturgy, in worship, in service and in belief, may only ever by you. In a modern world where idols appear in all kinds of shapes and forms, this remains my prayer. And, Lord, let that commitment be one of love, not one of fear or even only dull obedience.

* *The Eye of Apollo.*

8 OCTOBER

God is our refuge and strength, an ever-present help in trouble. Therefore we will not fear, though the earth give way and the mountains fall into the heart of the sea, though its waters roar and foam and the mountains quake with their surging . . . He says, 'Be still, and know that I am God' (Psalm 46:1-10 *NIV*)

A rush and crash like the reversed rush of a rocket was cloven with a strident and incessant yelling. Five people rushed into the gate of the mansions as three people rushed out, and for an instant they all deafened each other. The sense of some utterly abrupt horror seemed for a moment to fill half the street with bad news – bad news that was all the worse because no one knew what it was. Two figures remained still after the crash of commotion: the fair priest of Apollo on the balcony above, and the ugly priest of Christ below him.

At last the tall figure and titanic energy of Flambeau appeared in the doorway of the mansions and dominated the little mob. Talking at the top of his voice like a fog-horn, he told somebody or anybody to go for a surgeon; and as he turned back into the dark and thronged entrance his friend Father Brown dipped in insignificantly after him. Even as he ducked and dived through the crowd he could still hear the magnificent melody and monotony of the solar priest still calling on the happy god who is the friend of fountains and flowers.

Father Brown found Flambeau and some six other people standing round the enclosed space into which the lift commonly descended. But the lift had not descended. Something else had descended; something that ought to have come by a lift. For the last four minutes Flambeau had looked down on it; had seen the brained and bleeding figure of that beautiful woman who denied the existence of tragedy. He had never had the slightest doubt that it was Pauline Stacey; and, though he had sent for a doctor, he had not the slightest doubt that she was dead.*

* *The Eye of Apollo.*

QUITE A SKILL, Lord – to remain still even in the midst of commotion. It's one I'd like to cultivate, with your help and tuition. In a high-speed world where commotions come and go with a fair bit of regularity, ranging from domestic matters to international concerns, when all around gives way, let my heart be calm, knowing that, in it all, you are God.

9 OCTOBER

He was despised and rejected by men, a man of sorrows and acquainted with grief (Isaiah 53:3 *ESV*)

[Flambeau] could not remember for certain whether he had liked her or disliked her; there was so much both to like and dislike. But she had been a person to him, and the unbearable pathos of details and habit stabbed him with all the small daggers of bereavement.

He remembered her pretty face and priggish speeches with a sudden secret vividness which is all the bitterness of death. In an instant like a bolt from the blue, like a thunderbolt from nowhere, that beautiful and defiant body had been dashed down the open well of the lift to death at the bottom.

Was it suicide? With so insolent an optimist it seemed impossible. Was it murder?*

THOSE HORRIBLE DAGGERS of bereavement, Lord, which sharply cut the heart of the bereaved into a thousand pieces. Man of Sorrows, be close to those who are shocked and newly-bereft today, and whose minds, in the early stages of grief, are racing frantically with unanswerable questions. Help them, I pray, as they too remember the faces of their loved ones, dearly departed.

* *The Eye of Apollo.*

10 OCTOBER

Live in harmony with one another (Romans 12:16 *NIV*)

'Prophet,' [Father Brown] said, presumably addressing Kalon, 'I wish you would tell me a lot about your religion.'

'I shall be proud to do it,' said Kalon, inclining his still crowned head.*

LOVING GOD, IF the alternatives are suspicion, mistrust, conflict and alienation, then let there be dialogue between representatives of different faiths. We may not agree – we probably shan't – but we can learn from one another as we talk. Draw us together in that way, I pray; not in a spirit of compromise, but of honest and constructive communication. That has to be a good option. To that end, bless and guide your people who are engaged in inter-faith dialogue.

* *The Eye of Apollo.*

11 OCTOBER

All have sinned and fall short of the glory of God (Romans 3:23 *NIV*)

In the long and startled stillness of the room the prophet of Apollo slowly rose; and really it was like the rising of the sun. He filled that room with his light and life in such a manner that a man felt he could as easily have filled Salisbury Plain. His robed form seemed to hang the whole room with classic draperies; his epic gesture seemed to extend it into grander perspectives, till the little black figure of the modern cleric seemed to be a fault and an intrusion, a round, black blot upon some splendour of Hellas.

'We meet at last, Caiaphas,' said the prophet. 'Your church and mine are the only realities on this earth. I adore the sun, and you the darkening of the sun; you are the priest of the dying and I of the living God. Your present work of suspicion and slander is worthy of your coat and creed. All your church is but a black police; you are only spies and detectives seeking to tear from men confessions of guilt, whether by treachery or torture. You would convict men of crime, I would convict them of innocence. You would convince them of sin, I would convince them of virtue.'*

AN INTERESTING SPEECH, Lord, yet at the heart of which is a denial of any kind of sinful nature. Christian doctrine, though, clearly teaches that humanity is a fallen species, tainted by sin. Yet, we are also shown a marvellous remedy for that problem in Christ, the second Adam, our Redeemer. We have our innocence, and we rejoice in that, but we realise it is an imparted virtue, thanks to our crucified God. I have no other argument: it is enough that Jesus died for me.

* *The Eye of Apollo.*

12 OCTOBER

Jesus did many other things as well. If every one of them were written down, I suppose that even the whole world would not have room for the books that would be written (John 21:25 *NIV*)

'Only a month or two ago [said Father Brown] a certain Brazilian official died in England, having quarrelled with Olivier and left his country. He was a well-known figure both here and on the Continent, a Spaniard named Espado; I knew him myself, a yellow-faced old dandy, with a hooked nose. For various private reasons I had permission to see the documents he had left; he was a Catholic, of course, and I had been with him towards the end . . . five or six common exercise books filled with the diary of some English soldier. I can only suppose that it was found by the Brazilians on one of those that fell. Anyhow, it stopped abruptly the night before the battle.'*

I AM CURIOUS, Lord Jesus, to know about those parts of your life and ministry that are not recorded in Scripture. As with the exercise books in the story, I can't help feeling there is so much more that could have been documented. However, I thank you for what I do know of your remarkable life; your incarnation, your three years of public ministry, your crucifixion, burial and resurrection. Despite my curiosity, Lord, that is enough, for the account of your life that does exist is an account of my salvation.

* *The Sign of the Broken Sword.*

13 OCTOBER

When Jesus had cried out again in a loud voice, he gave up his spirit (Matthew 27:50 *NIV*)

'The account of that last day in the poor fellow's life was certainly worth reading. I have it on me; but it's too dark to read it here, and I will give you a resume.'*

HOW PAINFUL AND how poignant it is, Lord Jesus, that anyone picking up a Bible or even only a New Testament has access to the account of your last day; a dark story indeed, but one that is quite gloriously laced all through with astonishing grace. Even in your agony, you granted pardon to the thief beside you. You prayed forgiveness over those who had crucified you and were mocking your agony. With aching lungs and parched lips, you declared the work of (my) redemption complete and irrevocable. Speak to me as I read the account again, that I may learn afresh of Calvary's reality. Wonderful words of love. Lord, make Calvary real to me.

* *The Sign of the Broken Sword.*

14 OCTOBER

No temptation has overtaken you that is not common to man. God is faithful, and he will not let you be tempted beyond your ability, but with the temptation he will also provide the way of escape, that you may be able to endure it (1 Corinthians 10:13 *ESV*)

'There is this about such evil [said Father Brown, to Flambeau], that it opens door after door in hell, and always into smaller and smaller chambers. This is the real case against crime, that a man does not become wilder and wilder, but only meaner and meaner.'*

INCREMENTAL SIN, LORD – one thing leading to another, in other words, as the sinner becomes more daring and brazen, excited by newer and newer possibilities. I guess that's the nature of temptation; Satan will tempt with a tit-bit that seems relatively innocuous, before adding to the menu, so to speak, until the hapless individual is caught in sin that escalates and enlarges. Redeeming God, in your mercy reach out to those who find themselves increasingly trapped, even if the original guilt is theirs. Let them find a way out, however deeply enmeshed they might be. However deep the pit, your grace runs deeper.

* *The Sign of the Broken Sword.*

15 OCTOBER

The Lord is the Spirit, and where the Spirit of the Lord is, there is freedom (2 Corinthians 3:17 *NIV*)

'[Cheerfulness] is a cruel religion,' said the priest, looking out of the window. 'Why couldn't they let him weep a little, like his fathers before him? His plans stiffened, his views grew cold; behind that merry mask was the empty mind of the atheist. At last, to keep up his hilarious public level, he fell back on that dram-drinking he had abandoned long ago. But there is this horror about alcoholism in a sincere teetotaller: that he pictures and expects that psychological inferno from which he has warned others. It leapt upon poor Armstrong prematurely, and by this morning he was in such a case that he sat here and cried he was in hell, in so crazy a voice that his daughter did not know it. He was mad for death.'*

SUCH A DREADFUL plight, Heavenly Father; to have to live as a caricature, a parody, of oneself; feeling the daily need to keep up a pretence of happiness, even when quite the opposite is true. And, then, to resort to using alcohol as a prop; gradually making a sad situation much worse. Lord of mercy and compassion, look upon those wearing masks today, and build up within them the courage to be themselves. Dissolve the façade, I pray, and bring freedom. Help those who, for whatever reason, are trapped, pretending to be what they are not. Set them free.

* *The Three Tools of Death.*

16 OCTOBER

There is nothing better for people than to be happy and to do good while they live. That each of them may eat and drink, and find satisfaction (Ecclesiastes 3:12, 13 *NIV*)

Miss Harrogate was specially radiant and ready for conversation on this occasion; and her family had fallen into the easier Continental habit, allowing the stranger Muscari and even the courier Ezza to share their table and their talk. In Ethel Harrogate conventionality crowned itself with a perfection and splendour of its own. Proud of her father's prosperity, fond of fashionable pleasures, a fond daughter but an arrant flirt, she was all these things with a sort of golden good-nature that made her very pride pleasing and her worldly respectability a fresh and hearty thing.*

A SIMPLE PRAYER today, Father God: thank you for good company, for friends who share my table from time to time, or allow me to share theirs. Thank you for conversation, and wit, and vivacity; all gifts that make up life's rich tapestry.

* *The Paradise of Thieves.*

17 OCTOBER

The citizens of Shechem set an ambush for Abimelech on the hilltops and robbed everyone who passed that way (Judges 9:25 *NLT*)

They were in an eddy of excitement about some alleged peril in the mountain path they were to attempt that week. The danger was not from rock and avalanche, but from something yet more romantic. Ethel had been earnestly assured that brigands, the true cut-throats of the modern legend, still haunted that ridge and held that pass of the Apennines . . .

'Now that sort of thing,' observed the banker weightily, 'would never be allowed in England; perhaps, after all, we had better choose another route. But the courier thought it perfectly safe.'

'It is perfectly safe,' said the courier contemptuously. 'I have been over it twenty times. There may have been some old jailbird called a King in the time of our grandmothers; but he belongs to history if not to fable. Brigandage is utterly stamped out.'

'It can never be utterly stamped out,' Muscari answered; 'because armed revolt is a recreation natural to southerners. Our peasants are like their mountains, rich in grace and green gaiety, but with the fires beneath. There is a point of human despair where the northern poor take to drink – and our own poor take to daggers.'*

THERE'S NO PRAYER needed today, Lord. The moral of the story is clear. The point is plain enough!

* *The Paradise of Thieves.*

18 OCTOBER

When I am afraid, I put my trust in you (Psalm 56:3 *NIV*)

'A poet is privileged,' replied Ezza, with a sneer. 'If Signor Muscari were English he would still be looking for highwaymen in Wandsworth. Believe me, there is no more danger of being captured in Italy than of being scalped in Boston.'

'Then you propose to attempt it?' asked Mr Harrogate, frowning.

'Oh, it sounds rather dreadful,' cried the girl, turning her glorious eyes on Muscari. Do you really think the pass is dangerous?'

Muscari threw back his black mane. 'I know it is dangerous:' he said. 'I am crossing it tomorrow.'*

GRANT ME COURAGE and resolve, Lord God, for situations I have to face that frighten me; for encounters with people by whom I feel threatened. In any sphere of life that is dangerous, Lord – practically or emotionally – then I am not ashamed to confess that I stand in need of help. Come with me, my God, when duty calls.

* *The Paradise of Thieves.*

19 OCTOBER

When he, the Spirit of truth, comes, he will guide you into all the truth. He will not speak on his own; he will speak only what he hears, and he will tell you what is yet to come (John 16:13 *NIV*)

Flambeau was peering into the house with a visage as white as a sheet. The occupant of the room was standing with his back to him, but in front of a looking-glass, and had already fitted round his face a sort of framework of rank red hair, hanging disordered from the head and clinging round the jaws and chin while leaving the mocking mouth uncovered. Seen thus in the glass the white face looked like the face of Judas laughing horribly and surrounded by capering flames of hell. For a spasm Flambeau saw the fierce, red-brown eyes dancing, then they were covered with a pair of blue spectacles. Slipping on a loose black coat, the figure vanished towards the front of the house. A few moments later a roar of popular applause from the street beyond announced that Dr Hirsch had once more appeared upon the balcony.*

THINGS (AND PEOPLE) aren't always what they seem, Lord. Our eyes and our senses can play tricks. We imagine all kinds of things, believing them to be quite real, only to later realise we are mistaken. How easily our minds deceive us! We could swear an oath that we had seen something, when in actual fact we might not have done. It's not that we are lying or deliberately dealing in untruths, it's just that imagination is a powerful force. Help us, then, Holy Spirit, to be very sure of what is true and reliable in terms of our spiritual convictions. Speak clearly to us about such things, for we need to get those right above all else.

* *The Duel of Dr Hirsch.*

20 OCTOBER

I would rather be a doorkeeper in the house of my God than dwell in the tents of wickedness (Psalm 84:10 *ESV*)

The door was opened to them by an aged servant or 'dresser', whose broken-down face and figure and black shabby coat and trousers contrasted queerly with the glittering interior of the great actress's dressing-room. It was fitted and filled with looking-glasses at every angle of refraction, so that they looked like the hundred facets of one huge diamond – if one could get inside a diamond. The other features of luxury, a few flowers, a few coloured cushions, a few scraps of stage costume, were multiplied by all the mirrors into the madness of the Arabian Nights, and danced and changed places perpetually as the shuffling attendant shifted a mirror outwards or shot one back against the wall. [Captain Cutler and Sir Wilson Seymour] both spoke to the dingy dresser by name, calling him Parkinson, and asking for the lady as Miss Aurora Rome.

Parkinson said she was in the other room, but he would go and tell her. A shade crossed the brow of both visitors; for the other room was the private room of the great actor with whom Miss Aurora was performing, and she was of the kind that does not inflame admiration without inflaming jealousy. In about half a minute, however, the inner door opened, and she entered as she always did, even in private life, so that the very silence seemed to be a roar of applause, and one well-deserved. She was clad in a somewhat strange garb of peacock green and peacock blue satins, that gleamed like blue and green metals, such as delight children and aesthetes, and her heavy, hot brown hair framed one of those magic faces which are dangerous to all men, but especially to boys and to men growing grey.*

* *The Man in the Passage.*

IT'S INTERESTING TO note, Lord, that in this narrative, the dresser is addressed only by his surname. He does not appear to qualify for any other title or token of respect or status. The attention in this story is placed firmly upon Miss Aurora Rome! No matter; the psalmist has his priorities right! So much better to be a doorkeeper (dresser) in your house, Lord, than to attempt to take centre stage. One of the lowliest roles in your Kingdom is a position of prestige and honour, such a privilege it would be! With that in mind, may the main protagonist in the account of my life be you, Lord God.

21 OCTOBER

The word of God is alive and active. Sharper than any double-edged sword, it penetrates even to dividing soul and spirit, joints and marrow; it judges the thoughts and attitudes of the heart (Hebrews 4:12 *NIV*)

[Miss Aurora Rome] greeted both men with the beaming and baffling smile which kept so many males at the same just dangerous distance from her. She accepted some flowers from Cutler, which were as tropical and expensive as his victories; and another sort of present from Sir Wilson Seymour, offered later on and more nonchalantly by that gentleman. For it was against his breeding to show eagerness, and against his conventional unconventionality to give anything so obvious as flowers.

He had picked up a trifle, he said, which was rather a curiosity, it was an ancient Greek dagger of the Mycenaean Epoch, and might well have been worn in the time of Theseus and Hippolyta. It was made of brass like all the Heroic weapons, but, oddly enough, sharp enough to prick anyone still. He had really been attracted to it by the leaf-like shape; it was as perfect as a Greek vase. If it was of any interest to Miss Rome or could come in anywhere in the play, he hoped she would —*

AN UNUSUAL GIFT, Lord! Of significance and worth, no doubt. How much better, though, for someone to receive the gift of a Bible, or a New Testament, especially perhaps in a country where the Bible is forbidden and outlawed. With that in mind, I pray today for societies and groups who endeavour to reach people all across the world with copies of the Scriptures; Bible distributors and all who seek to place such gifts in the hands of those who might never otherwise even see them. Bless them! Is there anything I can to do assist such distribution?

* *The Man in the Passage.*

22 OCTOBER

The heart is deceitful above all things, and desperately sick; who can understand it? (Jeremiah 17:9 *ESV*)

'I reckon you'll be shocked,' replied Greywood Usher, 'as I know you don't cotton to the march of science in these matters. I am given a good deal of discretion here, and perhaps take a little more than I'm given; and I thought it was an excellent opportunity to test that Psychometric Machine I told you about. Now, in my opinion, that machine can't lie.'

'No machine can lie,' said Father Brown; 'nor can it tell the truth' . . .

'You always forget . . . that the reliable machine always has to be worked by an unreliable machine.'

'Why, what do you mean?' asked the detective.

'I mean Man,' said Father Brown, 'the most unreliable machine I know of. I don't want to be rude; and I don't think you will consider Man to be an offensive or inaccurate description of yourself.'*

A TRUTH THAT is somewhat unpalatable, Lord, yet one that helps me if I am willing to take it on board and turn to you for heart surgery. Help me to want what you want, I pray. Turn my heart increasingly to your will. This needs to be your work, I think, with my cooperation.

* *The Mistake of the Machine.*

23 OCTOBER

After many days had gone by, there was a conspiracy among the Jews to kill him, but Saul learned of their plan. Day and night they kept close watch on the city gates in order to kill him. But his followers took him by night and lowered him in a basket through an opening in the wall (Acts 9:23-25 *NIV*)

Usher read the headlines, 'Last-Trick's Strayed Revellers: Mirthful Incident near Pilgrim's Pond.' The paragraph went on: 'A laughable occurrence took place outside Wilkinson's Motor Garage last night. A policeman on duty had his attention drawn by larrikins to a man in prison dress who was stepping with considerable coolness into the steering-seat of a pretty high-toned Panhard; he was accompanied by a girl wrapped in a ragged shawl. On the police interfering, the young woman threw back the shawl, and all recognized Millionaire Todd's daughter, who had just come from the Slum Freak Dinner at the Pond, where all the choicest guests were in a similar deshabille. She and the gentleman who had donned prison uniform were going for the customary joy-ride' . . .

Mr Usher found a strip of a later paper, headed, 'Astounding Escape of Millionaire's Daughter with Convict. She had Arranged Freak Dinner. Now Safe in –'

Mr Greenwood Usher lifted his eyes, but Father Brown was gone.*

A GREAT ESCAPE! Ingenious in its way. Quite an object lesson, Lord – as is today's Bible reading – in deploying one's own resources and wit. That's not to dispense with prayer, not at all, but simply a reminder to use the brain you have given me in order to figure out my options – not to wait on you for specific guidance on every single matter under the sun, I mean. Help me if I'm drifting off course with an idea, Lord, but for quite a

* *The Mistake of the Machine.*

few things I think it's right to think things through and come to an informed decision without overmuch spiritual deliberation. Pray. Think. Act. Will that do, Lord, on the basis that I'm commending all things to you anyway?

24 OCTOBER

So, if you think you are standing firm, be careful that you don't fall! (1 Corinthians 10:12 *NIV*)

'One summer afternoon [said Christabel Carstairs], when I had promised to go shrimping along the sands with Philip, I was waiting rather impatiently in the front drawing-room, watching Arthur handle some packets of coins he had just purchased and slowly shunt them, one or two at a time, into his own dark study and museum which was at the back of the house. As soon as I heard the heavy door close on him finally, I made a bolt for my shrimping-net and tam-o'-shanter and was just going to slip out, when I saw that my brother had left behind him one coin that lay gleaming on the long bench by the window. It was a bronze coin, and the colour, combined with the exact curve of the Roman nose and something in the very lift of the long, wiry neck, made the head of Caesar on it the almost precise portrait of Philip Hawker. Then I suddenly remembered Giles telling Philip of a coin that was like him, and Philip wishing he had it. Perhaps you can fancy the wild, foolish thoughts with which my head went round; I felt as if I had had a gift from the fairies. It seemed to me that if I could only run away with this, and give it to Philip like a wild sort of wedding-ring, it would be a bond between us for ever; I felt a thousand such things at once.'*

THE POWERFUL, ALL-CONSUMING, headstrong rush of temptation's giddy hour! When I'm tempted to do wrong, keep me resolute, keep me strong. Above all, Lord, never let me fall into complacency, whereby I assume some kind of invulnerability.

* *The Head of Caesar.*

25 OCTOBER

They brought the coin, and he asked them, 'Whose image is this? And whose inscription?' 'Caesar's,' they replied. Then Jesus said to them, 'Give back to Caesar what is Caesar's and to God what is God's' (Mark 12:16, 17 *NIV*)

'Then there yawned under me, like the pit, the enormous, awful notion of what I was doing; above all, the unbearable thought, which was like touching hot iron, of what Arthur would think of it. A Carstairs a thief; and a thief of the Carstairs treasure! I believe my brother could see me burned like a witch for such a thing, But then, the very thought of such fanatical cruelty heightened my old hatred of his dingy old antiquarian fussiness and my longing for the youth and liberty that called to me from the sea.

Outside was strong sunlight with a wind; and a yellow head of some broom or gorse in the garden rapped against the glass of the window. I thought of that living and growing gold calling to me from all the heaths of the world – and then of that dead, dull gold and bronze and brass of my brother's growing dustier and dustier as life went by. Nature and the Carstairs Collection had come to grips at last.'*

HOW INTRIGUING IT is to note the all-too-familiar pattern of temptation being followed closely by whispered thoughts of self-justification; a kind of reasoning and logic whereby a sinful act is excused and made to sound as though it were the right thing to do. What a tactic that is, on Satan's part; to play with one's mind and to gradually seduce. Help me, I pray, to see right through that psychological strategy, and to live on the straightest terms possible, handling my business with probity and accountability.

* *The Head of Caesar.*

26 OCTOBER

Peter came to Jesus and asked, 'Lord, how many times shall I forgive my brother or sister who sins against me? Up to seven times?' Jesus answered, 'I tell you, not seven times, but seventy-seven times' (Matthew 18:21, 22 *NIV*)

'Nature is older than the Carstairs Collection. As I ran down the streets to the sea, the coin clenched tight in my fist, I felt all the Roman Empire on my back as well as the Carstairs pedigree. It was not only the old lion argent that was roaring in my ear, but all the eagles of the Caesars seemed flapping and screaming in pursuit of me. And yet my heart rose higher and higher like a child's kite, until I came over the loose, dry sand-hills and to the flat, wet sands, where Philip stood already up to his ankles in the shallow shining water, some hundred yards out to sea. There was a great red sunset; and the long stretch of low water, hardly rising over the ankle for half a mile, was like a lake of ruby flame. It was not till I had torn off my shoes and stockings and waded to where he stood, which was well away from the dry land, that I turned and looked round. We were quite alone in a circle of sea-water and wet sand, and I gave him the head of Caesar.'*

THE DEED IS done! The crime is committed! Temptation has won the day! Oh how wonderful, though, Lord Jesus, that, however many times we fall and give in, you are always prepared to accept a sincere apology, and to pardon. You keep no record of wrongs. You delight in mercy. The reality is, we will mess up and yield to the tempter's power time and again over the years. Our fallen nature rears its ugly head. The greater reality, though, is that your grace has no measure, whether we are up to our ankles in sin or up to our eyes in it. Hallelujah! What a Saviour!

* *The Head of Caesar.*

27 OCTOBER

Be on your guard against all covetousness (Luke 12:15 *ESV*)

[Father Brown asked] 'What is there wrong about a miser that is not often as wrong about a collector? What is wrong, except . . . thou shalt not make to thyself any graven image; thou shalt not bow down to them nor serve them, for I . . . but we must go and see how the poor young people are getting on.'

'I think,' said Flambeau, 'that in spite of everything, they are probably getting on very well.'*

AN INTERESTING COMPARISON, Lord! A miser is generally thought to be selfish and something of a hoarder, whereas a collector (of coins, for example) is, equally generally, applauded and respected for their careful protection of valuable artefacts. Father Brown's question throws that open to debate! Are there things in my life, Lord, that perhaps I justify accumulating, without considering the possibility of miserliness? If there is, I'd like to know! Meanwhile, as I wait for you to show me, I'll continue with my everyday business, just like Father Brown and his young people!

* *The Head of Caesar.*

28 OCTOBER

When Jehu came to Jezreel, Jezebel heard of it. And she painted her eyes and adorned her head and looked out of the window (2 Kings 9:30 *ESV*)

'Very good wine,' said Father Brown, gravely lifting his glass, 'but, as you see, a very bad wine-bibber. I most sincerely beg your pardon': for he had spilt a small spot of wine on the table-cloth.

He drank and put down the glass with a composed face; but his hand had started at the exact moment when he became conscious of a face looking in through the garden window just behind the Admiral – the face of a woman, swarthy, with southern hair and eyes, and young, but like a mask of tragedy.*

THAT WOULD BE enough to make anyone spill a drop of their drink, Lord, a face suddenly looking in through the window, yet in Jezebel's case, her appearance at a window was part of a premeditated plan, to catch Jehu's attention. Who might be watching me today, Lord, whether or not I am aware of it? Who might be studying my movements and conduct? And, by the same token, who might be trying to catch my eye for some nefarious reason? In all these ways, Lord, whether I am being watched or whether someone is intent on side-tracking me, help me to remain alert, and to respond only as you would have me do. May those peering into my life, so to speak, see only Christ, and may those plotting any mischief sense your hand of deterrent.

* *The Perishing of the Pendragons.*

29 OCTOBER

Remove the dross from the silver (Proverbs 25:4 *NIV*)

'The mist's rising from the river,' said the staring Flambeau.

Almost as he spoke the huge figure of the hairy gardener appeared on a higher ridge of the trenched and terraced lawn, hailing them with a brandished rake and a horribly bellowing voice. 'Put down that hose,' he shouted; 'put down that hose and go to your – '

'I am fearfully clumsy,' replied the reverend gentleman weakly; 'do you know, I upset some wine at dinner.' He made a wavering half-turn of apology towards the gardener, with the hose still spouting in his hand. The gardener caught the cold crash of the water full in his face like the crash of a cannon-ball; staggered, slipped and went sprawling with his boots in the air.

'How very dreadful!' said Father Brown, looking round in a sort of wonder. 'Why, I've hit a man!'*

AN ULTERIOR MOTIVE, Lord – that's a fascinating moral principle! Father Brown had every intention of soaking the gardener with water, but only because he probably suspected him of foul play and ill intent. Motives matter to you, Heavenly Father, maybe more than actions; the reasons behind my deeds. For example, if I give a sandwich to a beggar in hopes of some kind of reward, either in this world or the next, then my motivation is askew, even though the sandwich is appreciated; my action is altruistic and possibly, therefore, means very little in your sight, despite a hungry individual having been fed. Keep an eye on my motives, please, Holy Spirit, and always let me know if my silver is mixed with dross.

* *The Perishing of the Pendragons.*

30 OCTOBER

The message of the cross is foolishness to those who are perishing, but to us who are being saved it is the power of God (1 Corinthians 1:18 *NIV*)

'Put a feather with a fossil and a bit of coral and everyone will think it's a specimen [observed Father Brown]. Put the same feather with a ribbon and an artificial flower and everyone will think it's for a lady's hat. Put the same feather with an ink-bottle, a book and a stack of writing-paper, and most men will swear they've seen a quill pen.'*

SO MUCH DEPENDS upon perspective, Lord, and what we want to see. One person, an atheist, for example, can look at the cross, and see only folly, whereas a believer will see the beautiful emblem of redemption for the whole world; yet, it is exactly the same object set before both of them. As I thank you for showing me salvation, I pray once again for those whose perspective means they haven't yet seen the Saviour. May they come to do so, by your grace.

* *The Perishing of the Pendragons.*

31 OCTOBER

Christ loved us and gave himself up for us, a fragrant offering and sacrifice to God (Ephesians 5:2 ESV)

In a moment [Father Brown] began to laugh a little. 'This wood must be rotten,' said Flambeau. 'Though it seems odd it should bear me, and you go through the weak place. Let me help you out.'

But the little priest was looking rather curiously at the corners and edges of the wood alleged to be rotten, and there was a sort of trouble on his brow. 'Come along,' cried Flambeau impatiently, still with his big brown hand extended. 'Don't you want to get out?'

The priest was holding a splinter of the broken wood between his finger and thumb, and did not immediately reply. At last he said thoughtfully: 'Want to get out? Why, no. I rather think I want to get in.' And he dived into the darkness under the wooden floor so abruptly as to knock off his big curved clerical hat and leave it lying on the boards above, without any clerical head in it.

Flambeau looked once more inland and out to sea, and once more could see nothing but seas as wintry as the snow, and snows as level as the sea. There came a scurrying noise behind him, and the little priest came scrambling out of the hole faster than he had fallen in. His face was no longer disconcerted, but rather resolute, and, perhaps only through the reflections of the snow, a trifle paler than usual.

'Well?' asked his tall friend. 'Have you found the god of the temple?' 'No,' answered Father Brown. 'I have found what was sometimes more important. The Sacrifice.'

'What the devil do you mean?' cried Flambeau, quite alarmed.*

THAT'S SOMETHING OF a frightening scenario, Lord; a dark place, the location of sacrifice. But then, you would know all about that, my Saviour. You were willing to be frightened (terrified) for my sake, as you approached the terror of the cross in order to actually become the ultimate sacrifice. Such love. This is my God.

* *The God of the Gongs.*

1 NOVEMBER

Let us then with confidence draw near to the throne of grace (Hebrews 4:16 *ESV*)

Both Flambeau and Father Brown have often confessed that, in all their (often outrageous) adventures, nothing had so chilled their blood as that voice of an ogre, sounding suddenly out of a silent and empty inn.

'My cook!' cried the proprietor hastily. 'I had forgotten my cook. He will be starting presently. Sherry, sir?'

And, sure enough, there appeared in the doorway a big white bulk with white cap and white apron, as befits a cook . . .

[Father Brown] increased his surprise that the hotel proprietor should answer the call of the cook, and not the cook the call of the proprietor. But he reflected that head cooks are proverbially arrogant; and, besides, the host had come back with the sherry, and that was the great thing.*

A MISUNDERSTANDING OF prayer, Father God, common amongst believers and sceptics alike, is that you are at our beck and call, as though you were some kind of heavenly vending machine only there to bail us out or supply the goods. Forgive that mistake, Lord, because it is quite a sad distortion of the true and much warmer nature of relational dialogue whereby a Father and his children spend time in rewarding communion. Take me deeper into the mystic union of prayer.

* *The God of the Gongs.*

2 NOVEMBER

Search me, O God, and know my heart: try me, and know my thoughts: And see if there be any wicked way in me, and lead me in the way everlasting (Psalm 139:23, 23 *KJV*)

The man with the motionless face . . . was a quiet, well-featured fellow, rather sallow; his dark clothes had nothing distinctive about them, except that his black necktie was worn rather high, like a stock, and secured by a gold pin with some grotesque head to it. Nor was there anything notable in the face, except something that was probably a mere nervous trick – a habit of opening one eye more narrowly than the other, giving the impression that the other was larger, or was, perhaps, artificial.*

QUITE POSSIBLY, LORD, a body language expert would read all sorts of things into such a distinctive facial expression, and arrive at certain conclusions. Psychological profiling is a big deal in modern detective work, and looms large in the corporate world too. That's fine, as far as it goes, but my personal priority, Lord, is to be known by you, the ultimate expert. Examine me this day, I pray.

* *The God of the Gongs.*

3 NOVEMBER

When the archangel Michael, contending with the devil, was disputing about the body of Moses, he did not presume to pronounce a blasphemous judgment, but said, 'The Lord rebuke you' (Jude 1:9 *ESV*)

'I am never surprised,' said Father Brown, 'at any work of hell.'*

ALMIGHTY GOD, THERE is, I assume, an inevitability about the fact that the spiritual forces of evil will seek to disarm and attack your people (perhaps especially new converts). This can be a brutal conflict – hence, maybe, Father Brown's lack of surprise at the hellish tactics deployed. I simply commend myself, in the context of today's Bible verse, and all who are under particular attack at this time, to your care and protection. Fight on our behalf, I pray.

* *The God of the Gongs.*

4 NOVEMBER

Elijah was afraid and ran for his life (1 Kings 19:3 *NIV*)

The motionless man continued to gaze at the sea, and the eyes in his head might have belonged to two different men. Then he made a movement of blinding swiftness.

Father Brown had his back to him, and in that flash might have fallen dead on his face. Flambeau had no weapon, but his large brown hands were resting on the end of the long iron seat. His shoulders abruptly altered their shape, and he heaved the whole huge thing high over his head, like a headsman's axe about to fall. The mere height of the thing, as he held it vertical, looked like a long iron ladder by which he was inviting men to climb towards the stars. But the long shadow, in the level evening light, looked like a giant brandishing the Eiffel Tower.

It was the shock of that shadow, before the shock of the iron crash, that made the stranger quail and dodge, and then dart into his inn, leaving the flat and shining dagger he had dropped exactly where it had fallen.

'We must get away from here instantly,' cried Flambeau, flinging the huge seat away with furious indifference on the beach. He caught the little priest by the elbow and ran him down a grey perspective of barren back garden.'*

GIVE ME THE wisdom to know when to run away and when to stand my ground, Lord. There is little virtue in staying put if it means I might be attacked, so if making a dash for it means I escape with only bruised pride, so be it. Teach me when to leave, and when to remain (in all kinds of ways).

* *The God of the Gongs.*

5 NOVEMBER

You perceive my thoughts from afar (Psalm 139:2 *NIV*)

'Well!' cried Cray, with wild eyes. 'I suppose you think I'm mad, like the rest?'

'I have considered the thesis,' answered the little man, composedly. 'And I incline to think you are not.'

'What do you mean?' snapped Cray quite savagely.

'Real madmen,' explained Father Brown, 'always encourage their own morbidity. They never strive against it . . . You are struggling against it. You want what no madman ever wants.'

'And what is that?'

'You want to be proved wrong,' said Brown.*

AN INTERESTING HYPOTHESIS, Heavenly Father. It causes me to ponder the fact that you, as my Creator, know all about my psyche, in more detail than anyone else could ever hope to. You know my moods, my ups and downs, my weaknesses and vulnerabilities, my strengths and powers. You know me better than I know myself. God of my inmost ways, I come to you.

* *The Salad of Colonel Cray.*

6 NOVEMBER

Salvation is found in no one else, for there is no other name under heaven given to mankind by which we must be saved (Acts 4:12 *NIV*)

'Well [explained Colonel Cray], these are the facts. The last day we were in an Indian city I asked Putnam if I could get some Trichinopoli cigars, he directed me to a little place opposite his lodgings. I have since found he was quite right; but 'opposite' is a dangerous word when one decent house stands opposite five or six squalid ones; and I must have mistaken the door. It opened with difficulty, and then only on darkness; but as I turned back, the door behind me sank back and settled into its place with a noise as of innumerable bolts. There was nothing to do but to walk forward; which I did through passage after passage, pitch-dark. Then I came to a flight of steps, and then to a blind door, secured by a latch of elaborate Eastern ironwork, which I could only trace by touch, but which I loosened at last. I came out again upon gloom, which was half turned into a greenish twilight by a multitude of small but steady lamps below. They showed merely the feet or fringes of some huge and empty architecture. Just in front of me was something that looked like a mountain. I confess I nearly fell on the great stone platform on which I had emerged, to realize that it was an idol. And worst of all, an idol with its back to me.'*

FABULOUS FICTION, LORD, but it does serve to highlight the importance of correct and precise instructions. A vague direction is almost as useless as no direction at all, and can even lead to problems. So be it in any walk of life; a musician in an orchestra looking to be conducted, for example, or an aeroplane pilot asking for permission to land. And how much more so in spiritual terms, Lord; truths that are not fudged or blurred, but are spelt out clearly, without much chance of misunderstanding (such as the

* *The Salad of Colonel Cray.*

one above). In my life, Lord, may I deliver and portray a clear, unambiguous route to heaven if and when my neighbour needs to know.

7 NOVEMBER

The name of the LORD is a fortified tower; the righteous run to it and are safe (Proverbs 18:10 *NIV*)

'It was hardly half human, I guessed; to judge by the small squat head, and still more by a thing like a tail or extra limb turned up behind and pointing, like a loathsome large finger, at some symbol graven in the centre of the vast stone back. I had begun, in the dim light, to guess at the hieroglyphic, not without horror, when a more horrible thing happened. A door opened silently in the temple wall behind me and a man came out, with a brown face and a black coat. He had a carved smile on his face, of copper flesh and ivory teeth; but I think the most hateful thing about him was that he was in European dress. I was prepared, I think, for shrouded priests or naked fakirs. But this seemed to say that the devilry was over all the earth. As indeed I found it to be.

"If you had only seen the Monkey's Feet," he said, smiling steadily, and without other preface, "we should have been very gentle – you would only be tortured and die. If you had seen the Monkey's Face, still we should be very moderate, very tolerant – you would only be tortured and live. But as you have seen the Monkey's Tail, we must pronounce the worst sentence, which is – Go Free."

'When he said the words I heard the elaborate iron latch with which I had struggled, automatically unlock itself: and then, far down the dark passages I had passed, I heard the heavy street-door shifting its own bolts backwards.

"It is vain to ask for mercy; you must go free," said the smiling man. "Henceforth a hair shall slay you like a sword, and a breath shall bite you like an adder; weapons shall come against you out of nowhere; and you shall die many times." And with that he was swallowed once more in the wall behind; and I went out into the street.' Cray paused; and Father Brown unaffectedly sat down on the lawn and began to pick daisies.*

* *The Salad of Colonel Cray.*

AN INTERESTING – AND challenging – contrast here, Lord. On the one hand, Colonel Cray frightened out of his wits by some kind of bizarre pseudo-spiritual experience, and on the other, an entirely unaffected Father Brown picking daisies. May my confidence in your great love and protection be such that I imitate the latter.

8 NOVEMBER

For the LORD comforts his people and will have compassion on his afflicted ones (Isaiah 49:13 *NIV*)

Then the soldier continued: 'Putnam, of course, with his jolly common sense, pooh-poohed all my fears; and from that time dates his doubt of my mental balance.'*

I HAVE NO right to behave as Putnam did, Lord. As I cannot possibly hope to know every detail of context and back-story regarding the way in which those around me behave, help me to err on the side of compassion and kindness.

* *The Salad of Colonel Cray.*

9 NOVEMBER

I am not ashamed of the gospel (Romans 1:16 *NIV*)

Father Brown threw away a daisy-chain he was making, and rose with a wistful look. 'Has Major Putnam,' he asked, 'got any Eastern curios, idols, weapons and so on, from which one might get a hint?' 'Plenty of those, though not much use, I fear,' replied Cray; 'but by all means come into his study.'

As they entered they passed Miss Watson buttoning her gloves for church, and heard the voice of Putnam downstairs still giving a lecture on cookery to the cook. In the Major's study and den of curios they came suddenly on a third party, silk-hatted and dressed for the street, who was poring over an open book on the smoking-table – a book which he dropped rather guiltily, and turned.

Cray introduced him civilly enough, as Dr Oman, but he showed such disfavour in his very face that Brown guessed the two men, whether Audrey knew it or not, were rivals. Nor was the priest wholly unsympathetic with the prejudice. Dr Oman was a very well-dressed gentleman indeed; well-featured, though almost dark enough for an Asiatic. But Father Brown had to tell himself sharply that one should be in charity even with those who wax their pointed beards, who have small gloved hands, and who speak with perfectly modulated voices.

Cray seemed to find something specially irritating in the small prayer-book in Oman's dark-gloved hand. 'I didn't know that was in your line,' he said rather rudely.

Oman laughed mildly, but without offence. 'This is more so, I know,' he said, laying his hand on the big book he had dropped, 'a dictionary of drugs and such things. But it's rather too large to take to church.' Then he closed the larger book, and there seemed again the faintest touch of hurry and embarrassment.*

* *The Salad of Colonel Cray.*

LORD JESUS, AS you have (rather astonishingly) never been ashamed of me, let me never be ashamed of you, or of my Bible, or of my creed. May I approach a curious world without embarrassment, in terms of my Christian witness.

10 NOVEMBER

Where two or three gather in my name, there am I with them (Matthew 18:20 *NIV*)

'I suppose,' said the priest, who seemed anxious to change the subject, 'all these spears and things are from India?'

'From everywhere,' answered the doctor. 'Putnam is an old soldier, and has been in Mexico and Australia, and the Cannibal Islands for all I know.' 'I hope it was not in the Cannibal Islands,' said Brown, 'that he learnt the art of cookery.' And he ran his eyes over the stew-pots or other strange utensils on the wall.

At this moment the jolly subject of their conversation thrust his laughing, lobsterish face into the room. 'Come along, Cray,' he cried. 'Your lunch is just coming in. And the bells are ringing for those who want to go to church.'

Cray slipped upstairs to change; Dr Oman and Miss Watson betook themselves solemnly down the street, with a string of other churchgoers.*

A LOVELY IMAGE, Lord; your people wending their way to worship. Meet with us as we do so, God of grace. Bless our times together in church.

* *The Salad of Colonel Cray.*

11 NOVEMBER

We all . . . are being transformed into his image with ever-increasing glory, which comes from the Lord (2 Corinthians 3:18 *NIV*)

'Anybody can be wicked – as wicked as he chooses. We can direct our moral wills; but we can't generally change our instinctive tastes and ways of doing things.'*

MAYBE FATHER BROWN has a point here, Lord? I don't know. What I do know, though, is that I believe in a God of transformation who can change the hearts of men, women and children. I believe in a God who can make love grow where once wickedness was planted. I believe in the potential of Christlikeness for any and all who wish to embrace it. This is my God.

* *The Strange Crime of John Boulnois.*

12 NOVEMBER

Do not nurse hatred in your heart (Leviticus 19:17 *NLT*)

'There were finger-prints on that sword; finger-prints can be detected quite a time after they are made if they're on some polished surface like glass or steel. These were on a polished surface. They were half-way down the blade of the sword. Whose prints they were I have no earthly clue; but why should anybody hold a sword half-way down? It was a long sword, but length is an advantage in lunging at an enemy. At least, at most enemies. At all enemies except one.'

'Except one,' she repeated. 'There is only one enemy,' said Father Brown, 'whom it is easier to kill with a dagger than a sword.' 'I know,' said the woman. 'Oneself.'

There was a long silence, and then the priest said quietly but abruptly: 'Am I right, then? Did Sir Claude kill himself?' 'Yes' she said, with a face like marble. 'I saw him do it.' 'He died,' said Father Brown, 'for love of you?' An extraordinary expression flashed across her face, very different from pity, modesty, remorse, or anything her companion had expected: her voice became suddenly strong and full. 'I don't believe,' she said, 'he ever cared about me a rap. He hated my husband.' 'Why?' asked the other, and turned his round face from the sky to the lady.

'He hated my husband because . . . it is so strange I hardly know how to say it . . . because . . .' 'Yes?' said Brown patiently. 'Because my husband wouldn't hate him.'

Father Brown only nodded, and seemed still to be listening; he differed from most detectives in fact and fiction in a small point – he never pretended not to understand when he understood perfectly well.*

THE DEATHLY POWER of hatred, Lord. May it find no resting place in my heart. Assist me to evict it as soon as it arrives, I pray, and not even to entertain it for a while.

* *The Strange Crime of John Boulnois.*

13 NOVEMBER

Haman boasted to them about his vast wealth, his many sons, and all the ways the king had honoured him and how he had elevated him above the other nobles and officials (Esther 5:11 *NIV*)

Mrs Boulnois drew near once more with the same contained glow of certainty. 'My husband,' she said, 'is a great man. Sir Claude Champion was not a great man: he was a celebrated and successful man. My husband has never been celebrated or successful; and it is the solemn truth that he has never dreamed of being so. He no more expects to be famous for thinking than for smoking cigars. On all that side he has a sort of splendid stupidity. He has never grown up. He still liked Champion exactly as he liked him at school; he admired him as he would admire a conjuring trick done at the dinner-table. But he couldn't be got to conceive the notion of envying Champion. And Champion wanted to be envied. He went mad and killed himself for that.'

'Yes,' said Father Brown; 'I think I begin to understand.' 'Oh, don't you see?' she cried; 'the whole picture is made for that – the place is planned for it. Champion put John in a little house at his very door, like a dependant – to make him feel a failure. He never felt it. He thinks no more about such things than – than an absent-minded lion. Champion would burst in on John's shabbiest hours or homeliest meals with some dazzling present or announcement or expedition that made it like the visit of Haroun Alraschid, and John would accept or refuse amiably with one eye off, so to speak, like one lazy schoolboy agreeing or disagreeing with another. After five years of it John had not turned a hair; and Sir Claude Champion was a monomaniac.'

'And Haman began to tell them,' said Father Brown, 'of all the things wherein the king had honoured him; and he said: 'All these things profit me nothing while I see Mordecai the Jew sitting in the gate.''*

* *The Strange Crime of John Boulnois.*

A STRANGE AMBITION, Lord – to want to be envied. I suppose that one is fundamentally about wanting the credit for oneself. In that respect, perhaps it's an ambition that is more common than we sometimes care to admit. Move me to a place, Lord, where I don't actually care who gets the credit, as long as you get the glory.

14 NOVEMBER

A heart at peace gives life to the body, but envy rots the bones (Proverbs 14:30 *NIV*)

'The crisis came,' Mrs Boulnois continued, 'when I persuaded John to let me take down some of his speculations and send them to a magazine. They began to attract attention, especially in America, and one paper wanted to interview him. When Champion (who was interviewed nearly every day) heard of this late little crumb of success falling to his unconscious rival, the last link snapped that held back his devilish hatred. Then he began to lay that insane siege to my own love and honour which has been the talk of the shire. You will ask me why I allowed such atrocious attentions. I answer that I could not have declined them except by explaining to my husband, and there are some things the soul cannot do, as the body cannot fly. Nobody could have explained to my husband. Nobody could do it now. If you said to him in so many words, 'Champion is stealing your wife,' he would think the joke a little vulgar: that it could be anything but a joke – that notion could find no crack in his great skull to get in by. Well, John was to come and see us act this evening, but just as we were starting he said he wouldn't; he had got an interesting book and a cigar. I told this to Sir Claude, and it was his death-blow. The monomaniac suddenly saw despair. He stabbed himself, crying out like a devil that Boulnois was slaying him.'*

DEEP IN THE human heart, feelings lie buried that grace can restore. What anguish, Lord. What an absurd and tragic conclusion to a very confused state of affairs. Lord, you know all our weaknesses, you know all our care; hear, and answer prayer.

* *The Strange Crime of John Boulnois.*

15 NOVEMBER

Do not put the LORD your God to the test (Deuteronomy 6:16 NIV)

'Who murdered him?' he roared. 'Your God murdered him! His own God murdered him! According to you, he murders all his faithful and foolish servants – as he murdered that one,' and he made a violent gesture, not towards the coffin but the crucifix.

Seeming to control himself a little, he went on in a tone still angry but more argumentative: 'I don't believe it, but you do. Isn't it better to have no God than one that robs you in this fashion? I, at least, am not afraid to say that there is none. There is no power in all this blind and brainless universe that can hear your prayer or return your friend. Though you beg Heaven to raise him, he will not rise. Though I dare Heaven to raise him, he will not rise. Here and now I will put it to the test – I defy the God who is not there to waken the man who sleeps for ever.'*

FEELINGS RUN HIGH, Lord, especially in times of loss and bereavement. We say things we probably don't mean, even though we feel we mean them at the time. Forgive our outbursts, Heavenly Father. You are a God of great mercy and understanding.

* *The Resurrection of Father Brown.*

16 NOVEMBER

Fear not, for you will not be put to shame; And do not feel humiliated, for you will not be disgraced (Isaiah 54:4 *NASB*)

Even as the priest spoke his face altered. His blinking eyelids shut suddenly and he stood up as if he were choking. Then he put one wavering hand as if groping his way towards the door.

'Where are you going?' asked the other in some wonder.

'If you ask me,' said Father Brown, who was quite white, 'I was going to pray. Or rather, to praise.'

'I'm not sure I understand. What is the matter with you?'

'I was going to praise God for having so strangely and so incredibly saved me – saved me by an inch.'

'Of course,' said Race, 'I am not of your religion; but believe me, I have religion enough to understand that. Of course, you would thank God for saving you from death.'

'No,' said the priest. 'Not from death. From disgrace.'*

THE GOD WHO saves. My God. My Saviour.

* *The Resurrection of Father Brown.*

17 NOVEMBER

Love is kind (1 Corinthians 13:4 *NIV*)

Although the little priest appeared to melt into the millions of New York next day, without any apparent attempt to be anything but a number in a numbered street, he was, in fact, unobtrusively busy for the next fortnight with the commission that had been given him, for he was filled with profound fear about a possible miscarriage of justice.*

HEAVENLY FATHER, THIS scenario makes me realise just how many people I might pass today who, although they melt into the crowd without meriting so much as a second glance, will quite possibly be carrying all sorts of burdens that no one, looking at them, would ever suspect. As we jostle along on the crowded pavements, or drive bumper-to-bumper on busy roads, keep me sensitive to that.

* *The Arrow of Heaven.*

18 NOVEMBER

Who are these that fly like a cloud, and like doves to their windows? (Isaiah 60:8 *ESV*)

Father Brown had asked, in an idle and conversational fashion, whether much flying was done in that district, and had told how he had at first mistaken Mr Merton's circular wall for an aerodrome.

'It's a wonder you didn't see any while we were there,' answered Captain Wain. 'Sometimes they're as thick as flies; that open plain is a great place for them, and I shouldn't wonder if it were the chief breeding-ground, so to speak, for my sort of birds in the future. I've flown a good deal there myself, of course, and I know most of the fellows about here who flew in the war; but there are a whole lot of people taking to it out there now whom I never heard of in my life. I suppose it will be like motoring soon, and every man in the States will have one.'

'Being endowed by his Creator,' said Father Brown with a smile, 'with the right to life, liberty, and the pursuit of motoring – not to mention aviation. So I suppose we may take it that one strange aeroplane passing over that house, at certain times, wouldn't be noticed much.'

'No,' replied the young man; 'I don't suppose it would.'*

THE ONWARD MARCH of progress, Lord! The relentless advance of science and technology! I thank you for those whose inventions and innovations have made life so much easier, whereby much of the old-fashioned drudgery of housework, for example, is alleviated. I thank you for those whose skill and expertise has brought forth the development of cars and aeroplanes, for example. There are, of course, serious environmental issues at stake, so I include those within my prayer too. Guide us, Heavenly Father, in ways that help us to develop our full, God-given, inventive potential, but in a manner that represents good stewardship.

* *The Arrow of Heaven.*

19 NOVEMBER

He was manifested in the flesh (1 Timothy 3:16 *ESV*)

[Father Brown] stood up abruptly, his face heavy with a sort of frown, and went on talking almost as if he were alone. 'It's the first effect of not believing in God that you lose your common sense and can't see things as they are. Anything that anybody talks about, and says there's a good deal in it, extends itself indefinitely like a vista in a nightmare. And a dog is an omen, and a cat is a mystery, and a pig is a mascot, and a beetle is a scarab, calling up all the menagerie of polytheism from Egypt and old India; Dog Anubis and great green-eyed Pasht and all the holy howling Bulls of Bashan; reeling back to the bestial gods of the beginning, escaping into elephants and snakes and crocodiles; and all because you are frightened of four words:

'He was made Man'.'*

I PRAY FOR those who worship animals, and carved, moulded images of animals. I think of some of the world's great religions, with millions of devotees kneeling before statues of snakes and elephants and monkeys and so on; none of whom can do anything at all about saving their souls. True and living God, have great mercy and draw them to yourself. I pray for those who share the gospel in such contexts.

* *The Oracle of the Dog.*

20 NOVEMBER

The wolf shall dwell with the lamb, and the leopard shall lie down with the young goat, and the calf and the lion and the fattened calf together; and a little child shall lead them. The cow and the bear shall graze; their young shall lie down together; and the lion shall eat straw like the ox. The nursing child shall play over the hole of the cobra, and the weaned child shall put his hand on the adder's den. They shall not hurt or destroy in all my holy mountain; for the earth shall be full of the knowledge of the Lord as the waters cover the sea (Isaiah 11:6-9 *ESV*)

The young man got up with a little embarrassment, almost as if he had overheard a soliloquy. He called to the dog and left the room with vague but breezy farewells. But he had to call the dog twice, for the dog had remained behind quite motionless for a moment, looking up steadily at Father Brown as the wolf looked at St Francis.*

WHAT A DELIGHTFUL prospect, Heavenly Father: paradise regained. Thank you for such terrific grounds for optimism. The best is yet to come!

* *The Oracle of the Dog.*

21 NOVEMBER

The man reached out his hand and took it (2 Kings 6:7 *NIV*)

'Dogs hate nervous people [said Father Brown]. I don't know whether they make the dog nervous, too; or whether, being after all a brute, he is a bit of a bully; or whether his canine vanity (which is colossal) is simply offended at not being liked . . .

Now I know you're awfully clever, and nobody of sense sneers at cleverness. But I sometimes fancy, for instance, that you are too clever to understand animals. Sometimes you are too clever to understand men, especially when they act almost as simply as animals. Animals are very literal; they live in a world of truisms. Take this case: a dog barks at a man and a man runs away from a dog. Now you do not seem to be quite simple enough to see the fact: that the dog barked because he disliked the man and the man fled because he was frightened of the dog. They had no other motives and they needed none.'*

O LORD! IS it sometimes the case that I overthink things? If so, forgive me, and teach me once again that lovely skill of simply receiving from you without complicating matters by asking too many questions! In simple trust . . .

* *The Oracle of the Dog.*

22 NOVEMBER

Search was made in the archives (Ezra 6:1 *NASB*)

Fiennes smiled as he answered, 'I wish you knew the secretary, Father Brown. It would be a joy to you to watch him make things hum, as he calls it. He made the house of mourning hum. He filled the funeral with all the snap and zip of the brightest sporting event. There was no holding him, after something had really happened. I've told you how he used to oversee the gardener as he did the garden, and how he instructed the lawyer in the law. Needless to say, he also instructed the surgeon in the practice of surgery.'*

AH, LORD, WHERE would we be without church secretaries and administrators! The gift of administration – not one to which many aspire, but a vocation that is probably crucial if a church is to run well. Bless them all as they oil the wheels of mission.

* *The Oracle of the Dog.*

23 NOVEMBER

Houses and wealth are inherited from parents, but a prudent wife is from the LORD (Proverbs 19:14 *NIV*)

[Father Brown continued] '[As] I went down the lanes leading to the Colonel's old place I met his daughter walking with Dr Valentine. She was in mourning, of course, and he always wore black as if he were going to a funeral; but I can't say that their faces were very funereal. Never have I seen two people looking in their own way more respectably radiant and cheerful. They stopped and saluted me, and then she told me they were married and living in a little house on the outskirts of the town, where the doctor was continuing his practice. This rather surprised me, because I knew that her old father's will had left her his property; and I hinted at it delicately by saying I was going along to her father's old place and had half expected to meet her there. But she only laughed and said: 'Oh, we've given up all that. My husband doesn't like heiresses.'*

THAT CAN BE a difficult transition, Heavenly Father; the progression from home life with one's parents to a new life with one's spouse. Likewise, the transition when one's parents die. God of all our circumstances, walk with us, hold us, guide us.

* *The Oracle of the Dog.*

24 NOVEMBER

The eye is the lamp of the body. If your eyes are healthy, your whole body will be full of light. But if your eyes are unhealthy, your whole body will be full of darkness. If then the light within you is darkness, how great is that darkness! (Matthew 6:22, 23 *NIV*)

Fiennes paused a moment before he replied. 'Dr Valentine took it in a curious way. Dr Valentine is a curious man. His appearance is rather striking but very foreign. He is young but wears a beard cut square; and his face is very pale, dreadfully pale – and dreadfully serious. His eyes have a sort of ache in them, as if he ought to wear glasses, or had given himself a headache with thinking; but he is quite handsome and always very formally dressed, with a top hat and a dark coat and a little red rosette. His manner is rather cold and haughty, and he has a way of staring at you which is very disconcerting.'*

INTRIGUING BIBLE VERSES, Lord. Divine Optician, I pray that your presence in my life will be seen by others as something (someone) full of light. Dwell within, so that others may see Christ in me.

* *The Oracle of the Dog.*

25 NOVEMBER

Here is a trustworthy saying that deserves full acceptance: Christ Jesus came into the world to save sinners – of whom I am the worst (1 Timothy 1:15 *NIV*)

'I've put it badly [said Father Brown], but it's true. No man's really any good till he knows how bad he is, or might be; till he's realized exactly how much right he has to all this snobbery, and sneering, and talking about 'criminals,' as if they were apes in a forest ten thousand miles away; till he's got rid of all the dirty self-deception of talking about low types and deficient skulls; till he's squeezed out of his soul the last drop of the oil of the Pharisees.'*

FATHER BROWN IS right, Lord.

* *The Secret of Father Brown.*

26 NOVEMBER

The Spirit of God dwells in you (Romans 8:9 *ESV*)

'I'm afraid,' said the American, in tones that were still doubtful, and keeping his eye on the priest rather as if he were a wild animal, 'that you'd have to explain a lot to me before I knew what you were talking about. The science of detection –' Father Brown snapped his fingers with the same animated annoyance. 'That's it,' he cried; 'that's just where we part company. Science is a grand thing when you can get it; in its real sense one of the grandest words in the world. But what do these men mean, nine times out of ten, when they use it nowadays? When they say detection is a science? When they say criminology is a science? They mean getting outside a man and studying him as if he were a gigantic insect: in what they would call a dry impartial light, in what I should call a dead and dehumanized light. They mean getting a long way off him, as if he were a distant prehistoric monster; staring at the shape of his 'criminal skull' as if it were a sort of eerie growth, like the horn on a rhinoceros's nose. When the scientist talks about a type, he never means himself, but always his neighbour; probably his poorer neighbour. I don't deny the dry light may sometimes do good; though in one sense it's the very reverse of science. So far from being knowledge, it's actually suppression of what we know. It's treating a friend as a stranger, and pretending that something familiar is really remote and mysterious. It's like saying that a man has a proboscis between the eyes, or that he falls down in a fit of insensibility once every twenty-four hours. Well, what you call 'the secret' is exactly the opposite. I don't try to get outside the man. I try to get inside the murderer. . . . Indeed it's much more than that, don't you see? I am inside a man. I am always inside a man, moving his arms and legs; but I wait till I know I am inside a murderer, thinking his thoughts, wrestling with his passions; till I have bent myself into the posture of his hunched and peering hatred; till I see the world with his bloodshot and squinting eyes, looking between the blinkers of his half-witted concentration; looking up the short and sharp perspective of a straight road to a pool of blood. Till I am really a murderer.'*

* *The Secret of Father Brown.*

HOW WONDERFUL IT is, gracious Holy Spirit, that you elect to live within my heart. You do not distance yourself from one such as I. Holy God, you inhabit my life, and you reside with me daily. You do not remain outside, staring at me from a long way off, but you impart your very presence, as my beloved guest. Thank you for such grace.

27 NOVEMBER

I acknowledge my sin unto thee, and mine iniquity have I not hid. I said, I will confess my transgressions unto the Lord; and thou forgavest the iniquity of my sin (Psalm 32:5 *KJV*)

Father Brown groaned. He put his head on his hands and remained a moment, as if full of a silent convulsion of thought. Then he lifted his head and said in a dull voice:

'Very well. I must tell the secret.'*

HOW GRACIOUS YOU are towards us, loving God. When we confess our sins, when we make confessional prayers, you do not reject us. Even though we are sometimes reluctant to confide in you, for fear of what you might think, you listen, you understand, you receive our confession. You do not dish out judgment or condemnation, but cleansing and mercy, representing a fresh start.

* *The Secret of Father Brown.*

28 NOVEMBER

The Lord was with Joshua, and his fame was in all the land
(Joshua 6:27 *NASB*)

Mr Chace had heard of Father Brown, and his tone faintly changed, as towards a celebrity. The interviewing instinct awoke, tactful but tense. If he did try to draw Father Brown, as if he were a tooth, it was done with the most dexterous and painless American dentistry.

They were sitting in a sort of partly unroofed outer court of the house, such as often forms the entrance to Spanish houses. It was dusk turning to dark; and as all that mountain air sharpens suddenly after sunset, a small stove stood on the flagstones, glowing with red eyes like a goblin, and painting a red pattern on the pavement; but scarcely a ray of it reached the lower bricks of the great bare, brown brick wall that went soaring up above them into the deep blue night. Flambeau's big broad-shouldered figure and great moustaches, like sabres, could be traced dimly in the twilight, as he moved about, drawing dark wine from a great cask and handing it round. In his shadow, the priest looked very shrunken and small, as if huddled over the stove; but the American visitor leaned forward elegantly with his elbow on his knee and his fine pointed features in the full light; his eyes shone with inquisitive intelligence. 'I can assure you, sir,' he was saying, 'we consider your achievement in the matter of the Moonshine Murder the most remarkable triumph in the history of detective science.'

Father Brown murmured something; some might have imagined that the murmur was a little like a moan.*

FAME! CELEBRITY! LET me know, Lord, please, if ever this world's empty glory is costing me too dear. Make me quick to deflect the attention back to you.

* *The Secret of Father Brown.*

29 NOVEMBER

I, the prisoner of the Lord, implore you to walk in a manner worthy of the calling with which you have been called (Ephesians 4:1 *NASB*)

Sir Leopold, in his height of good humour, even told the priest that though he himself had broader views, he could respect those whose creed required them to be cloistered and ignorant of this world.*

A PRAYER TODAY, Heavenly Father, for my Christian brothers and sisters whose vocation is to live sacrificially as monastics, ascetics and renunciants. Theirs is by no means an easy calling, even though in many ways they enter into years of spiritual privilege. May they know your rich blessing as they go about their days.

* *The Flying Stars.*

30 NOVEMBER

I am come that they might have life, and that they might have it more abundantly (John 10:10 *KJV*)

There were hollows and bowers at the extreme end of that leafy garden, in which the laurels and other immortal shrubs showed against sapphire sky and silver moon, even in that midwinter, warm colours as of the south. The green gaiety of the waving laurels, the rich purple indigo of the night, the moon like a monstrous crystal, make an almost irresponsible romantic picture; and among the top branches of the garden trees a strange figure is climbing, who looks not so much romantic as impossible. He sparkles from head to heel, as if clad in ten million moons; the real moon catches him at every movement and sets a new inch of him on fire. But he swings, flashing and successful, from the short tree in this garden to the tall, rambling tree in the other, and only stops there because a shade has slid under the smaller tree and has unmistakably called up to him.

'Well, Flambeau,' says the voice, 'you really look like a Flying Star; but that always means a Falling Star at last.'*

THAT'S A USEFUL perspective, Heavenly Father; to be reminded that even the brightest star must eventually die, however brightly it shines at its brilliant best. Even the fieriest comet does not blaze for ever. The stark truth is, life is followed by death (whether we like it or not). That being so, show me how best to live the life I have, the years I have been granted. What might that mean for me?

* *The Flying Stars.*

1 DECEMBER

The angel showed me a river with the water of life, clear as crystal, flowing from the throne of God and of the Lamb (Revelation 22:1 *NLT*)

Sir Leopold Fischer . . . still seemed struggling with portions of his well-lined attire, and at length produced from a very interior tail-coat pocket, a black oval case which he radiantly explained to be his Christmas present for his god-daughter.

With an unaffected vain-glory that had something disarming about it he held out the case before them all; it flew open at a touch and half-blinded them. It was just as if a crystal fountain had spurted in their eyes. In a nest of orange velvet lay like three eggs, three white and vivid diamonds that seemed to set the very air on fire all round them.

Fischer stood beaming benevolently and drinking deep of the astonishment and ecstasy of the girl, the grim admiration and gruff thanks of the colonel, the wonder of the whole group.*

IT'S HARD FOR me to imagine, Almighty God, that, one day, I will actually be living somewhere within proximity of that great crystal fountain you have established in the heavenly realms; it all seems so unreal. As I look out of my window and see pavements and roads and buildings, and lorries going by, I can scarcely envisage the life to come. Yet, it is true! The Bible tells me so. It'll be wonderful!

* *The Flying Stars.*

2 DECEMBER

The islanders showed us unusual kindness. They built a fire and welcomed us all because it was raining and cold (Acts 28:2 *NIV*)

The chestnut seller, turning up the collar of his coat, told him he should probably be moving shortly, as he thought it was going to snow. Indeed, the evening was growing grey and bitter, but Angus, with all his eloquence, proceeded to nail the chestnut man to his post.

'Keep yourself warm on your own chestnuts,' he said earnestly. 'Eat up your whole stock.'*

A STRANGE (HEARTLESS?) approach to someone struggling with the cold, Lord. Remind me of this story, the next time I see someone in similar circumstances. May my response be one of warmth.

* *The Invisible Man.*

3 DECEMBER

Those who guard their lips preserve their lives, but those who speak rashly will come to ruin (Proverbs 13:3 *NIV*)

'Well [said the young lady], I did what I've since thought was perhaps a silly thing. But, after all, these freaks were my friends in a way; and I had a horror of their thinking I refused them for the real reason, which was that they were so impossibly ugly. So I made up some gas of another sort, about never meaning to marry anyone who hadn't carved his way in the world. I said it was a point of principle with me not to live on money that was just inherited like theirs. Two days after I had talked in this well-meaning sort of way, the whole trouble began. The first thing I heard was that both of them had gone off to seek their fortunes, as if they were in some silly fairy tale.'*

O LORD! PROMISES made, in the heat of the moment, that can come back to bite us! Excuses offered, which are then exposed, leaving us embarrassed. Awkward moments, Lord. Forgive us our impetuousness, and help us to pause before we speak, and in the process save ourselves a lot of worry.

* *The Invisible Man.*

4 DECEMBER

The birds of the sky nest by the waters; they sing among the branches (Psalm 104:12 *NIV*)

All the corners of the sky were brightening into blue and silver; the birds were chattering in the tiny garden trees; so loud it seemed as if the trees themselves were talking.*

HOW OFTEN WE need such scenes to break into our days, Heavenly Father! Glimpses of beauty, when, perhaps, the daily routine seems somewhat monotonous, or when our responsibilities are arduous. We look up and notice the sky, the birds, the trees, and our spirits are lifted. Thank you for tokens of love like these. Cause us to look up often, for there us a tonic in the trees and a solace in the skies!

* *The Honour of Israel Gow.*

5 DECEMBER

When anxiety was great within me, your consolation brought me joy (Psalm 94:19 *NIV*)

Nature deserted me. I felt ill. I felt just as if I had done something wrong. I think my brain is breaking up; I feel some sort of desperate pleasure in thinking I have told the thing to somebody; that I shall not have to be alone with it if I marry and have children. What is the matter with me? . . . Madness . . . or can one have remorse, just as if one were in Byron's poems!*

LORD OF MERCY, life can take horrific turns at times, leaving us at our wits' end. No matter whether we have sown the seeds of our own undoing, or whether circumstances have conspired against us, come to us when we are at our most fragile. We might well be guilty, we might well have brought matters upon our own heads. We might be perfectly innocent. Either way, Lord Jesus, help us when we are frantic, when we think we might be going mad, and when we are experiencing days of utter despair. I pray this prayer for anyone facing such a predicament today.

* *The Wrong Shape.*

6 DECEMBER

The days of our years are threescore years and ten; and if by reason of strength they be fourscore years, yet is their strength labour and sorrow; for it is soon cut off, and we fly away (Psalm 90:10 *KJV*)

When the priest went forth again and set his face homeward, the cold had grown more intense and yet was somehow intoxicating. The trees stood up like silver candelabra of some incredible cold candlemas of purification. It was a piercing cold, like that silver sword of pure pain that once pierced the very heart of purity. But it was not a killing cold, save in the sense of seeming to kill all the mortal obstructions to our immortal and immeasurable vitality. The pale green sky of twilight, with one star like the star of Bethlehem, seemed by some strange contradiction to be a cavern of clarity. It was as if there could be a green furnace of cold which wakened all things to life like warmth, and that the deeper they went into those cold crystalline colours the more were they light like winged creatures and clear like coloured glass! It tingled with truth and it divided truth from error with a blade like ice; but all that was left had never felt so much alive. It was as if all joy were a jewel in the heart of an iceberg. The priest hardly understood his own mood as he advanced deeper and deeper into the green gloaming, drinking deeper and deeper draughts of that virginal vivacity of the air. Some forgotten muddle and morbidity seemed to be left behind.*

HOW SHALL WE approach our Homeward journey, Lord? That last day, when we sense our departure from this life and our impending arrival in the next. When we all get to heaven, what rejoicing there will be, when, soon, the muddle and morbidity of our years in this existence will be left behind, giving way to all that lies ahead. May we go forth, carrying the whispered reassurance in our hearts: it is well with my soul.

* *The Dagger with Wings.*

7 DECEMBER

The disciples were first called Christians (Acts 11:26 *ESV*)

'Why,' said Boyne, 'I should have thought that a rascal could pretty well profess any religion he chose.'

'Yes,' assented the other; 'he could profess any religion; that is he could pretend to any religion, if it was all a pretence. If it was mere mechanical hypocrisy and nothing else, no doubt it could be done by a mere mechanical hypocrite. Any sort of mask can be put on any sort of face. Anybody can learn certain phrases or state verbally that he holds certain views. I can go out into the street and state that I am a Wesleyan Methodist or a Sandemanian,* though I fear in no very convincing accent.'†

GOD OF GRACE and truth, let my relationship with you be uppermost in my spiritual thinking, from which all else will flow. Whichever church or denomination I prefer and choose to belong to, subsequently, is secondary; important, but secondary. Please keep me from confusing one with the other. Abide with me.

* An old Scottish sect.

† *The Dagger with Wings.*

8 DECEMBER

The company of the prophets said to Elisha, 'Look, the place where we meet with you is too small for us. Let us go to the Jordan, where each of us can get a pole; and let us build a place there for us to meet.' And he said, 'Go' (2 Kings 6:1, 2 *NIV*)

'I'm afraid I'm a practical man,' said the doctor with gruff humour, 'and I don't bother much about religion and philosophy.'

'You'll never be a practical man till you do,' said Father Brown.

'Look here, doctor; you know me pretty well; I think you know I'm not a bigot. You know I know there are all sorts in all religions; good men in bad ones and bad men in good ones. But there's just one little fact I've learned simply as a practical man, an entirely practical point, that I've picked up by experience, like the tricks of an animal or the trade-mark of a good wine. I've scarcely ever met a criminal who philosophized at all, who didn't philosophize along those lines of orientalism and recurrence and reincarnation, and the wheel of destiny and the serpent biting its own tail. I have found merely in practice that there is a curse on the servants of that serpent; on their belly shall they go and the dust shall they eat; and there was never a blackguard or a profligate born who could not talk that sort of spirituality. It may not be like that in its real religious origins; but here in our working world it is the religion of rascals; and I knew it was a rascal who was speaking.'*

CARPENTER-GOD, LET us dispel with the notion (the subtle lie) that your people – people of faith – are so heavenly minded so as to be of little or no practical use. It's an image of Christians that is wet, drippy and not at all true, yet one that often prevails. To that end, I pray for Christians who go about the outworking of their faith in immensely practical ways, engaged in professions that require

* *The Dagger with Wings.*

great skill in practicality; builders, plumbers, architects, bricklayers, and so on. Bless that kind of witness. I think especially perhaps of those undertaking construction projects on behalf of the poor and homeless. Give them your blessing as they go in your name.

9 DECEMBER

The getting of treasures by a lying tongue is a fleeting vapour (Proverbs 21:6 *ESV*)

'It began with his deceiving . . . with elaborate excuses and ingeniously detailed lies [said Father Brown]; but even that may have been, at the beginning, little more than the tall stories and tarradiddles* of the child who may say equally he has seen the King of England or the King of the Fairies. It grew strong in him through the vice that perpetuates all vices, pride; he grew more and more vain of his promptitude in producing stories of his originality, and subtlety in developing them.'†

THE EASIEST THING in the world in many ways, Lord – yet, potentially, the most deadly. A 'little' lie here, followed by another there, until a tangled web is weaved and extrication becomes increasingly difficult. Tracks have to be covered at every turn. Have mercy on those whose hearts have led them astray, Lord. Graciously help them back to the right path. Untangle them.

* Pretentious nonsense.

† *The Dagger with Wings.*

10 DECEMBER

It is better to go to a house of mourning than to go to a house of feasting, for death is the destiny of everyone; the living should take this to heart (Ecclesiastes 7:2 *ESV*)

'You will admit [said Dr Mulborough] I kept my promise; I have shown you something in the village considerably more creepy than a corpse; even a corpse stuffed with poison. The black coat of a parson stuffed with a blackmailer is at least worth noticing and my live man is much deadlier than your dead one.'

'Yes,' said the doctor, settling himself back comfortably in the cushions. 'If it comes to a little cosy company on a railway journey, I should prefer the corpse.'*

AN INTERESTING CONTEMPLATION, Lord: my own mortality. Stay with me as I contemplate that fact today. Help me think through its implications.

* *The Vampire of the Village.*

11 DECEMBER

You are to love those who are foreigners, for you yourselves were foreigners in Egypt (Deuteronomy 10:19 *NIV*)

'As a matter of fact,' went on Father Brown, 'there was a plainer and more glaring cause for suspicion. It concerned the Dark Lady of the Grange, who was supposed to be the Vampire of the Village. I very early formed the impression that this black blot was rather the bright spot of the village. She was treated as a mystery; but there was really nothing mysterious about her. She had come down here quite recently, quite openly, under her own name, to help the new inquiries to be made about her own husband. He hadn't treated her too well; but she had principles, suggesting that something was due to her married name and to common justice.'*

GOD OF JUSTICE and truth, I pray for those who bear the burden of the shadow of suspicion and mistrust. Specifically, today, I pray for refugees and economic migrants. I pray for those fleeing war in their homelands and desperately seeking safe havens. They are, Lord, all-too-often regarded as suspect and even unworthy, somehow. As they run for help and as they endeavour to settle in lands not their own, often using a second language they can barely grasp, may they find compassion. I ask your blessing on churches who have opened their doors in welcome. Give your support to such endeavours, I pray.

* *The Vampire of the Village.*

12 DECEMBER

Christ loved the church and gave himself up for her (Ephesians *5:25 ESV*)

'Our controversialists [said Father Brown] often complain that there is a great deal of ignorance about what our religion is really like. But it is really more curious than that. It is true, and it is not at all unnatural, that England does not know much about the Church of Rome. But England does not know much about the Church of England. Not even as much as I do. You would be astonished at how little the average public grasps about the Anglican controversies; lots of them don't really know what is meant by a High Churchman or a Low Churchman, even on the particular points of practice, let alone the two theories of history and philosophy behind them. You can see this ignorance in any newspaper; in any merely popular novel or play.'*

AH, LORD, YOUR imperfect Church, made up of all us imperfect people! How you love, despite all our flaws. You have greatly blessed England over the years. You have revived, you have delivered. Would you do so again? Have mercy.

* *The Vampire of the Village.*

13 DECEMBER

Some soldiers asked him, 'And what should we do?' He replied, 'Don't extort money and don't accuse people falsely – be content with your pay' (Luke 3:14 *NIV*)

The old man courteously waved Father Brown to a seat, which he took and sat there silent, staring blandly at the ceiling. But something made Mulborough feel that he could deliver his important news more impressively standing up. 'I feel,' he said, 'that you ought to be informed, as in some sense the spiritual father of this community, that one terrible tragedy in its record has taken on a new significance; possibly even more terrible. You will recall the sad business of the death of Maltravers; who was adjudged to have been killed with the blow of a stick, probably wielded by some rustic enemy.' The clergyman made a gesture with a wavering hand. 'God forbid,' he said, 'that I should say anything that might seem to palliate murderous violence in any case. But when an actor brings his wickedness into this innocent village, he is challenging the judgement of God.' 'Perhaps,' said the doctor gravely. 'But anyhow it was not so that the judgement fell. I have just been commissioned to conduct a post-mortem on the body; and I can assure you, first, that the blow on the head could not conceivably have caused the death; and, second, that the body was full of poison, which undoubtedly caused death.'

Young Hurrel Horner sent his cigarette flying and was on his feet with the lightness and swiftness of a cat. His leap landed him within a yard of the reading-desk.

'Are you certain of this?' he gasped. 'Are you absolutely certain that that blow could not cause death?' 'Absolutely certain,' said the doctor. 'Well,' said Hurrel, 'I almost wish this one could.' In a flash, before anyone could move a finger, he had struck the parson a stunning crack on the mouth, dashing him backwards like a disjointed black doll against the door. 'What are you doing?' cried Mulborough, shaken from head to foot with the shock and mere sound of the blow. 'Father Brown, what is this madman doing?' But Father Brown had not stirred; he was still staring serenely at the ceiling. 'I was waiting for him to do that,' said the priest placidly. 'I rather wonder he hasn't done it before.' 'Good God,' cried the doctor. 'I know we thought he was wronged in some ways; but to strike his father; to strike a clergyman and a non-combatant –''He has not struck his father; and he has not struck a clergyman,' said Father Brown. 'He has struck a blackmailing blackguard of an actor dressed up as a clergyman, who has lived on him like a leech for years. Now he knows he is free of the blackmail, he lets fly; and I can't say I blame him much. More especially as I have very strong suspicions that the blackmailer is a poisoner as well. I think, Mulborough, you had better ring up the police.'*

I PRAY FOR blackmailers, extortionists, and telephone scammers today, Lord. By your Spirit, mightily convict them of their wrongdoing, even as they operate.

* *The Vampire of the Village.*

14 DECEMBER

O God, thou hast taught me from my youth: and hitherto have I declared thy wondrous works. Now also when I am old and greyheaded, O God, forsake me not (Psalm 71:17, 18 *KJV*)

'I had a talk with the bank manager [said Father Brown], and as we were inquiring in confidence into a serious crime, under authority from the police, he told me the facts. The old clergyman has retired from parish work; indeed, this was never actually his parish. Such of the populace, which is pretty pagan, as goes to church at all, goes to Dutton-Abbot, not a mile away. The old man has no private means, but his son is earning good money; and the old man is well looked after. He gave me some port of absolutely first-class vintage; I saw rows of dusty old bottles of it; and I left him sitting down to a little lunch quite recherche in an old-fashioned style. It must be done on the young man's money.'*

MY PRAYERS TODAY, Heavenly Father, are for retired clergy. Bless them. I pray especially for any known to me personally. May they know your blessing in the evening of life.

* *The Vampire of the Village.*

15 DECEMBER

Whoever comes to me I will never drive away (John 6:37 *NIV*)

[Father Brown] was . . . well aware that his old religious communion could boast of several distinguished poisoners.*

IN ONE SENSE, that's the beauty of the Church, Heavenly Father. Holiness and righteousness are the goals, of course. So too righteousness and discipleship. However, if ever it ceases to be a place where poisoners and other sinners can turn to for pardon and counsel, then it has ceased to be that which beats with your heart of redemptive love. The vilest offender must always know of grace. May that be so in the church to which I belong.

* *The Vampire of the Village.*

16 DECEMBER

Peter opened his mouth, and said, Of a truth I perceive that God is no respecter of persons (Acts 10:34 *KJV*)

'Gentlemen,' [Father Brown] said, when he had resumed his seat, 'it was you who asked me to look into the truth about this puzzle; and having found the truth, I must tell it, without any pretence of softening the shock. I'm afraid anybody who pokes his nose into things like this can't afford to be a respecter of persons.'*

ONE OF THE guiding principles of the Christian faith, Lord, surely must be that whosoever will may come – to belief, to your Throne of Grace, to church, to Bible classes, to penitent forms and to altars. Squire and scavenger are, in the sense of both having souls that need to be saved, much the same proposition in your eyes. Prince and pauper may kneel before you together, aware of their mutual need of forgiveness. There is no distinction, and that's a marvellous element of authentic Christianity; the ground at the foot of the cross is level. We're all seeking the same Saviour, and there is no partiality in pardoning.

* *The Arrow of Heaven.*

17 DECEMBER

God, whose word I praise (Psalm 56:4 *NIV*)

'We know all millionaires are holy and sainted [growled Drage]; you can find it all in the papers next day, about how they lived by the light of the Family Bible they read at their mother's knee. Gee! if they'd only read out some of the things there are in the Family Bible, the mother might have been startled some. And the millionaire, too, I reckon. The old Book's full of a lot of grand fierce old notions they don't grow nowadays; sort of wisdom of the Stone Age and buried under the Pyramids. Suppose somebody had flung old man Merton from the top of that tower of his, and let him be eaten by dogs at the bottom, it would be no worse than what happened to Jezebel. Wasn't Agag hacked into little pieces, for all he went walking delicately?'*

LORD GOD, I cannot deny that these stories are found in the Bible. Nor do I wish to. They don't make for easy reading, but that's the beauty of your book, Lord; it reflects human life in all its gory truth; murder, vengeance, bloodshed – the lot! There is no whitewashing, no pretence, and no 'spin'. And that, for me, Lord, tells of a holy book that is authentic. I don't think I'd want a book of sugar-coated fairy tales that had nothing to do with real life, warts and all.

* *The Arrow of Heaven.*

18 DECEMBER

Great is your faithfulness (Lamentations 3:23 *ESV*)

Mr Norman Drage still confronted the world grimly behind his great goggles, which seemed somehow to cover his face like a dark musk of glass. But except for the goggles, his appearance had undergone a strange transformation . . .

He had . . ., as Father Brown had noted, been dressed up to the nines – up to that point, indeed, where there begins to be too fine a distinction between the dandy and the dummy outside a tailor's shop.

But now all those externals were mysteriously altered for the worse; as if the tailor's dummy had been turned into a scarecrow. His top hat still existed, but it was battered and shabby; his clothes were dilapidated; his watch-chain and minor ornaments were gone. Father Brown, however, addressed him as if they had met yesterday, and made no demur to sitting down with him on a bench in the cheap eating-house whither he was bound.*

LORD JESUS, HOW graciously and humbly you, the King of kings, make no demur to sitting down with any of us, lowly though we be. Your grace is always at its zenith. That is to say, you don't love us more when we are at our smartest or less when we are somewhat more dilapidated. Faithful God.

* *The Arrow of Heaven.*

19 DECEMBER

The chief cupbearer said to Pharaoh, 'I remember my offenses today. When Pharaoh was angry with his servants and put me and the chief baker in custody in the house of the captain of the guard, we dreamed on the same night, he and I, each having a dream with its own interpretation. A young Hebrew was there with us, a servant of the captain of the guard. When we told him, he interpreted our dreams to us, giving an interpretation to each man according to his dream (Genesis 41:9-12 *ESV*)

Though the Professor was limited to small doses of the stimulant of conversation, he concentrated most of it upon these interviews with his clerical friend. Father Brown had a talent for being silent in an encouraging way and Smaill was encouraged by it to talk about many strange things not always easy to talk about; such as the morbid phases of recovery and the monstrous dreams that often accompany delirium. It is often rather an unbalancing business to recover slowly from a bad knock on the head; and when the head is as interesting a head as that of Professor Smaill even its disturbances and distortions are apt to be original and curious. His dreams were like bold and big designs rather out of drawing, as they can be seen in the strong but stiff archaic arts that he had studied; they were full of strange saints with square and triangular haloes, of golden out-standing crowns and glories round dark and flattened faces, of eagles out of the east and the high headdresses of bearded men with their hair bound like women.*

WHAT A FASCINATING gift, Lord – the interpretation of dreams. This causes me to realise, Almighty God, that you are as alert and as active when I am sleeping and dreaming as you are when I am awake. That's a reassuring thought. By day and by night, whether I am conscious or unconscious, you are my unsleeping God.

* *The Curse of the Golden Cross.*

20 DECEMBER

Precious in the sight of the Lord is the death of his saints (Psalm 116:15 *NIV*)

'You have seen his body [said Father Brown]. You haven't seen him – the real living man; but you have seen his body all right. You have stared at it hard by the light of four great candles . . . lying in state like a Prince of the Church in a shrine built before the Crusade.'*

THOSE WHO HAVE gone before, Eternal God; those whose bodies lie, entombed now, in churches and cathedrals, whose names are marked with honour and respect. To dust, their weary mortal frames have returned. For all the saints, for their stories, and for their example, I give you thanks. I hope to live up to them.

* *The Curse of the Golden Cross.*

21 DECEMBER

My God is my rock, in whom I take refuge, my shield and the horn of my salvation. He is my stronghold, my refuge and my saviour – from violent people you save me (2 Samuel 22:3 *NIV*)

'Well,' answered Race, 'I suppose you were astonished at being knocked on the head.'

Father Brown leaned over to him and said in a low voice, 'I was astonished at not being knocked on the head.'

Race looked at him for a moment as if he thought the knock on the head had been only too effective; but he only said: 'What do you mean?'

'I mean that when that man brought his bludgeon down with a great swipe, it stopped at my head and did not even touch it. In the same way, the other fellow made as if to strike me with a knife, but he never gave me a scratch. It was just like play-acting. I think it was.'*

LORD OF HOSTS, I pray for those of your people who are engaged in dangerous situations today; military padres, for example, who minister your love in theatres of conflict, or Christians whose calling takes them into areas of gang warfare where knives and guns are the order of the day. Those are special ministries, Lord, and those people need your special protection.

* *The Resurrection of Father Brown.*

22 DECEMBER

The LORD bless you (Numbers 6:24 *NIV*)

He came tumbling down the steps, the people flinging themselves before him to implore his blessing.

'Bless you, bless you,' said Father Brown hastily. 'God bless you all and give you more sense.'*

WHAT AN AMUSING sort of blessing, Lord! Nevertheless, thank you for those who bless me in all kinds of ways. With the best will in the world, it's so easy to dispense those words, 'bless you', without (sometimes, inadvertently) realising their full meaning, perhaps casually over the phone or as someone is leaving the house: 'to ask God to look favourably upon'. So today, Lord, I ask you to look favourably upon my family and loved ones, and those I care for. I ask you to look favourably upon my friends. Bless them, bless them, according to their circumstances and present needs.

* *The Resurrection of Father Brown.*

23 DECEMBER

As soon as he came near the camp and saw the calf and the dancing, Moses' anger burned hot (Exodus 32:19 *ESV*)

In the midst of all this tornado of beatitude was a little man struggling to be heard. His voice was small and faint, and the noise was deafening. He made weak little gestures that seemed more those of irritation than anything else. He came to the edge of the parapet above the crowd, waving it to be quiet, with movements rather like the flap of the short wings of a penguin. There was something a little more like a lull in the noise; and then Father Brown for the first time reached the utmost stretch of the indignation that he could launch against his children.

'Oh, you silly people,' he said in a high and quavering voice; 'Oh, you silly, silly people.'*

AN ANGRY PRIEST, Lord! (Perhaps exasperated is a better word?) How trying it must be at times, for a priest/minister/vicar to cope with all the complex demands of ministry without occasionally wanting (needing) to let off steam and say what they really think. Bless my priest/minister/vicar at such times, Lord, I pray! In addition, surround them with people with whom they feel comfortable offloading – that'll help.

* *The Resurrection of Father Brown.*

24 DECEMBER

No longer drink only water, but use a little wine for your stomach's sake (1 Timothy 5:23 *NKJV*)

Eckstein was a fussy little man with fuzzy hair and pince-nez, who was wildly anxious that the priest should not only try some of his celebrated medicinal port, but should let him know where and when he would drink it, in acknowledging its receipt. The priest was not particularly surprised at the request, for he was long past surprise at the lunacies of advertisement. So he scribbled something down and turned to other business which seemed a little more sensible. He was again interrupted, by a note from no less a person than his political enemy Alvarez, asking him to come to a conference at which it was hoped that a compromise on an outstanding question might be reached; and suggesting an appointment that evening at a cafe just outside the walls of the little town. To this also he sent a message of acceptance by the rather florid and military messenger who was waiting for it; and then, having an hour or two before him, sat down to attempt to get through a little of his own legitimate business. At the end of the time he poured himself out a glass of Mr Eckstein's remarkable wine and, glancing at the clock with a humorous expression, drank it and went out into the night.*

A MILDLY CONTENTIOUS issue, Lord – should Christians drink alcohol or remain teetotal? There are credible points of view on both side of the discussion, all of which go to demonstrate the worth and value of happy disagreement. May your Church always be a community, Lord, in which differing opinions are welcomed and respected, covering all kinds of subjects. I pray for my own church in that regard.

* *The Resurrection of Father Brown.*

25 DECEMBER

'If you are the Messiah,' they said, 'tell us.' Jesus answered, 'If I tell you, you will not believe me, and if I asked you, you would not answer' (Luke 22:67, 68 *NIV*)

The third witness called by Sir Walter Cowdray was the little Catholic clergyman, so little, compared with the others, that his head seemed hardly to come above the box, so that it was like cross-examining a child.

But unfortunately Sir Walter had somehow got it into his head (mostly by some ramifications of his family's religion) that Father Brown was on the side of the prisoner, because the prisoner was wicked and foreign . . .

Therefore he took Father Brown up sharply whenever that proud pontiff tried to explain anything; and told him to answer yes or no, and tell the plain facts without any jesuitry. When Father Brown began, in his simplicity, to say who he thought the man in the passage was, the barrister told him that he did not want his theories.*

LORD JESUS, YOU know all about an unfair and biased trial in a courtroom – a 'kangaroo court' in which the verdict is probably decided long before any actual deliberations. I think today of believers who are called to stand trial for their faith, in countries where Christianity is brutally outlawed. The likelihood is, their prison sentences are already prescribed; bribed jurors and corrupt judges handling their cases. Even if your people are allowed to have their say, it will probably be ignored. Bless those who are imprisoned and standing trial for their witness, Lord; may they find solace in knowing that you stand alongside them.

* *The Man in the Passage.*

26 DECEMBER

Since we are surrounded by such a great cloud of witnesses, let us throw off everything that hinders and the sin that so easily entangles. And let us run with perseverance the race marked out for us (Hebrews 12:1 *NIV*)

Father Brown and Parkinson were left alone, and they were neither of them men with a taste for superfluous conversation.

The dresser went round the room, pulling out looking-glasses and pushing them in again, his dingy dark coat and trousers looking all the more dismal since he was still holding the festive fairy spear of King Oberon.

Every time he pulled out the frame of a new glass, a new black figure of Father Brown appeared; the absurd glass chamber was full of Father Browns, upside down in the air like angels, turning somersaults like acrobats, turning their backs to everybody like very rude persons.

Father Brown seemed quite unconscious of this cloud of witnesses.*

I SHOULD IMAGINE, Heavenly Father, that most of us, to be honest, are, like Father Brown, quite unconscious of the cloud of witnesses that surrounds us. For all that, it's still quite a thought! We may not understand exactly what it means, but it reminds us that we are by no means alone. On the contrary, we could imagine we are being cheered along and encouraged, from on high. Thank you for their support!

* *The Man in the Passage.*

27 DECEMBER

He has planted eternity in the human heart (Ecclesiastes 3:11 NLT)

'By the way,' went on Father Brown, 'don't think I blame you for jumping to preternatural conclusions. The reason's very simple, really. You all swore you were hard-shelled materialists; and as a matter of fact you were all balanced on the very edge of belief – of belief in almost anything. There are thousands balanced on it today; but it's a sharp, uncomfortable edge to sit on. You won't rest till you believe something; that's why Mr Vandam went through new religions with a tooth-comb, and Mr Alboin quotes Scripture for his religion of breathing exercises, and Mr Fenner grumbles at the very God he denies. That's where you all split; it's natural to believe in the supernatural. It never feels natural to accept only natural things.'*

I THINK FATHER Brown is right, Lord. He's on to something. Despite every denial and despite every resistance, there is something within human beings that means we lean towards you, or, at least, towards the supernatural and the spiritual. We are curious regarding the possibility that there is more to our existence than meets the eye, and we suspect there very well might be. Again, Heavenly Father, I return to prayer for those I love and care for, who deny your existence and show no interest in faith. In your mercy, soften their hearts and nudge them towards new conclusions.

* *The Miracle of Moon Crescent.*

28 DECEMBER

The God of peace will soon crush Satan under your feet (Romans 16:20 *ESV*)

'I don't think I quite understand,' observed the millionaire, curiously.

'I don't think you do,' said Father Brown, with simplicity.

'You say this thing was done by spiritual powers. What spiritual powers? You don't think the holy angels took him and hung him on a garden tree, do you? And as for the unholy angels – no, no, no. The men who did this did a wicked thing, but they went no further than their own wickedness; they weren't wicked enough to be dealing with spiritual powers. I know something about Satanism, for my sins; I've been forced to know. I know what it is, what it practically always is. It's proud and it's sly. It likes to be superior; it loves to horrify the innocent with things half understood, to make children's flesh creep. That's why it's so fond of mysteries and initiations and secret societies and all the rest of it. Its eyes are turned inwards, and however grand and grave it may look, it's always hiding a small, mad smile.'

He shuddered suddenly, as if caught in an icy draught of air.*

THIS IS THE icy, shuddering reality, Almighty God: we are engaged in a spiritual battle with the forces of evil. Such warfare is as real as the planet we live on and the air we breathe, and is as Father Brown describes it; our enemy is horrifyingly wicked, who will stop at nothing to oppose and destroy all that is good and lovely. There are, however, two sides to every story, and the glorious truth is that Satan is already defeated. This conflict, as fierce as it can be, represents his death throes, for Jesus has conquered and we are merely awaiting the culmination of his ultimate triumph. Thanks be to God!

* *The Miracle of Moon Crescent.*

29 DECEMBER

Search the Scriptures (John 5:39 *ESV*)

'I only mean that the police are stupid in thinking they can leave out the psychological element in these things [said the professor]. Well, of course, the psychological element is everything in everything, though it is only just beginning to be understood. To begin with, take the element called personality. Now I have heard of this priest, Father Brown, before; and he is one of the most remarkable men of our time. Men of that sort carry a sort of atmosphere with them; and nobody knows how much his nerves and even his very senses are affected by it for the time being. People are hypnotized – yes, hypnotized; for hypnotism, like everything else, is a matter of degree; it enters slightly into all daily conversation: it is not necessarily conducted by a man in evening-dress on a platform in a public hall.'*

I DON'T THINK hypnotism has anything to do with it, Lord, but there is without question a psychological element to religion and faith. Psychology, that is, in terms of a reasoned, thought-out belief; a confidence in Christ that stems from a process of rational consideration. Lord, preserve us from intellectual laziness and from a religious expression that has failed to engage the mind.

* *The Miracle of Moon Crescent.*

30 DECEMBER

Choose this day whom you will serve (Joshua 24:15 *ESV*)

Father Brown rapped sharply on the stove with the short pipe he was about to fill; one of his very rare spasms of annoyance contracted his face.

'No, no, no,' he said, almost angrily; 'I don't mean just a figure of speech. This is what comes of trying to talk about deep things. . . . What's the good of words . . .? If you try to talk about a truth that's merely moral, people always think it's merely metaphorical. A real live man with two legs once said to me: 'I only believe in the Holy Ghost in a spiritual sense.' Naturally, I said: 'In what other sense could you believe it?' And then he thought I meant he needn't believe in anything except evolution, or ethical fellowship, or some bilge.'*

PHILOSOPHICAL DISCUSSIONS REGARDING the nature of spiritual matters have their place, Lord. It's good that we approach you with our minds as well as our hearts . . . but not quite so good if we find ourselves going round and round in seemingly endless philosophical circles! At some point, Lord, we need to make a decision; to consider the arguments, to look at the information set before us, and to decide, one way or the other. Today, then, I pray for those who philosophise without reaching a conclusion, and for those who procrastinate. In your mercy, Father God, let us all make a personal, definite response to today's challenge, be that afresh or anew; to stand for Christ, and Christ alone.

* *The Secret of Father Brown.*

31 DECEMBER

And, in conclusion, we share together the Lord's Prayer, a unifying prayer for Christians of all denominations, all around the world:

Our Father,
who art in heaven,
hallowed be thy name;
thy kingdom come;
thy will be done on earth as it is in heaven.
Give us this day our daily bread;
and forgive us our trespasses as we forgive those who trespass
against us;
and lead us not into temptation,
but deliver us from evil.
Amen.

Or, as Father Brown himself might prefer to pray:

Pater noster,
qui es in caelis,
sanctificetur nomen tuum.
Adveniat regnum tuum.
Fiat voluntas tua, sicut in caelo et in terra.
Panem nostrum quotidianum da nobis hodie,
et dimitte nobis debita nostra sicut et nos dimittimus
debitoribus nostris.
Et ne nos inducas in tentationem,
sed libera nos a malo.
Amen.